D1112643

CHANNEL SHORE

CHANNEL SHORE

FROM THE WHITE CLIFFS
TO LAND'S END

TOM FORT

**SIMON &
SCHUSTER**

London · New York · Sydney · Toronto · New Delhi

First published in Great Britain by Simon & Schuster UK Ltd, 2015
A CBS COMPANY

Copyright © 2015 by Tom Fort

This book is copyright under the Berne Convention.
No reproduction without permission.
All rights reserved.

The right of Tom Fort to be identified as the author
of this work has been asserted by him in accordance with sections
77 and 78 of the Copyright, Designs and Patents Act, 1988.

All photographs © Jason Hawkes

Map © Colin Midson

1 3 5 7 9 10 8 6 4 2

Simon & Schuster UK Ltd
1st Floor
222 Gray's Inn Road
London WC1X 8HB

www.simonandschuster.co.uk

Simon & Schuster Australia, Sydney
Simon & Schuster India, New Delhi

A CIP catalogue record for this book
is available from the British Library

Hardback ISBN: 978-1-4711-2972-8
eBook ISBN: 978-1-4711-2974-2

The author and publishers have made all reasonable efforts
to contact copyright-holders for permission, and apologise
for any omissions or errors in the form of credits given.
Corrections may be made to future printings.

Typeset in the UK by M Rules
Printed and bound by CPI Group (UK) Ltd, Croydon, CR0 4YY

To local historians, past, present and future

CONTENTS

Contents

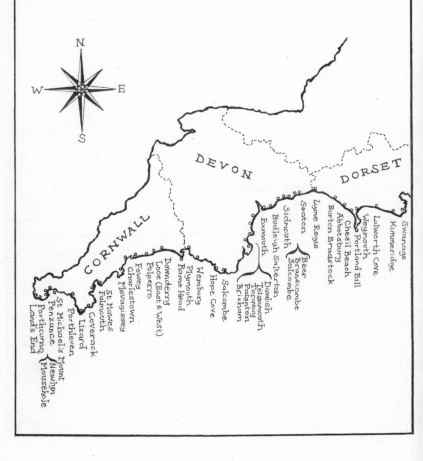

A MAP OF THE CHANNEL SHORE
INCLUDING (ALMOST) EVERY LOCATION
VISITED BY THE AUTHOR, TOM FORT

N
W   E
S

DEVON

DORSET

CORNWALL

Swanage
Kimmeridge
Lulworth Cove
Weymouth
Portland Bill
Chesil Beach
Abbotsbury
Burton Bradstock
Lyme Regis
Seaton
Beer
Branscombe
Sidmouth
Salcombe
Budleigh Salterton
Exmouth
Dawlish
Teignmouth
Torquay
Paignton
Brixham
Downderry
Looe (East & West)
Polperro
Fowey
Charlestown
Mevagissey
Wembury
Plymouth
Rame Head
Hope Cove
Salcombe
St Mawes
Falmouth
Coverack
Lizard
Porthleven
St Michael's Mount
Penzance
Newlyn
Porthcurno
Mousehole
Land's End

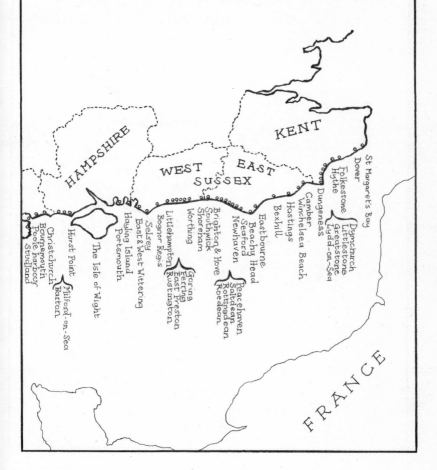

FROM ST MARGARET'S BAY IN KENT VIA SUSSEX, HAMPSHIRE DORSET & DEVON, TO LAND'S END IN CORNWALL

HAMPSHIRE

KENT

WEST

EAST

SUSSEX

St Margaret's Bay
Dover
Folkestone
Hythe
Greatstone
Littlestone
Lydd-on-Sea
Dymchurch
Dungeness
Camber
Winchelsea Beach
Bexhill
Hastings

Eastbourne
Beachy Head
Seaford
Newhaven
Brighton & Hove
Shoreham
Southwick
Worthing
Littlehampton
Bognor Regis
Selsey
East & West Wittering
Hayling Island
Portsmouth

Peacehaven
Saltdean
Rottingdean
Roedean
Goring
Ferring
East Preston
Rustington

The Isle of Wight

Hurst Point
Milford-on-Sea
Barton
Christchurch
Bournemouth
Poole harbour
Studland

FRANCE

PREFACE

A July day, and I am in a deckchair under an umbrella on the beach at Bournemouth, near the pier. It is hot, but English hot, not Mediterranean or Aegean; a tolerable, friendly heat. The sky is blue, brushed by high cirrus, the sea pale-blue topaz. The golden sand which runs for miles is parcelled out evenly between low wooden breakwaters.

Everyone is here: the old, in invalid chairs or sunk in deckchairs beneath faded sunhats, toddlers tottering across the sand in disposable nappies sagging with sea water, girls with stomach piercings glinting against nut-brown skin, lads with bony chests in long trunks larking around in inflatables, children on body boards making the best of amiable waves. I watch a dark-skinned woman, fully dressed with just her hands, feet and head showing, dive and twist in the water. She comes out grinning, squeezing the water from her long black hair. In front of us a Polish couple are tenderly intent on their child. A dozen languages mingle over the sand.

Elsewhere the world is tearing itself apart in the normal way. But here the offshore breeze is suffused with the contentment of those lucky enough to be alive and relishing the perfection of an English summer's day at the seaside.

A generation ago they told us the seaside holiday was dying and would soon pass away like Empire Day and the Morris Traveller and tinned apricots with evaporated milk and other curious relics. Cheap air travel, package holidays, guaranteed sun, sand and blood-warm sea – that was what the British holidaymaker wanted; not shabby amusement arcades, moth-eaten donkeys, rancid fish-and-chips, hatchet-faced boarding-house landladies, a wind-whipped sea the colour of breeze blocks and colder than the Mr Whippy squirming from stainless steel spouts in the ice-cream stalls.

But the seaside holiday clung obstinately to life. People realised that when the sun shone – which it tended to do more often and more potently than when I was a little boy, shivering in my shorts at Middleton-on-Sea – our beaches could hold their own against those of the Côte this and the Costa that. They were free, open to anyone, easy to get to. The sea was bracing rather than freezing, and although there might be jellyfish, they were not huge and red with terrifying bunches of tentacles, and the water did not spawn banks of bright-green algal jelly. And some of our seaside towns had charms of their own and had learned to please.

I love to be beside the sea, and to be in it, not too deep. But being out on it in anything other than a proper ferryboat or a flat calm makes me tense. I do not like the currents, the depths, the way fierce tides invade at the gallop. Waves with foaming crests make me nervous.

We used to have holidays on a small island on the west coast of Scotland. It was in the mouth of a long sea loch and was consequently swept by vigorous tidal currents, as well as being subject to the normal boisterous weather of those parts. On one occasion we set off down the loch for a picnic. The wind picked up and the water became choppy. At my suggestion we decided to turn back, into the wind and the waves. My sister, sitting in the bow, reported water coming through the planks as well as over the prow. I gripped the handle of the outboard as if the future of the human race depended on it, and we made it back to the bay in front of the house. Looking out half an hour later I observed that the boat had vanished at its mooring, leaving only the painter attached to the buoy as evidence that it had ever existed.

On another occasion I went with one of my brothers to the mainland to get lobsters. Fortunately we were piloted by one of the island's permanent inhabitants, who did it all the time. While we were engaged with the crustacea the wind turned into the east and gathered strength considerably, so that by the time we set off back to the island the waves were charging ahead of us in long, implacable lines, the breaking crests flattened and whipped into the air by the wind. 'This is exhilarating,' my brother shouted as we rode one wave and then the next. I felt ill with fear.

I am a landsman. My nervousness of the sea is not something I am proud of, but it's best to accept these limitations. It followed that when I came to write this Channel story it would be from a land-based perspective, of one looking out to sea with feet planted on firm rock, or sand or earth. The idea for it was not mine, but came from a film-maker, Harry Marshall of Icon Films, who wanted to make a sequence of programmes about the Channel and what it means to us, and thought I might make a suitable presenter. The project was eventually aborted – the deep thinkers at the BBC decided it would tread ground sacred to the long-running *Coast*. But by then I had been thoroughly seduced by the prospect of a personal exploration of that strip of land beside the waterway that, more than any other, has formed our sense of who we are.

So I went alone, free from the tyranny of filming, from Kent to Cornwall – down Channel. I was curious to know what it was about our Channel shore that was so special and indispensable; that drew some people and held them and called them back even when they had taken themselves off somewhere else. It was pretty straightforward to work out why some – like myself – chose to take their holidays beside the sea. More interesting, to my way of thinking, were those who chose to live within sight and sound and smell of the Channel shore: some born to it, many others pulled that way later in their lives by an insistent force.

As I made my way south-west over the course of the summer of 2013, I came to appreciate the nature of that force as I never had while just on holiday. Those who take their week or fortnight by the sea, or flit to and from their holiday homes, scrape the surface. If the weather is kind, they are happy; if not, they return home resentful, as if somehow they had been misled or let down. For those who live there, the whole point is the bad weather with the good, the richness of variation, the endless change in mood and colour and texture. They tend to be not so interested in the blatant pleasures of the summer season. They wait for the transients to depart to reclaim their kingdom.

I tried, as far as my circumstances permitted, to experience something of the Channel out of season. I was in Bournemouth in January, Torquay and Eastbourne in February, Penzance in March. But the main part of my exploration was undertaken over May, June and July 2013, by bicycle. I pedalled in stages, at no great speed, from St Margaret's Bay in Kent to Land's End – a total distance, taking in diversions, backtrackings, circuitous inland detours and so forth, of 675 miles. I was lucky, in that it was a fine summer after two dismal ones, which made for generally comfortable cycling, at least until I reached the strenuous hills of Devon and Cornwall. Much more important, the sunshine showed the places I went through and lingered in to advantage, and put their people in good humour, and me in good humour.

The cycling was a means to an end. This is not a two-wheeled epic of lung-bursting ascents (though there were times when I thought my lungs might burst) and hair-raising descents (though there were times when my hair would have stood on end if I had that kind of hair). Being on a bicycle is a good way to see, breathe, stop, talk, contemplate – quick enough to make a longish journey manageable, slow enough to absorb it properly.

So I pedalled and freewheeled and sometimes pushed. I stopped to look and to accost strangers and ask them why they liked to be beside the sea. I followed trails that made me curious – some were dead ends, some led somewhere, some gave me answers.

I do not live by the sea or anywhere near it, and at my time of life I am disinclined ever to move again. But having finished this journey, having breathed the air and watched the waves and listened to and felt the rhythms of the sea that beats against our English Channel shore, I can see the point in a way that I never did before.

1

DOVER PORT

There is no fuss, no fanfare, nothing to tell anyone that this is where our most familiar and important waterway begins and ends. The invisible line between the North Sea and the English Channel touches shore in Kent at Leathercote Point. There is a memorial on the clifftop there which honours the part played by the Dover Patrol during the 1914–18 war in protecting the passage of troops and supplies to and from France. But the inscriptions do not mention that this is where the Channel is born.

That is the way with water. The boundaries between seas are necessarily unseen and self-evidently fluid. The International Hydrographic Organization has determined that the eastern limit of the Channel extends from Leathercote Point in Kent to the defunct Walde lighthouse just east of Calais. The currents flow and the waves sweep across it as easily as the ships and yachts. Who marks the imaginary divide, or pauses to wonder when, exactly, they are no longer in the North Sea but the Channel, or the other way round?

In contrast, the facing coasts of England and France proclaim the separation between the two countries. The Channel is twenty miles wide at the Straits of Dover, and in clear weather each coastline is easily visible from the other. But their proximity serves to define their separateness rather than obscure it.

In large part the story of the Channel has been determined by these two geographical imperatives: the fixed opposition of the seaboards of England and France, and the unfettered waterway between, opening to the North Sea one way and the Atlantic the other. The destinies of both nations have been shaped to a remarkable degree by these unalterable forces and the interaction between them.

There used to be a hotel beside the beach at St Margaret's Bay, which is the easternmost (and northernmost) settlement on the English side of the Channel. It was built in the 1880s and was called the Lanzarote, presumably a marketing ploy to suggest a climate comparable with that of the Canary Islands many hundreds of miles away to the south. The charms of the bay were celebrated by Charles George Harper in *The Kentish Coast*, one of the many travelogues churned out by this energetic journalist in the immediate pre-First World War period.

'The spirit of the place is elusive and refuses to be captured and written down and printed,' he wrote down and had printed in 1914. 'Those who want to be amused – that great *desideratum* of the brainless and uncultivated – will not come to St Margaret's Bay. I do not think a motor car has ever been down here, which is so much to the good.'

The Lanzarote was subsequently renamed, more prosaically but aptly, the Bay Hotel. In the 1930s it was joined at the eastern end of the bay by a cluster of smart white beach houses. During the 1939–45 war the Army annexed the whole place for training, as a result of which the hotel and the Excelsior Tearooms and various bungalows nearby were wrecked and shattered by gunfire, and had to be demolished. But the smart houses, although damaged, were salvageable, and in 1945 the playwright Noël Coward took a lease on the last one.

It was called White Cliffs. 'I don't think I can fail to be happy here,' he said. The house was squeezed onto a ledge between the sea and the foot of the chalk cliff. There was just enough room for the chickens required to provide Coward's daily breakfast egg, but not for a garden. Then, as now, cliff falls were a hazard and after the appalling later winter of 1947 he spent £2000 (£70,000 in today's money) having the chalk above the house shored up.

Coward treasured the seclusion and peace, the view of the grey shingle beach and the water, the noise of the sea lapping or beating at the wall below his bedroom window. Although his heyday as a dramatist was by then over, he was busy on a host of projects. He was also enormously rich, and willing and able to entertain with a lavishness that was exceptional at that austere time. Among the stars who came to White Cliffs to feast and frolic were Spencer Tracy and his lover, the famously hale and hearty Katharine Hepburn, who amused the locals by swimming in the sea every day whatever the weather.

To protect his privacy Coward arranged for his mother, his secretary Cole Lesley and his friend, the thriller writer Eric Ambler, to take the leases on the houses closest to his. Even so, the attractions of St Margaret's Bay became, in his view, its undoing. The road brought cars and the cars brought trippers to gawp at Coward and his glamorous guests. He complained that the beach was 'crowded with noisy *hoi polloi*'. In 1951 he was told he could return to Goldenhurst, his house in Romney Marsh, which the Army had requisitioned during the hostilities.

The many – the English translation of hoi polloi – continue to descend on the bay in force at holiday time, filling the car park and crowding the stony beach. But I came midweek in early April and it was very quiet, just me and my bike and a few dog walkers and a girl who'd opened up the tea kiosk at an opportune moment. There was no wind at all. The sea was flat calm, bathed in a milky haze that made it impossible to see any distance out to sea or to tell where sea ended and sky began.

The girl at the kiosk who made my tea lived in Dover. She liked the job. 'It calms you down being here,' she said. 'Just looking out at the sea helps when you're stressed. Course it's heaving in the season but a day like today is perfect.'

I wandered along to look at Coward's house. It was empty and silent, the pale yellow shutters closed. It looked in good order, as if it had survived the ravages of sea and storm pretty well, but the house next door was showing signs of wear and tear, its plasterwork stained and its metal window frames spotted with rust. The cliff behind seemed menacingly close.

Coward had the lease of White Cliffs transferred to his friend Ian Fleming, who with his lover and later wife, Ann Rothermere, had been a frequent guest. Fleming's gift to St Margaret's Bay was to set much of the action of his third James Bond story, *Moonraker*, there and thereabouts.

A few years ago, when on holiday in Italy, I came upon a paperback copy of *Moonraker*, and was curious enough to reread it. An early passage sets the tone. Bond is bowling along the Deal road on his way to engineer the downfall of the card cheat and closet Nazi, Sir Hugo Drax. A Special Branch officer, Gala Brand, has been assigned to help him, and as he steers the Aston Martin Bond ponders her career notes – 'distinguishing marks: mole on upper curvature of right breast' – and lets his mind roam.

A later sunbathing session, presumably involving close investigation of the mole, is interrupted by a cliff fall triggered by one of Drax's murderous henchmen. Bond and Gala Brand make it to the Granville Hotel above the beach at St Margaret's – later demolished and replaced by a block of smart apartments – for a hot bath and 'rest', followed by 'delicious fried soles and Welsh rarebit'.

The story ends with the rocket intended by Sir Hugo to blow up Buckingham Palace being ingeniously redirected into the Channel to destroy the Russian submarine in which Drax and his evil entourage are fleeing. To Bond's irritation, Miss Brand declines his offer to accompany him to France for further exploration of her distinguishing marks, so that she can go and marry her policeman fiancé. Bond consoles himself with the knowledge that by deploying his amazing sexual magnetism to thaw her oh-so-English frigidity, he has eased the path to shared marital bliss.

The book has the whiff of uncollected food waste about it. Fleming's way with Bond's women is comically voyeuristic – 'the wrap-over bodice just showed the swell of her breasts which were as splendid as Bond had guessed from the measurements on her record sheet.' The story itself, energised by a rabid hatred of Germans focussed on the ridiculous caricature villain Drax, is vintage Bulldog Drummond, redeemed only somewhat by Fleming's evident affection for the Kent coastline and the bay where he made his home for a while.

* * *

Dover cliffs

The path to Dover passes South Foreland lighthouse on the seaward side. The lighthouse's days of guiding mariners through the Strait and away from the ships' graveyard of the Goodwin Sands are long gone. It is now heritage, and very neat and white and National Trust. A little way on, the bastions of Dover Castle showed above the skyline. I met a couple from Folkestone who said they often came to walk this way. 'It's the sense of freedom you get up here on the cliffs,' the wife said. 'And of being so close to France and Paris,' he added.

He was right. The French coast is as close here as it gets, although I never saw it.

Dover port

The cliffs extend to the eastern limit of the port, so that Dover and its main business are revealed suddenly and completely. Announcements of the ferry departure and arrival times in French and English float melodiously above the ceaseless dissonant grinding and hissing of gears and brakes and roaring of diesel engines as the mighty movers of goods manoeuvre themselves around the approaches to the ferries. The roads in and out, the A2 and the A20, make no concessions to gracious living. Their function is to shift heavy traffic as quickly as possible, and the buildings near them shake and reverberate with the sound and fury of forty-ton loads.

As the main Channel port, Dover does not need another role. During the nineteenth century it had pretensions to become a resort, and built an array of gleaming hotels and terraces and crescents of stuccoed mansions with balconies framed by ornate ironwork. Dickens stayed in a house in Camden

Crescent, just back from the seafront, for three months in 1852 to work on *Bleak House*. He found Dover 'not quite to my taste, being too bandy (I mean too musical, no reference to its legs) and infinitely too genteel ... but the sea is very fine and the walks very remarkable.'

Victorian Dover was badly knocked about by German bombs and shells between 1940 and 1944. The work of further wrecking the town has been actively pursued by planners and developers ever since. In the 1950s the prime position on the seafront was filled by a huge slab of flats known as the Gateway. At the time it was considered rather daring and contemporary – Pevsner talked of it presenting 'a bold face to the sea' – but the passing of time has not been kind to it and the sheer size of the dingy brown façade with its clutter of balconies overwhelms everything around.

Schemes to clear up the muddle of the town centre have come and gone. Some did not get beyond the drawing board. Others – such as the one involving the building of the famously hideous and now derelict Burlington House office block in the 1960s – were partially realised, then abandoned once their awfulness became apparent. In the 1990s the council proudly opened an audio-visual extravaganza called the White Cliffs Experience to show that Dover could attract more than truckers and passing continental holidaymakers. It flopped and was turned into the Dover Discovery Centre, which squats unappealingly but at least usefully beside the London road.

Wholesale redevelopment is now promised again, although seasoned observers and cynics are not holding their breath. Meanwhile a grandiose plan for the western fringes of the town, to include 500 houses, a 'retirement village', a conference hall and the inevitable heritage centre, has been waved through by the government despite howls of outrage from conservation bodies including the National Trust and Natural England. The council leader wittered something about the transformation of fields into a housing estate 'unlocking the economic potential of our heritage assets', words which should strike a chill into Dovorian hearts.

Looking out from a plinth in front of the Gateway flats is a bust of the man who first swam the narrow divide with France. Matthew Webb, his body daubed with porpoise fat, reached Calais on 25 August 1875 to be welcomed with a rendition of 'Rule Britannia' from the crew of the Royal Mail's packet service, which happened to be leaving harbour at the same time. He had been in the water for almost twenty-two hours and because of the tides and currents had covered thirty-nine miles, almost twice the actual distance. In the process Webb became a national hero and instituted a classic of endurance that has drawn legions of swimmers from all over the world ever since.

Poor Webb! He was a hero, but also an early victim of what we now know as the cult of celebrity. In the first few months after his conquest of the Channel a testimonial fund raised £2500 for him, and he toured the country to describe his exploits in his rolling Shropshire accent. But, as the invitations dried up and the money began to run out, he realised that he was defined by his swim and that alone, so swim he must. He embarked upon a programme of races and endurance challenges which put his physique under severe strain. After one challenge he coughed blood, and his brother, a doctor, warned him that he was asking too much of his body. Webb's response was to announce that he would swim the rapids and whirlpools below Niagara Falls. A friend told him he would not come back alive. 'Don't care,' Webb replied. 'I want money and I must have it.'

He lasted nine minutes before being dragged down for the last time. His shattered body, identified by a blue anchor tattooed on his right arm, was recovered eight miles downstream. He had a gash to the top of his head that had penetrated to his brain.

It is no coincidence that of the more than 1300 swimmers from around the world to have crossed the Channel, a bare half-dozen have been French. Their lack of enthusiasm for following in Webb's powerful breast strokes is symptomatic of a wider indifference. To us it is the English Channel, to them it is merely La Manche, The Sleeve. French writers have hardly bothered with it as an entity. The nineteenth-century historian Jules Michelet – a fierce critic of all things Anglo-Saxon – said he was saddened that 'this expanse of freedom' should belong to another nation, but he did not dispute the claim.

This French complaisance is understandable. England may be the ancient enemy, but France's borders are open to armies and influences from all directions. Historically the first duty of England's rulers and the first priority of England's security strategy has been to keep watch and hold sway over the Channel, whereas France's enemies have come from every point of the compass.

Geological accident also contributed significantly to England's primacy. The Pleistocene upheaval that separated Britain from continental Europe left the southern coast of England with a succession of deeply indented inlets and flooded estuaries to serve as anchorages for warships. In contrast the French Channel coast had no deep-water sanctuaries from the storms and the fierce currents that swirled around the offshore reefs. During the Napoleonic Wars Britain had Portsmouth and Falmouth from which to launch and supply its navy. The French had only Brest, outside the Channel and comparatively simple to blockade.

Most of the decisive events in our external history have involved the Channel in one key way or another. Julius Caesar crossed it to threaten invasion, and the army of Claudius to effect it. The monk Augustine came through the Strait of Dover to bring Christianity to Kent. Duke William of Normandy sailed from Barfleur in the late summer of 1066 to make landing near Hastings. Edward III, his son the Black Prince and Henry V all led their armies the other way en route to their great victories at Crécy, Poitiers and Agincourt. The Armada sailed up the Channel in 1588, the first act in England's salvation and Spain's catastrophe. Charles II arrived in Dover in 1660 to claim his crown. Twenty-eight years later William of Orange brought his fleet into Brixham in Devon to depose James II and ensure England remained Protestant. In 1805, with his armies massed at Boulogne, Napoleon ordered Admiral Villeneuve to leave Cádiz to make the Channel safe for the invasion – Villeneuve got as far as Trafalgar. In 1940 Hitler ordered the Luftwaffe to clear the skies over the Channel and bomb the Channel ports in preparation for Operation Sea Lion, the invasion of Britain. Four years later those Channel ports dispatched the D-Day invasion forces to liberate Europe.

These crises all contributed to shaping the nation and our awareness of who we are. They have also cemented the place of the Channel in that awareness as both our principal defence against our enemies and the visible symbol of our separateness from Europe. The novelist William Golding detected what he called 'a hard core of reserve' in our attitude to crossing that divide. 'The waters of the Channel have run for too many years in our blood,' he wrote.

But our apprehension is subtly various. Throughout our history the Channel has been both bulwark and transport route. When the occasion has demanded, we have generally been able to turn it into a formidable defence. Yet our rulers and their armies and navies have come and gone across it, as have our traders. For the great majority of the past two thousand years the Channel has been far more important as our connection with mainland Europe, enabling us to do business, conduct diplomacy, export and absorb cultural and philosophical influences.

Our conception of the Channel is not one thing or the other, but a composite derived from multiple roles. The defence role is now defunct – no invader need ever cross the Channel again. Nevertheless, and despite the Tunnel, it continues to define and stand for our detachment from our neighbours. Travelling overland in mainland Europe, it is now extremely easy to overlook borders. It is not so easy to miss Portsmouth Harbour or the Dover cliffs.

2

A MERE DITCH

Dover Castle

Dover is flanked by two mighty defence installations, neither of
which has ever played any useful active role in defending the
realm. To the east is Dover Castle, the biggest in the country,
which has stood for 800 years. Facing it across the town is the
Western Heights, a labyrinth of redoubts, gun emplacements,

underground shafts and chambers and magazines excavated and constructed to resist Bonaparte's invasion.

In days long past, poor people – the lighter the better – descended the cliffs below Dover Castle to collect the fleshy green leaves of rock samphire. Pickled, it was highly regarded in a salad; the seventeenth-century diarist John Evelyn recommended soaking the leaves in brine before bottling – 'then it will keep very green' he wrote.

Rock samphire, *Crithmum maritimum*, grows in the fissures of chalk cliffs. It should not be confused with sea or marsh samphire, which belongs to a wholly different family of plants and is used these days as a fancy accompaniment to fish. Shakespeare was familiar with the hazardous business of collecting it; a late scene in *King Lear* is set in 'the country near Dover' in which Edgar leads the blinded Gloucester close to the cliff edge where 'halfway down / hangs one that gathers samphire – dreadful trade!'

The dreadful trade died out in the nineteenth century. But a ghostly echo has been deployed for heritage purposes at Samphire Hoe, a country park created halfway between Dover and Folkestone from the chalky earth excavated by the Channel tunnellers. I cycled down to it quite by accident, thinking I was on the path to Folkestone. It has all the usual features – nature trail, cycleway, sea-wall path, hides for looking at birds, wheelchair ramps, visitor centre, café – and a squad of well-intentioned volunteers ready to steer you in the direction of the nesting sites of stonechats or the haunts of peregrine falcons or the meadowland where the shy spider orchid raises its curiously shaped brown head. I suspect that, were you to attempt to climb in search of samphire with a knife in your hand, you would be detained and reminded that conservation rather than consumption is the current orthodoxy.

I had a rest on a seat outside Folkestone's parish church, dedicated to St Mary and St Eanswythe, a virtuous Kentish nun. I intended, once I got my strength back, to go inside and inspect the wealth of memorials. There is one to Folkestone's most famous son, William Harvey, who first described the circulation of blood. I liked the sound of another, by the Reverend John Langhorne in memory of his brother, with these affecting lines: 'If life has taught me aught that asks a sigh / 'tis but like thee to live, like thee to die.'

However, the door was locked and there was nothing to say where a key might be obtained. There was a notice announcing that the 8 a.m. Holy Communion had been 'discontinued until further notice'. The roof of the aisle was hidden by scaffolding and sheets of plastic, behind which a pair of workmen applied hammers and nails. Two cider drunks were showering each other with abuse and spittle in one part of the churchyard. Multiple deposits of dog shit compounded the general air of abandonment.

A tour of Folkestone's much-publicised Creative Quarter did little to lift the spirits. The transformation of the heart of old Folkestone into an enclave of bright, trendy boutiques and bars and galleries began a decade ago, and has often been held up as a shining example of how small-scale, grass-roots initiatives can spark a renewal of commercially moribund seaside communities. It was applauded and rightly so, but the limitations of the model were plain to see, with at least a quarter of the shops empty or about to be empty, and customers sparsely distributed along the cobbled streets.

Folkestone Harbour

In September 2000 Folkestone ceased to be a cross-Channel port. The opening of the Tunnel and the concentration of ferry services on Dover dealt the town a blow from which it has not yet recovered. The impact is most evident in the wasteland that has spread to the west of the old terminal. This stretch of seafront, in front of the vast Grand Burstin Hotel, used to be filled by the garish and cheerful Rotunda fun park, complete with boating pool, rollercoaster, dodgems, amusement park and Castle Dracula – all now swept away as if they had never been. The hotel is left, with its 481 en-suite bedrooms and an impressive collection of scathing TripAdvisor comments. Across the road are derelict buildings, a skatepark rich in graffiti and wide, empty spaces of cracked concrete, with the grey shingle, the black breakwaters and the grey sea beyond.

The chant from those who care about Folkestone is regeneration. There is a plan, naturally. There is always a plan, sometimes even a Masterplan. Norman Foster presented a Masterplan for Folkestone's decayed seafront some years ago. It envisaged a marina, a university campus, 1400 homes, a revived ferry connection with France, even a lighthouse, plus the usual hotels/restaurants/leisure-and-conference facilities. It perished; a victim of the recession, it was said.

It has been replaced by another plan, not a Masterplan this time, the work of Sir Terry Farrell. His vision concentrates on housing – beach houses nearest the sea, so-called 'dune' houses behind, mews houses behind them, town houses at the back, flats to one side – with the retail and visitor attraction stuff woven in and around. The local MP, Damian Collins, called it 'very exciting', adding perceptively, 'Rome was not built in a day and nor will this be.'

The spectacle of seaside towns grappling with the future tends to be a discomfiting one. The sequence is familiar: a decline in tourist trade matched by a decline in other local employment; mounting social problems of health, crime and deprivation; neglect of long-standing and well-loved buildings and landmarks in favour of rubbishy hotels and gimcrack leisure centres; the development of hideous and badly constructed shopping malls. The common feature is a childish faith in 'the big project', the Masterplan, a vast and colossally expensive vision of destruction and rebuilding offered on a take-it-or-leave-it basis by a shadowy alliance of investors with an eye on congratulatory media coverage and a heady rate of return.

It was not always thus. In 1920 a government inspector was sent to Folkestone to conduct a public inquiry into the council's proposal to borrow £10,000 to finance a facelift for its prime seafront asset, the clifftop park known as The Leas. The plan included building a zigzag path down to the beach, the replacement of seats, strengthening the cliff face and planting many shrubs and plants. The Mayor told the gathering that failure to act would enable other resorts to get ahead of Folkestone. But there were dissenting voices. A clergyman said the shrubs would not survive the gales. A Captain Wilson said that he spoke as an Irishman whose property in Ireland had gone to pieces, and now his rates were to be used to pay for fanciful and unnecessary extravagances.

The inspector approved the plan, and although the cost rose to £13,000, there were few in Folkestone who dared complain when, seven years later, George V's third son, Prince Henry, opened the majestic Leas Cliff Hall. There was immense civic pride, and unanimous agreement with the words delivered by the Prince: 'Municipal spirit and local patriotism are praiseworthy and beneficent things when they are directed to the care of a town which seems to be the model and example of what a seaside town should be.'

The doyen of seaside historians, Professor John Walton, has provided a characteristically astute analysis of what has gone wrong in a handbook called *Coastal Regeneration in English Resorts*. Walton points out that the period between 1870 and 1939 saw local municipal government at its strongest and most self-confident, nourishing proud traditions of public service and local expertise. The role of councils was well-understood: to promote a vigorous, locally owned and run private sector, backed by first-rate public services.

The rot set in post-war, with the pursuit by successive national governments of a campaign to erode local independence and extend and strengthen central control. Walton accepts that this process cannot be reversed. But he sees at least a partial reassertion of local autonomy and civic pride as the key to success in bringing downtrodden seaside towns back to life. However, local leaders need to learn some difficult lessons. Regeneration should not mean bulldozing what is left from the past to replace it with something different, but reviving and revitalising what Walton calls 'identities', which are treasured and recognised and capable of creating employment.

Walton emphasises a truth that should be obvious, but has often been lost in the fog of panic and unreal expectation: that there is no point in losing genuinely distinctive and notable buildings if you have nothing better to put in their place. Local authority leaders need to resist the lure of the big project, sold to them with the promise of solving all problems at a stroke. At the same time they need to rid themselves of the desire to leave some kind of mark on the communities they serve, and the hunger for favourable media coverage. They should look after existing residents and regular visitors, including those of pensionable age often overlooked in the past but now an increasingly important economic and social force, and give them priority over the pursuit of seductive but often imaginary new markets.

Folkestone would do well to heed Professor Walton's wisdom.

Sandgate

The town is badly let down by the seafront, but up behind The Leas are leafy avenues and crescents that retain a certain elegance and air of comfortable living. They merge imperceptibly into Sandgate, so I wasn't aware of having left one for the other until I noticed several front windows displaying a sticker: 'Sandgate says No to Unrestricted Development'. I met an elderly, white-haired man striding vigorously along the pavement and asked him if Sandgate took a dim view of speculative developers. Very, he answered. So you come down on them like a ton of bricks? I ventured. Harder, he said, smiling.

Sandgate has been a favoured seaside resort for a long time. The *Kentish Gazette* reported in 1809 that 'the lodgings are full ... Purdey's Library, recently fitted up with an elegant reading-room, has become very fashionable ... The balls at Strood's Rooms, which are every fortnight, have been fully attended . . . the sea-bathing is of the greatest perfection.' A visitor in the same year said 'it has an air of neatness which cannot be exceeded.' Sandgate is still distinctly neat and clean, with a fine esplanade for taking a stroll. The sea looked grey and unappetising to me, but my acquaintance said his wife swam often. I asked him what he liked about the place. 'I like the space of the sea,' he said. 'With the land so steep behind, you need the openness in front.'

It is agreeable to note that intensely respectable Sandgate's most notable resident was the extremely unrespectable H. G. Wells. He came to live there with his wife Jane in 1898, first renting a cottage directly on the beach, then a semi-detached villa in Castle Road, and finally moving into Spade House, a splendid example of English vernacular style with massive chimneys, steep slate roof, broad eaves and sloping buttresses designed for him by Charles Voysey. By 1903 Jane had given birth to two sons, after which – according to Wells – sexual activity between them ceased.

'I have never been able to discover,' he mused much later, 'if my interest in sex is more than normal.' It was certainly keen. During the building of Spade House Wells had affairs with the writer Violet Hunt and with Rosamund Nesbit, officially the daughter of the children's writer E. Nesbit although in fact born to the family governess. Many other liaisons followed, including one with the exponent of 'stream of consciousness' fiction, Dorothy Richardson, whose 'interestingly hairy body' Wells recalled with more affection than 'her vein of evasive, ego-centred mysticism.'

Sandgate was evidently good for Wells' creative juices. He is hardly read today, but in his time he was the best-known popular novelist in the land, and several of his tales – including *Love and Mr Lewisham*, *The History of Mr Polly* and *Kipps* – were partially or wholly written within sight and sound of the Channel. It was Wells' notorious affair with the Fabian feminist Amber Reeves – 'a great storm of intensely physical sexual passion and desire', he recalled with relish – that precipitated his move from Sandgate to Hampstead. He never came back, and Spade House has for some years fulfilled a more sedate and suitable role as a nursing home.

In addition to other outlets for his energies, H. G. Wells was a keen cyclist. He would write in the morning and pedal off in the afternoon to explore the Kent countryside and drop in on one or other of his literary friends who lived within striking distance – among them Ford Madox Ford, Joseph Conrad and Henry James. Wells sometimes inserted cycling scenes into his fiction – a key scene in *Kipps* has the hero being rammed at a junction in Folkestone by another cyclist in knickerbockers whose intervention changes the course of his life.

Zooming down the hill from Spade House, I felt an affinity with Wells, and made a kind of promise, not yet fulfilled, to have a crack at him. On the esplanade I came upon a memorial bust of Sir John Moore, the hero of Corunna and the subject of what Byron considered one of the finest odes in the English language:

Not a drum was heard, not a funeral note,
As his corse to the rampart we hurried;
Not a soldier discharged his farewell shot
O'er the grave where our hero we buried.

We buried him darkly at dead of night
The sods with our bayonets turning,
By the struggling moonbeam's misty light,
And the lanthorn dimly burning.

It is stirring stuff, written by a young Irish clergyman, Thomas Wolfe, in the finest tradition of celebrating military fiascos in heroic stanzas. Moore was fatally wounded by a cannonball as his army sought to escape by sea from the port of Corunna after a desperate retreat across the mountains of northern Spain in the winter of 1809. He lived long enough, his ribs, left arm, breast and shoulder all shattered, to be told that the bulk of his men had managed to get away safely.

Seven years earlier Moore had been given command of the newly built army training camp at Shorncliffe Redoubt, on the high ground above Sandgate. From outside his tent Moore was able to look across at Boulogne and see the fires of the 120,000-strong invasion force assembled by Napoleon. Bonaparte himself stalked the opposing clifftop, telescope in hand: 'I have seen the English coast as clearly as one sees the Calvary from the Tuileries,' he stated. 'It is a ditch which will be leaped whenever one has the boldness to try.'

It is not recorded what Sir John Moore had to say as he stared across from the other side; being a Scot by birth, probably not much. Understatement was the British way. 'My lords, I do not say that the French cannot come,' Lord St Vincent, commander of the Channel fleet, famously reported to the Admiralty. 'I only say that they cannot come by sea.' Napoleon had two thousand transports ready, but no warships to protect them. In July 1805 he ordered the Grand Army to prepare to invade, and sent word to Admiral Villeneuve in Cádiz: 'Sail, do not lose a moment . . . England is ours . . . we will avenge six centuries of insults and shame.' A month later the Emperor addressed his men: 'Brave soldiers, you are not going to England. The Emperor of Austria, bribed with English gold, has declared war on France. New laurels await beyond the Rhine.'

* * *

Hythe is at least as respectable as Sandgate, possibly more so. Its wavy old High Street is lined by unimpeachably genteel shops, so that the appearance of an Iceland food store comes as a shock, as if one had stumbled on a knocking-shop. I came across no deposits of dog shit at all, a sure indicator of a community with the highest standards of behaviour.

Having left my rucksack with my very respectable landlady, I took the cycle path along the Royal Military Canal to West Hythe. As one would expect, it is a very well-behaved path, keeping company beneath the shade of willows and alders with the still, brown, duck-infested water.

It is curious to think that it and all the pleasant land around, with its villages and hamlets, was covered by the sea within the era of modern history – say, when Henry went off to thrash the French at Agincourt. At West Hythe the ruins of St Mary's Church stand beside what is now a quiet country lane just north of the canal. It is five miles from the sea. Yet it used to stand on the edge of the harbour serving the port of Hythe, one of the original Cinque Ports given charters under Henry II and his son, King John, to trade and defend the realm.

Of the original five, only Dover and Hastings are still by the sea. The others – Hythe, Romney and Sandwich – have against their will retreated well inland, as have the so-called 'Antient Towns' of Rye and Winchelsea that were appointed to support the original Cinque Ports. At the time of Julius Caesar's landing, the sea probably reached what is now a line of hills that stretches in a sweeping inland curve between Hythe and Hastings. But it was a very shallow sea, and the relentless depositing of silt by one sluggish river after another combined with the accumulation of sand and shingle pushed east by the prevailing winds eventually repelled the sea and turned the bay into a marsh, and later – assisted by artificial drainage – into a dry and fertile strip of land.

The process was disputed by the ports, which depended on their sea trade. Romney, Hythe, Rye and Winchelsea all made strenuous, expensive and unavailing efforts to keep their harbours open. The last to give up the struggle was Rye, which as late as the 1760s was still striving to divert the flow of the river Rother away from its harbour. Long before that, however – certainly by the time Elizabeth I came to the throne in 1558 – the Cinque Ports had ceased to perform any useful service to the Crown. The once-important post of Lord Warden became purely honorary, and in 1828 the salary that went with it was withdrawn. But there were still perks, among them the use of the official residence, Walmer Castle.

It is alleged that another was a *droit du seigneur* – also known in French as a *droit de jambage* or 'right of the leg' – over the daughters of the keepers of lighthouses along the stretch of coast once controlled by the Ports. It is further alleged that this right was exercised by Winston Churchill, who was Lord

Warden between 1941 and his death in 1965, and that this accounted for the unusual incidence of Churchill lookalikes along the south coast. When I say 'it is alleged', I have to admit that the source of these allegations is my eldest brother, a notable storehouse of arcane facts. When challenged he insisted that he had read about it many years ago in the correspondence pages of the *Guardian* but could be no more precise than that. I have spent many hours scouring histories of the Cinque Ports detailing the privileges and duties of the Lord Warden, and I have not come across a shred of evidence to support my brother's contention, which I am reluctantly forced to conclude is not true.

* * *

In May 1804 William Pitt was restored as Prime Minister of a Britain convulsed with fear of a French invasion. The Duke of York, the vocal if not exactly battle-hardened commander-in-chief of British forces, pressed for a defensive system to thwart the Grand Army. In September of that year Pitt ordered the construction of what became known as the Martello Towers at intervals of six hundred yards along the stretch of coast closest to France.

At the same time serious consideration was given to a proposal to flood the whole of Romney Marsh to block a French advance. Pitt agreed with the Duke that this would be impracticable, but that security would be enhanced by constructing a canal sixty feet wide and nine feet deep to run in a loop twenty-eight miles long from just west of Folkestone to just east of Hastings.

That October Pitt himself addressed a meeting of Romney

Marsh landowners. He convinced them that even if the nightmare of invasion never came to pass, the canal would improve drainage, alleviate floods and provide irrigation, thereby enhancing the yield and value of their land. After a slow start, the canal was dug as far as Rye by 1806 and completed three years later. The seventy-four Martello Towers along the eastern Channel were built over roughly the same period, by the end of which the danger of the French army arriving on our shores had receded out of sight. Neither the towers nor the canal ever served any military role and the combined cost of one-and-a-half million pounds – a huge slice of the defence budget – caused them to be much mocked. The social reformer and fierce radical William Cobbett called the towers 'ridiculous . . . a monument to the wisdom of Pitt', and was far from alone in wondering 'how the French who had so often crossed the Rhine and the Danube were to be kept back by a canal thirty feet wide at the most.'

But the farmers were happy. The canal and its attendant network of cuts, ditches and sluices kept the saltwater from surging inland when storms coincided with high tides, and retained the freshwater when needed to serve the stock and crops. Until 1939 sheep predominated on the Marsh, but during the Second World War the transformation to arable was effected and these days less than a tenth is pasture. The Royal Military Canal has become a precious leisure and heritage asset. It accommodates all manner of healthy pastimes – cycling, fishing, canoeing, bird-watching – and is fitted out with dinky footbridges and picnic sites and weatherproof panels conveying interesting historical titbits.

As for the Martello Towers, those squat, ugly, brown relics, some have been cleared away after falling into disrepair. But many survive – why would they not, with cannon-proof walls ten feet thick? A few have been converted into private houses; the rest stand as reminders of that unimaginably remote time when invasion talk panicked the nation.

3

DUNGIE

Dymchurch

One of the key control points for the Romney Marsh drainage system is the sluice on the sea wall between Hythe and Dymchurch. Guarded by the Dymchurch Redoubt, which was built at the same time as the Martello Towers, it is a cheerless spot on a murky morning with the breeze coming off a leaden sea.

Immediately to the east is the Hythe Firing Range, where generations of infantry soldiers have been taught how to shoot straight. It and its beach are generally forbidden territory for the public at large, although at the weekend the red warning flags are sometimes lowered and people can trudge along the shingle foreshore.

Further east still is Hythe Beach, where the famously peculiar Lord Rokeby was accustomed to bathe. I think even Lord Rokeby would have thought twice about taking a dip on the morning I passed through. It was high tide, and the sea was lapping hungrily at the blocks of Norwegian granite piled along the wall. I met two Bulgarian women huddled in thick coats against the wind. They were staying with their children at the New Beach holiday park, one of two spread across the flat land behind. 'The pictures showed sand,' one of them wailed. 'Where is sand?' I said they would have to wait a few hours until the tide went out. 'It is so cold,' she said, smiling bravely. They had come in April instead of May because a caravan sleeping six cost £180 for the week instead of £400.

A week behind the Dymchurch sea wall in April? I wished them luck and pedalled on. The wall is not a thing of beauty but it makes a satisfactorily flat and firm cycleway, as well as protecting the holiday parks from sea invasion.

Halfway to Dymchurch I saw an angler on the shingle in the lee of his umbrella. He fished most days, he told me, and ate fish every day. You look well on it, I said. I'm seventy-three, he said, inviting congratulation. He'd had a flounder and a couple of dogfish the day before and now had hopes of a bass, with the wind shifting into the west and warming the water. He asked me where I was heading. When I told him he nodded encouragingly. Yeah,

Dungie, he said, good spots for bass at Dungie if you knew your way around. And fish-and-chips. He advised me to go to the Pilot. Best fish-and-chips around.

The most handsome house in Dymchurch − not a fierce competition − is the one used for holidays by E. Nesbit. The household, outwardly highly proper in the Edwardian way, seethed with hidden currents and passions. It comprised Edith Nesbit, by then an acclaimed writer of stories for children, her husband Hubert Bland, several children and a governess. H. G. Wells, a frequent visitor, observed of Bland that he 'presented himself as a Tory . . . he was publicly emphatic for social decorum, punctilio, the natural dependence of women and the purity of the family.' In reality he was, like Wells, an irrepressible philanderer, and two of the children were his by the governess, including Rosamund, whom Wells seduced.

Among other visitors were a brother and sister, Russell and Sybil Thorndike. They came with their mother, who liked Dymchurch so much she bought a pair of coastguard cottages on the sea. They both became actors, but Russell was eclipsed in fame by his sister, and anyway much preferred writing stories. He loved the village and set a series of popular adventure stories in and around Dymchurch and the marsh behind. His hero was Doctor Syn, a clergyman who somewhat loses his moral bearings when his wife goes off with his best friend, and takes to a life of smuggling and general derring-do.

The first adventure, *Doctor Syn: a Tale of the Romney Marsh*, appeared in 1915 and ended with the hero's death, harpooned through the neck by a mute mulatto. Twenty years later, his acting career in abeyance, Russell Thorndike returned to the errant cleric and provided him with an incident-packed earlier life spread over six more tales. Bestsellers in their day, they have long since gone the way of other swashbuckling literature in the Scarlet Pimpernel genre. But the character is still celebrated every other year in Dymchurch's Day of Syn when villagers dress up in eighteenth-century costume to re-enact skirmishes between smugglers and revenue men and parade to the church for evensong and a good old-fashioned sermon.

Present-day Dymchurch's attractions include a small amusement park, a storm-battered Martello Tower with a glass-covered viewing platform and the beach below the concrete wall. On that basis it advertises itself as a Children's Paradise, which might be pushing it. The wall continues as far as Littlestone, where I had to divert onto the A259 coast road, which passes an interminable line of bungalows and villas comprising the seaward side of Littlestone, Greatstone and Lydd-on-Sea, all indistinguishable one from another. Ahead is Dungeness, the skyline ruled by the brooding bulk of its famous power stations.

There is a disused gravel pit behind the strip settlement of Greatstone where you can, with considerable difficulty, inspect one of the more curious relics of the coastal defence system patched together in the years before 1939. Sound mirrors, otherwise known as acoustic defences or Listening Ears, were the brainchild of a now-forgotten pioneer in the science of sound waves, William Sansome Tucker. While stationed in Belgium during the 1914–18 war, Tucker noticed that the report of an artillery shell being fired at a distance was followed by a draught of cold air being expelled from a mousehole near his bed. He experimented with a device which registered the pressure waves from artillery fire on a platinum wire stretched across a hole.

Dungie

From this he developed a microphone able to fix the position of enemy guns and determine how big they were and in which direction they were aimed.

Listening Ears

After the war Tucker was appointed Director of Acoustical Research at RAF Biggin Hill, where he worked on designing and building concave concrete walls fitted with microphones to detect enemy aircraft approaching over the Channel. These grew from a modest twenty feet in width to the monster 200-feet wall at Greatstone, which was backed up by two circular dishes supported on concrete standings. The Greatstone Listening Ear was in position by 1929. It worked, up to a point, but the operatives experienced difficulty in distinguishing between the sound waves created by aircraft and those of ships, or indeed road traffic.

While Tucker wrestled with these problems, investigations of a different kind were being carried out at the Radio Research Station at Ditton Park near Slough. These culminated in 1935 in a memorandum to the government from the station's director, Robert Watson-Watt, entitled 'Detection and Location of Enemy Aircraft by Radio Methods'. Radar was born, and at a stroke Doctor Tucker's sound mirrors were redundant. His plea for the two systems to be combined, with a chain of massive mirrors at sixteen-mile intervals from Norfolk to Dorset, was dismissed. The order was given for the existing sound mirrors to be destroyed, but through bureaucratic inertia they survived. Several still stand, mute and massive, their concrete stained and crumbling, like monuments built by some ancient civilisation for purposes lost in time.

It is a strange place, Dungeness, not like anywhere else. It is triangular, shaped rather like the blade of a turfing spade, with its sharp end thrust out into the Channel. Its position means that it acts as a trap for the shingle shifted east along the shore by the prevailing wind-driven movement of water. The result is that the nose of the Ness, built up by the recruitment of shingle, is inclined to push ever further out. The south side of the triangle, immediately in front of the nuclear power stations, Dungeness B and the now-redundant Dungeness A, is exposed to the full force of the longshore drift and, if left to its own devices, rapidly erodes. For a long time it has been necessary to transfer enormous quantities of shingle from the eastern to the southern shore to save the power stations from being devoured by the sea.

The water is deep off the beach and the tidal currents are

swift. Big ships can come in close, but the low profile of the land can spell trouble when visibility is poor. There has been a succession of lighthouses, five in all. The most recent, black and white like a tubular liquorice sweet, was installed in 1961. In clear weather its light is visible twenty-five miles away.

Before and despite the lighthouses, Dungeness was a byword for danger among mariners. The most outrageous of the many disasters overtook a passenger ship, the *Northfleet*, on the night of 22 January 1873. With 400 passengers and crew bound for Hobart, Tasmania, she was at anchor two miles off the Ness when she was struck amidships on the starboard side by a steamship going at full speed. She immediately began to list and the watch frantically hailed the vessel that had rammed her, appealing for help. The steamer, subsequently identified as the *Murillo*, a Spanish cargo ship, backed off and sailed away into the darkness.

The *Northfleet* sank within an hour; only two of the seven lifeboats were successfully launched. Forty-three out of the 44 children on board, and 41 of the 42 women, were drowned. Altogether 291 people – most of them emigrants seeking a new life on the far side of the world – lost their lives. There was a huge fuss in Parliament, but the owners of the *Murillo* denied responsibility and in the absence of an extradition treaty between Britain and Spain there was little to be done. Eight months after the disaster, the *Murillo* was arrested off Dover, impounded and subsequently sold for £7500, the proceeds going to offset some of the insurance claims.

For many centuries this great, bare expanse of shingle ridges, scoured and scourged by the winds, was cut off from the outside world, inhabited by a few families of inbreds who lived in huts and scraped an existence from fishing and the detritus washed up on their shore. The arrival of two outside fishing clans – one from Cornwall, the other French in origin – began to change the Ness. The fishing, mainly for herring, became more organised. Permanent dwellings were built, low against the shingle, thick-walled to withstand the storms. In time the railway arrived, and with it employees of the Southeastern Railway Company. Some of them liked the wildness and remoteness of the place and acquired surplus train carriages and dragged them across the stones to a spot they fancied, and either lived there or came for holidays.

This democratic and spontaneous settlement pattern established the character of the Ness that endures, with inevitable modifications, today. The guiding principle is randomness. The hundred or so dwellings are scattered about as if they were toy houses thrown by a childish hand. There is no common architectural style. There are just cabins, shacks, chalets, call them what you will. A few of the original railway carriages survive, generally incorporated into expanded residences. Black is the predominant colour and rectangular box the predominant shape. But Dungeness allows for white and splashes of colour, expanses of untreated wood, curves and sharp angles, and the odd old-fashioned caravan.

Everything is open. There are no drives or fences or hedges or enclosing walls. The gardens – most famously the garden created by the film director and designer, Derek Jarman – have no secrets. Paradoxically – given the absence of visible boundaries between properties – freedom of movement for visitors is severely restricted. The place is peppered with signs declaring that this track or that, or this patch of shingle or that, is private, and warning of the risk to life and limb posed by winches and cables put on the beach to get boats in and out of the sea.

This fixation with privacy is combined, somewhat awkwardly, with the need to pull in as many visitors as possible to keep the local economy afloat. The lighthouses, the power stations, the terminus of the Romney and Hythe Steam Railway, the bird and plant life, the views and the general weirdness of the place make Dungeness a potent visitor attraction. Most of the cabins are second homes and/or holiday lets. Where once upon a time railway waggons changed hands for a tenner, the going price for a property in Dungeness these days is anything from £250,000 upwards.

The legacy of the fishing heritage is very visible along the shore. Rusted winches rise from the shingle. Drums of cable lie on their sides, frozen by rust, leaking red onto the stones. The shells and skeletons of old boats are framed against the sky. A tiny handful of working boats survive. I was cycling cautiously around trying to find someone prepared to talk to me about the place when I was hailed from a window by one of the skippers (I think he was also the chairman of the residents' association, although we did not get as far as exchanging names).

'Do you want something?'

'I'm writing a book about the Channel.' I tried to explain what it was supposed to be about, then asked him if he lived permanently at Dungeness.

'All my life.'

'Why here?'

'I'm a fisherman.'

'Are you still fishing?'

'Yes.'

'Commercially?'

(Pitying look) 'We're all commercial.'

'Have you been fishing recently?'

'This morning.'

'Any luck?'

'Four boxes of sole.'

'Dover sole?'

(More intense pitying look) 'Yes.'

'Where do they go?'

'France.'

The window shut, which I took to be a sign that the interview was over.

The ride from Dungeness to the nearest inland settlement, Lydd, is not scenic. The flat road cuts through Denge Beach, which is not a beach at all but a windswept wasteland of stones and scrub, and Denge Marsh, which stopped being a real marsh centuries ago.

Painters and writers used to rhapsodise about the magic of Romney Marsh and its coast. Paul Nash, who lived and painted at Dymchurch for a while, wrote of watching 'the eastern sky darken against the dyked flats . . . the strange unity of sea, sky and earth that grows unnoticed at this time and place.' Ford Madox Ford, who lived near Winchelsea for much of the decade between 1901 and 1910, urged those coming to the Marsh to leave maps behind, or risk losing the 'sense of magic'. Ford loved the 'brooding silence, an inconceivably self-centred abstraction', but even he found the south-east corner between Lydd and Dungeness 'the Marsh at its most desolate . . . almost soilless, nearly always parched and brown.'

I pedalled strenuously into an unremitting headwind past low banks and drifts of open shingle fringed by patches of scrub grass, gravel pits gouged and then left without any thought of landscaping and pallid fields grazed by a few sheep and horses in a manner suggesting they had been forgotten or abandoned until their natural terms expired. To the left, lines of pylons extended north from the power stations like skeletal robots on a secret and sinister mission. To the east an opposing army of wind turbines rotated their pale limbs in a slow, monotonous ballet.

The road back to the sea skirts the perimeter of Lydd Ranges, which occupy a wedge of foreland between Dungeness and Camber. Mile after mile of chain-link fencing surmounted by razor wire and frequent warnings to keep out, backed up by red flags, made for dreary cycling. I reflected that wherever the magic of Romney Marsh had once resided, and whatever its elements were, it had been thoroughly erased before I got there.

Magic of a different kind, uncelebrated in literature, is found by some at Camber Sands. On fine summer days, so I was told, the roads and car parks are clogged, and as many as 30,000 people disport themselves across a vast expanse of sand and frolic in the opaque, safe sea.

In the 1920s plotlanders started arriving at Camber dragging railway waggons, old buses and trams, caravans and shacks on trailers. They were searching for a different way of life, away from the smoke and noise of the city and the proximity of neighbours and strangers. They were ordinary people – shop-keepers, traders, small-time entrepreneurs, struggling artists – who simply wanted a place on the fringe to be free and left in peace. They paid £25 for a hundred feet of sand facing the sea, which was enough. There were no planning regulations then, no council planning departments. You could go where you wanted and, within reason, live as you liked.

The plotland movement took off in various parts of the country, inland and by the sea. The story of its short-lived flowering was told by Dennis Hardy and one of the founding fathers of the gentle, pastoral, English style of anarchism, Colin Ward, in their book *Arcadia For All*. They saw the plotlanders as innocent and unconscious anarchists, claiming a place on land that was unwanted and useless for agriculture and creating, through hard work and inventiveness, strong, organic communities held together by bonds of friendship and interdependence.

In 1947 the Town and Country Planning Act became law. It was the first systematic step towards imposing state control on what could be built where, and it killed off the plotland movement, as it was intended to do. But, as Hardy and Ward pointed out, the spirit behind it is immortal and continues to find occasional expression even in these regulation-stuffed, form-filled days. At Jury's Gap, a settlement just east of Camber, several of the bungalows along the road retain something of the plotland ethos. One, in pale-blue clapperboard and shaped like three sheds nailed together, had a verandah, in front of which an old chap was energetically strimming the grass. He told me he had moved there for one reason: it was cheap. 'Do you like my sea view?' he asked with a laugh, pointing at the sea defence between him and the Channel.

I hoisted my bike onto it and set off towards Camber. Yellow waves broke onto the distant sea edge. Beyond, kitesurfers were slicing through the breakers at incredible speed, sails taut against the gusting breeze. Every now and then one would take off altogether, turning and twisting in the air, then float down to the surface again.

Kitesurfing is banned at Camber Sands itself because of the danger of the wires slicing somebody's head off. At the café on the beach I had a bacon sandwich and a mug of tea. The bloke running it said he'd come to Camber for the fishing. He'd always planned to end up by the sea; on quiet days like this he spent a lot of time staring out from the windows, thinking of cod and bass. The scene always changes, he said, but it's always the same as well. 'You can never get tired of looking at the sea. Winter's best, and spring and autumn. Summer's for business.'

Steep dunes of yellow sand held together by marram grass and chestnut paling rear up between the beach and the road. I asked my friend in the café if any of the original railway carriages were still around. He pointed at the dunes. 'There's at least one buried in there,' he said.

A little further west, skirting Winchelsea Beach, I bumped into an old fairground man walking his dog. He and his family had once run the amusement park opposite the entrance to the caravan park. 'It did well in the seventies,' he reminisced. 'Then it went downhill, then it went through the floor.' It was the electronic age that did for it. Kids used to come to the park to play video games, then they got them on their home computers. 'Now it's all iPads.' He shook his head. 'Still, mustn't grumble. It's still a great place to live. You can't beat the sea air.'

4

CONCRETE KING

Warrior Square, Hastings

Considering its reputation as a premier seaside sinkhole, Hastings is a pleasant surprise. Its old town is quaint and full of charm. Its imposing seafront, in spite of various eyesores and aberrations, retains much of its stuccoed elegance, enough to recall the confidence and pride of its Victorian builders.

It has the swish and striking black-clad Jerwood Gallery, the distinctive black weatherboarded Net Shops, and a fishing fleet that, although drastically reduced from what it once was, still fishes and gives the town the flavour of having a working port. It has a splendidly shabby Gothic library, a treasure store of information about Hastings' long history. It has the Marine Court apartment block, which was built to look like a Cunard liner berthed on land, magnificently self-assured in its day although now getting somewhat scruffy. It even has a silver statue of a giant whelk.

Inevitably Hastings has its disfigurements. In the 1990s it gave up its fine old cricket ground in exchange for a dull shopping centre like every other dull shopping centre. Its pier – now being restored – has long been a wrecked, scorched, skeletal symbol of neglect. The arcade of shops below and to the front of the glorious Pelham Crescent has been permitted to sink into

Pelham Crescent, Hastings

a scandalous state of decay and tackiness, as has the extravagant pile, part renaissance palace, part French château, that is the former Palace Hotel, now Palace Court.

Successive generations of planners and their masters have much to answer for in Hastings as in other seaside towns. But sometimes you have to feel for them. In the case of Hastings the most intractable challenge in terms of crumbling infrastructure facing the local authority is the legacy of the man who did more than any other to restore – for a brief, golden period – the status that the town had enjoyed in the nineteenth century.

When Sidney Little was interviewed for the post of Hastings Borough Engineer in 1926, he told his prospective employers that he had walked around the town and found it shabby and decayed. What Hastings needed, he declared, was 'to be dragged into the twentieth century'. They took a leap of faith with Little, gave him the funds he needed and he repaid them amply.

He began by upgrading the sea defences and building a new pavilion for the bowling green. He had the tramways along the seafront ripped up and installed Britain's first underground car park. He completely rebuilt the seafront promenade on two levels. The covered lower walkway incorporated semicircular bastions with sliding glass windows to keep off the rain and the spray and a 500-seat heated sun lounge with a floor patterned in Jarrah. Set into the back wall were millions of fragments of smashed bottles of coloured glass that winked and glittered kaleidoscopically when the sun was reflected off the sea.

The cost of the seafront project was £150,000, perhaps £8 million today. At the same time Little was busy working his way through a further £100,000 on refurbishing and enlarging the

White Rock Swimming Baths, originally built as Turkish baths in the 1870s. This reopened in June 1931, complete with a blue-and-yellow bathers' deck, a two-tier viewing gallery for 400 people enclosed by a bronze ballustrade, and an entrance lit by two giant semi-circular copper-glazed windows. The main pool, tiled in white and green, was 165 feet long and 37 feet wide. A passage led to smaller chambers containing a foam pool and a saltwater pool with seaweed.

Little then turned his attention to the swimmers of St Leonard's, the well-bred western extension of Hastings. The St Leonard's outdoor pool was conceived and constructed on a heroic scale: 100 yards long, 30 wide, with a 10-metre high-diving board, terraces to seat 200 and space around for 2000 to sunbathe. In 1936 two more underground car parks were opened by the Transport Minister, Leslie Hore-Belisha, who told his audience that they 'celebrated the enterprise that has put Hastings in the forefront of all seaside towns.'

In retrospect it's easy to see that Sidney Little's ambitions for Hastings were out of proportion to its needs. During the war he was seconded to the MOD and helped develop the concrete Mulberry harbours used for the D-Day landings. In 1946 he returned to the south coast to take up the reins again. But everything had changed or was changing. Little drew up a plan to raze much of the town centre and replace it with a new one built – like his promenade – on two levels. It was rejected, as was a proposal to extend the promenade east and clear out the fishing port in favour of an amusement park.

Little retired in 1950. His day was done; so too – broadly speaking – was the age of big spending by seaside local author-ities on prestigious public works. It did not take long for changing times and habits and the sea to take their toll on Sidney Little's bequest to Hastings.

He was known as the Concrete King. Like many architects and other planners of his time, Little embraced reinforced concrete as the answer to all the twentieth century's building challenges. But the British seaside weather has a habit of searching out concrete's inherent flaw. Where the salt spray touches the steel implants, it corrodes. The rust eats into and degrades the concrete, which stains and over time cracks and crumbles. Preventing corrosion and keeping the concrete sound demand constant and expensive maintenance.

Much of Sidney Little's work in Hastings has been erased or just abandoned. The mighty St Leonard's pool was turned into a holiday camp, and eventually filled in and demolished. The sun lounge at the front of the promenade was torn down. The White Rock Baths are shut off and mouldering away. The glass

Hastings fishing boats

screens along the front of Bottle Alley have long gone and the ceiling is pitted with holes where the concrete has been devoured by damp. The pillars are flaky, spotted with brown, the floor slabs are cracked, wet, uneven.

For bad, if understandable, reasons, Hastings Council has consistently shied away from tackling any of this, preferring instead to hire consultants to draw up improbable schemes and hold extended public consultations on them. A choice example of this familiar species of dithering was the 2005 Hastings and Bexhill Seafront Strategy. This took the form of a lavishly illustrated publication stuffed with stale jargon of the 'nodes of activity ... multi-purpose function space ... area-wide action ... zones of change ... public realm improvements ... renewal initiatives ... design strategies' type.

Bottle Alley, for instance, was to be transformed (these people only ever think in terms of transformation, usually radical transformation) into 'a covered space' to be filled with studios, craft workshops, 'market-style accommodation', retail outlets, café. The spending envisaged by the authors of this futile document was comically divorced from reality. 'In all more than £35 million will be spent by 2013,' they warbled, but 2013 has come and gone and the wind still whistles around the pockmarked pillars on Bottle Alley.

The example of Hastings Pier should alert the town's leaders to the peril of continued inertia. Built in the 1870s to a design by Eugenius Birch, the prince of pier builders, Hastings Pier flourished for half a century, declined for half a century and was then left to rot until a fire in 2010 reduced it to a blackened shell. In that condition it seemed somehow to sum up and symbolise all Hastings' well-documented problems of social deprivation, unemployment, crap schools, vandalism, drug use, violence and so forth.

The pier's restoration has cheered the town up no end. True, the £14 million budget is not coming from the council but is being provided from lottery funding. But Hastings' leaders need to realise that unless the rebirth of the pier is followed by the salvation of what is salvageable from the Concrete King's legacy – certainly the promenade and Bottle Alley, possibly the White Rock Baths – a huge opportunity will have been lost, for which they will not be easily forgiven.

The signing of the Entente Cordiale between England and France in April 1904 signalled the formal end to 900 years of hostility and suspicion between the nations. But Hastings was ahead of the game; it had already concluded its own *entente*. As the site of the battle that delivered the England of old into French hands, Hastings led the way in putting ancient antagonisms to rest.

The initiative was organised by a prominent Hastings citizen, Edward Clarke, a passionate Francophile (the *Hastings and St Leonard's Observer* said of him that he spoke French as a native and English with a French accent). On a visit to Normandy Clarke had met a distinguished aristocrat, the Marquis de la Rochethulon et Grente, and got talking with him about Anglo-French relations, then going through a sticky patch because of colonial rivalries in North Africa. The Marquis was president of the Souvenir Normand, a high-minded body established to promote links with European peoples who, at one time or another, had come under Norman influence.

Clarke saw an opportunity to 'dispel by friendly discourse

the cloud that for several years has hovered over our relations with France.' The upshot was the arrival in Hastings in August 1903 of a delegation from the Souvenir Normand led by the Marquis de la Rochethulon and the Vicomte Jehan Soudan de Pierrefitte. The English could not match their visitors in nomenclature – the delegation was welcomed by Clarke and the Mayor, Alderman Tree. But in nobility of purpose they were well-matched.

The visit was extensively reported in the local press and secured coverage in the national newspapers. The main events were the inspection of the battlefield north-west of the town and the unveiling of a commemorative stone near the altar in the ruins of Hastings Abbey. That evening the guests were treated to a performance in the Abbot's Hall of a musical pageant especially composed by the Vicomte Soudan de Pierrefitte (described by the *Hastings and St Leonard's Weekly Mail and Times* as 'having the slight stoop and faraway look in the eyes that one generally associates with artists and poets').

Before returning to France, the visitors were given an extensive tour of Hastings itself, including the seafront. According to the *Mail and Times*, there was disapproval of the summer dresses on display, which some considered 'thin, insufficient and unsuitable'. Nevertheless cordiality persisted and the following year the newly formed Hastings branch of the Souvenir Normand were entertained in Rouen. In 1906 Hastings played host again, one of the highlights being a battle on the pier fought with confetti and what Edward Clarke called 'thorough heartiness and goodwill'.

I'm glad to say that the Hastings branch of the Souvenir Normand continues the pioneering work of Edward Clarke to this day. Exactly how it does so I'm afraid I cannot say, as the secretary was extremely guarded about its activities when I telephoned her. But it's heartening to know that Hastings still sets an example in promoting 'friendship and cordiality where once had festered mistrust and enmity'. It cannot be a coincidence that, since Alderman Tree and the Marquis clasped hands, we have never fought the French again. Edward Clarke was right when he looked forward to a time 'when chivalry will be more concerned with raising up than striking down, when Englishmen and Frenchmen will shake hands instead of fists, when the bayonet will be replaced by the branch and the apple blossom.'

* * *

Bexhill and the De La Warr Pavilion

There is a long, gentle slope into Bexhill from the east. The coast road runs through a wide stretch of closely mown grass abundantly provided with wooden benches placed in memory of departed Bexhillians and sat on by those destined to follow in due course.

Hastings has distinction and problems. Bexhill, in comparison, has few problems and no distinction – apart, that is, from its one glory and claim to attention, the extraordinary De La Warr Pavilion. I own to being something of a philistine about architecture – I can see the point without being stirred in my spirit – but even I was startled by the beauty and brilliance of Mendelsohn and Chermayeff's pleasure house.

Almost equally startling is its incongruity. The hope, when it was commissioned in 1933, was that it would light the way to a new Bexhill, and lift it from the mediocrity of what one critic called 'the rococo redness of that terrible town'. The Pavilion was to be complemented by a lido and a pier in a general aesthetic rebirth, but it did not happen. Eighty years on, the Pavilion is spiritually more isolated than ever, the mediocrity of its surroundings enhanced rather than diminished.

The people of Bexhill do not seem bothered. To judge from the letters page in the *Bexhill Observer*, affection for the town's only celebrated landmark is lukewarm at best, and there is an undercurrent of resentment over the £500,000-a-year support it gets from the council. Bexhill has long been something of a joke because of the large numbers of elderly people who choose to live there. They do so for sound reasons that have very little to do with the De La Warr Pavilion. They like the benches and the neat cream and crimson shelters, the silver painted railings, the smart beach huts, the easy walks, the air, the general spick-and-spanness, above all the feeling of safeness.

I met a couple who had retired to Bexhill from Cambridge, where he had spent forty-five years working for the gas board.

Weather permitting, they walked one-and-a-half miles along the seafront in one direction every day, and one-and-a-half miles back. 'You can never get bored by the sea,' she said, and the sea answered with a soft, percussive sigh. They had no opinions about the Pavilion but plenty on the subject of Hastings. 'We like it here because there's no trouble,' he said. 'Not like Hastings.' Trouble meant youths and teenage girls, and youths and teenage girls meant spitting, swearing, shouting, fighting and worse.

I talked to a lady of mature years who was sitting on a bench on the colonnade warming herself in the pale sunshine. She had come from Belfast in the 1980s. Why Bexhill? 'I love the Pavilion,' she said (so someone does). 'And the peace and the calm. After Belfast.'

Apart from the Pavilion there is not a lot of historical interest in Bexhill, if you discount the house where Eddie Izzard was brought up and the house in Station Road where the first genius of television, John Logie Baird, died in 1946. But there is a rather handsome railway station, built of red brick, with a canopy at the front and a cheerful pyramidal roof and lantern above. Inside is a waiting room with comfortable sofas and bookcases filled with romantic historical fiction and detective stories, which tells you something about Bexhill-on-Sea.

5

EMPRESS OF WATERING HOLES

Eastbourne Pier before the fire

'There is no more beautiful spot on the south coast than Eastbourne ... everywhere the eye is enchanted ... many of the busiest thoroughfares would console a Parisian *flâneur* for the loss of his beloved *boulevards*.' The eye in question, somewhat rosy, belonged to a Victorian journalist and dramatist, George

Robert Sims, who fell under the spell of the town as a school-boy there.

Eastbourne has survived changing times and fashions pretty well, and it would be a churlish soul who could not take pleasure in its handsome and handsomely looked-after seafront. In my view it has one major failing: its deplorable hostility towards bicycles and cyclists, who are banned from even a sliver of the wide esplanade and forced onto the pestilential main road.

I stayed a night in the Langham, the last of the substantial stuccoed hotels before the eastern end of the front gives way to red brick villas converted to guesthouses and B & Bs. The hotel was extremely well run, staffed by friendly and attentive Eastern Europeans, and alluringly priced (in February) at £37 for a bedroom with a view of the sea and breakfast. Being there set me thinking about hotel names and their mysterious resonances.

Eastbourne's grandest hotel is the Grand, which is so grand that 'gentlemen' must still wear a jacket and tie to have dinner there. 'Langham', I would suggest, is a middling kind of name. One does not expect the same degree of deep-carpeted class at the Langham as at the Grand; or indeed as at the Imperial, the Chatsworth, the Burlington or the Cumberland (none of which I have been inside). Why Cumberland should be classier than Alexandra I cannot say, but it is. No disrespect to the west coast of Scotland but the Oban cannot hope to aspire to the status of the Cavendish, nor the Heatherleigh to that of the Claremont.

The hotel with the most arresting name is the Big Sleep, which was once part-owned by the American actor John

Malkovich. This connection, worked on by imaginative journalism, gave rise to a rumour that he was thinking of becoming an Eastbourne resident. This in turn inspired the council's 'cabinet member for tourism' to urge that a Hollywood-style 'Welcome To Eastbourne' banner should be placed on the landward approach. Fortunately for Eastbourne, wiser counsels prevailed.

The Langham is owned and run by a dapper marathon-running fanatic, Neil Kirby. He came to Eastbourne from the Grosvenor in London, where he was general manager. Kirby put £3 million of his own and borrowed money into retrieving the Langham from ruinous decay. He and his wife had toiled night and day to turn it round, and they had won.

The secret of success, he told me, lay in pricing, investing and getting the right staff. Every once in a while he went across the road to study the Langham's façade and note down the signs of wear. Nothing puts prospective guests off more thoroughly than letters missing from the hotel's name and chunks of plaster from the stucco. Two-thirds of his rooms were occupied over the winter, he said; the Grand's occupancy over the same period was a third. He ran a ladies' lunch club, a jazz club, a pudding and wine club, lunchtime cabaret – anything within reason to bring locals in and make the place feel busy. When I was there they had a big group from a church in London, with an entertainer each night. The performer for that evening wandered through while I was chatting to Kirby, who broke off to remind him to eschew the blue when it came to the jokes.

Eastbourne fishing boats

In the morning I wandered east past the guesthouses and B & Bs. Most had 'No Vacancies' signs up, which made me think Eastbourne must be doing remarkably well for winter trade until I discovered that this was just a polite way of letting on that they were closed until spring.

At the shabby end of Royal Parade I came across Eastbourne's fishing fleet pulled up onto the shingle amid heaps of lobster and crab pots and netting, coils of rope, stacks of plastic and polystyrene fish boxes, rusted barrels, anchors and chains, winches and cable – all the proper paraphernalia of the business, properly jumbled up. On the road was the headquarters of Southern Head Fishing, where a million quid's worth of locally caught fish and shellfish changes hands each year.

I looked at the board outside. Dover sole, lemon sole, dabs, whiting, hake, brill, turbot, cod, plaice, scallops – it was a fish-eater's paradise, at prices to make the mouth water. Outside, three blokes were loading sacks of whelks onto a trailer. It was 9.30 in the morning and they had already returned from emptying 800 pots stuffed with this humble crustacean. I am a pretty keen consumer of shellfish, anything from lobster and crab down to clams and cockles and even the occasional winkle. But whelks? I've tried them and I can live without them – unlike the people of South Korea. This load was destined for sorting and freezing in King's Lynn, and shipment to Seoul.

That's a lot of whelks, I observed acutely. There's plenty out there, one of the blokes said. And cuttlefish, we're just starting on them. Plus the Dover sole and the rest of them. It was heartening to hear a story of marine abundance for a change.

Somehow wet fish and the smell of fish and the hard lives of fishermen seem not quite to fit the Eastbourne image, which perhaps is why the boats are kept out of sight. Eastbourne is about respectability and tidiness and restrained behaviour and taking your time. It has miles of smart blue railings, and equally smart cream and blue shelters at regular intervals. There are benches, hundreds of benches, possibly thousands of benches, arranged to give views of the sea and the massed ranks of petunias and begonias in the meticulously tended seafront beds and the lines of hebe and lavender and other decorous shrubs.

Eastbourne has its seafront, the most consistently tasteful of all seafronts. Its very handsome pier was severely damaged in a fire in July 2014, but – Eastbourne being Eastbourne – it will surely return to its former glory before too long. It has a

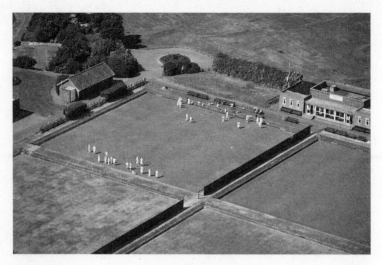

Bowls in Eastbourne

marvellous bandstand, domed in blue with a pillared colonnade. It has tennis, a lot of tennis and bowls, and county cricket. It has fine churches and many fine houses and remarkably few architectural horrors. It also has, in Camilla's Bookshop, one of the few old-fashioned secondhand bookshops left in the south of England, a warren of book-lined passages and chambers that celebrates – or perhaps it should be commemorates – the toil of an army of scribes.

Remarkably, the town has managed to remain faithful in the important respects to the principles of its founding fathers and patrons. The historian David Cannadine argued persuasively in his study *Lords and Landlords* that these were, in the main, pecuniary rather than philanthropic. The Cavendishes, who owned the land, needed the money from rents for the upkeep of Chatsworth and their other drainingly expensive estates. The motives of the Eastbourne worthies were also largely financial, but it was in the interests of both parties to obscure the real purpose of the contract between them, and portray it as an exercise in benevolence.

Whenever the 7th Duke of Devonshire appeared in Eastbourne – which was as infrequently and briefly as was consistent with his role there – the worthies made sure that the town abased itself before him. The opening by him of the new drainage system in 1867 inspired, in Cannadine's words, 'general rejoicing, with shops closed, streets decorated and a procession of townsfolk accompanied by the band of the Sussex 19th Rifle Corps.' An illuminated address was presented to the Duke expressing 'on behalf of the middle classes, tradesmen and inhabitants generally . . . our sincere admiration of those noble qualities which so pre-eminently distinguish Your Grace.' At the celebratory dinner, the Vicar of Eastbourne toasted 'our excellent patron, our genial saint of Eastbourne', words greeted with loud applause.

Deafening cheers, applause and expressions of undying gratitude greeted the Duke whenever he deigned to show his long-whiskered face, whether to launch the new lifeboat, open the pier or lay the foundation stone for Eastbourne College. His death in 1891 plunged Eastbourne's council leaders into a deep well of official grief. They passed a motion recording that it was to his 'liberality and forethought' that the town owed its pre-eminent position among seaside resorts. His generosity, public spirit and warm interest in the welfare of his tenants (rather than their rents) would long be remembered, the motion concluded.

The Eastbourne brand was clearly defined – 'this town is primarily one that appeals to the best social grades,' one of its many aldermen declared. The first priority of every council was the defence and promotion of the brand, and to that end they applied themselves unswervingly to the task of cleansing Eastbourne from anything that might smack of the vulgar or cheap. 'Niggers'[*sic*], blind men with begging bowls, beach performers, vendors of fruit, sweetmeats and ice-cream, hawkers, distributors of handbills and newspapers, barking dogs, pierrots, ventriloquists and phrenologists were all banned from the seafront; as were loud music, late-night motoring, picture palaces, sixpenny dinners and whelk stalls. A London newspaper that dared to criticise Eastbourne's profusion of bylaws was accused by the *Eastbourne Herald* of 'an ill-mannered attack on the Duke of Devonshire'.

In addition to respectability, rectitude and retirement, Eastbourne is or used to be notable for an abnormal concentration of boys' preparatory schools. Something in the air or the sea must have been deemed especially conducive to the training of young minds and bodies. The genteelness of the surroundings was a distinct asset. It meant that the pupils were unlikely to be troubled or set upon by rough lower-class lads; also that the masters were less exposed to the temptations of gambling or consorting with tarts.

Of these schools, one was more written about, mythologised and demonised than any other institution of its kind, in a manner all the more remarkable because it lasted no more than forty years before being destroyed by fire. St Cyprian's in Summerdown Road was founded at the turn of the nineteenth century by Lewis Vaughan Wilkes and his young wife Cicely to educate young boys into their version of muscular Christianity and prepare them for life at the top public schools, particularly Eton and Harrow.

Known as Sambo and Flip (never to their faces), they were clearly unforgettable. Five well-known twentieth-century figures – the writers George Orwell, Cyril Connolly and Gavin Maxwell, the photographer and designer Cecil Beaton and the golfing journalist Henry Longhurst – chose to record their impressions of the couple and the 'vast gabled redbrick house' – as Longhurst remembered it – at the western edge of town.

Cyril Connolly later came to regret the way he had mocked and vilified the Wilkeses in his *Enemies of Promise*. But Connolly's account of the miseries he suffered at St Cyprian's was tame in comparison with Orwell's. His extended essay about his schooldays, *Such, Such Were The Joys*, portrayed the Wilkeses as monsters of sadistic intent. He accused them of setting out to make his young self feel like a worm. He was ugly. He was poor. He smelt. He was weak. 'I was damned,' he wrote. 'I was an unattractive boy. St Cyprian's made me so.'

However, there must be a strong suspicion that Orwell dramatised and distorted formative experiences to explain and excuse aspects of himself that he disliked. A childhood friend who saw him frequently during the school holidays failed entirely to recognise this self-portrait when it was published; she suggested perceptively that Orwell had made St Cyprian's a scapegoat for the sickness and disappointment that afflicted him much later.

Cecil Beaton and Gavin Maxwell were also miserable in Eastbourne, although Maxwell had the grace to concede that he was 'too much of an oddity' to be happy anywhere. The one corrective to this picture of torment was provided by Henry Longhurst in his breezy memoir *My Life and Soft Times*. Unlike the others, Longhurst was a hearty. He loved sport and swimming in the freezing sea and excursions with Flip among the brambles and wildflowers on the Downs, with a bottle of ice-cream soda at the end. 'There was much to be revelled in,' he wrote, 'and if it lasts in the memory so long there must have been something in it.' He remained in touch with Flip long after St Cyprian's had closed – 'my respect for her grew and grew till I realised that she was undoubtedly the outstanding woman in my life.'

Longhurst's affection extended to Eastbourne itself. Another whose fondness for the town endured was Andrew Cavendish, the 11th Duke of Devonshire, who celebrated its charms for the benefit of the *Oldie* magazine. 'I like everything about Eastbourne,' he wrote. 'I like the pier. I like the theatre. You can take a boat trip round the lighthouse. There's a miniature railway and, best of all, really good military bands. You can't beat the English seaside.'

I could see his point, despite the scandalous prejudice against cycling. In the course of the day I walked from the fishmongers in the east along the front and up Beachy Head in the west and most of the way back. I thought that if I lived in Eastbourne, somewhere not too far from the front, I would not get tired of the walking. When I got old I would not be able to manage Beachy Head, but I would still have the flat promenade with the sea on one side and the fine mansions on the other, and the pier and the bandstand and the flower beds, and people to look at and benches on which to park my increasingly shrivelled backside.

It would not be so bad, I thought. And when I got very old, who knows – there might be someone to push me in my wheelchair and tuck a blanket around my withers and pause to let me watch an angler cast a lugworm for a plaice or a dab, and hear the waves hiss against the shingle.

Beachy Head

And if it all became too much for me, Beachy Head is very conveniently situated. Why waste time and effort and money hauling yourself off to Dignitas in Switzerland when you have the third or fourth most popular suicide destination in the world (depending on which table you consult) on your doorstep?

Each year roughly twenty people kill themselves at Beachy Head, most by jumping, a few by driving off the road and across the springy turf and over the edge of the 530-foot sheer drop. Many more come with some kind of self-destructive urge and either change their minds for themselves or are coaxed away by members of the Beachy Head Chaplaincy Team who patrol the clifftop.

Why Beachy Head? It is a safe bet; few survive the fall. It is extremely accessible. It is unfenced. It is famous, almost mythic. The guaranteed presence of Christian do-gooders ready to listen and console might have something to do with it. Imitative suicide is a well-documented global phenomenon, and nowhere in Britain can rival Beachy Head's celebrity status. The White Cliffs of Dover, for instance – just as potentially lethal – record an average of one suicide a year.

A pathologist who reviewed the statistics for the *British Medical Journal* detailed the cases of four women who had survived suicide attempts. Two said they would try again. One was physically restrained from leaving hospital to return to Beachy Head. One said the attraction was that it was always available and required no preparation – all you had to do was keep walking.

The first time I went there, it was a warm and sunny August bank-holiday afternoon. The car parks were packed, the paths were ceaselessly trod, the place swarmed with people doing what people do on sunny bank-holiday afternoons: sauntering, sitting, lying, playing with the dog, leaving litter, picnicking, going around in irregular circuits beginning and ending at the car park. Death seemed inconceivable on such an occasion, although most Beachy Head suicides do occur in the summer, and no one can go there without having it in their mind that they might see something dreadful.

For some unaccountable reason, April is the least popular month. I don't know about February, but the place has a very different atmosphere about it on a dark late-winter afternoon with a surging grey sea and a sky bulging with rain clouds. I was alone as I shuffled fearfully towards the void and peered over. Below me the sea licked and sucked hungrily at the black rocks spilled along the foot of the white cliff.

I would not say that, in general, I am particularly suggestible or prey to fancy. But I will testify that I felt a distinct and scary seductiveness in the emptiness above the devouring swell of the sea, a pulling at my being that terrified and entranced me. That boundary between land and air, between known and unknown, seemed haunted by the spirits of those who had jumped, calling others to follow.

Near the bottom of the cliff is a cave – now blocked and filled by falls of rock – known as Darby's Hole. This was probably excavated in the first instance by smugglers and used to store contraband. But it acquired its name from the eighteenth-century vicar of the inland parish of East Dean, the Reverend Jonathan Darby. After the smuggling gang was broken up by the authorities, he cleared the cave and on stormy nights would hang lanterns in the mouth to warn mariners in pre-lighthouse days of the perils of Beachy Head, and to provide a shelter for victims of shipwreck.

There is no reason whatever to doubt the essence of the story. But legend can be very unkind to those unable to defend themselves. Somehow another version of Parson Darby's motivation took root, an antique whispering game alleging that his real reason was to have a refuge from the nagging tongue of Mrs Darby. This ridiculous canard – why would anyone in his right mind laboriously maintain two chambers with a connecting staircase just to have peace from his spouse? – has been endlessly recycled in guidebooks through the ages. For instance E. V. Lucas, a perfectly respectable essayist and literary bod, repeated it in his generally splendid *Highways and Byways in Sussex* without a thought for Mr Darby and his reputation.

The boldness of Beachy Head and the wildness of its setting have moved many of poetical inclination, among them Charlotte Smith, whose sonnets were apparently admired by Coleridge and Wordsworth. Her verses on Beachy Head are fairly representative of the genre:

> *On thy stupendous summit, rock sublime*
> *That o'er the Channel roared . . .* [etc., etc.]

To plumb something of the mystery of the place I suggest turning instead to a marvellous essay called *The Breeze on Beachy Head* by Richard Jefferies, a great haunter of the south coast whose short life, dogged by poverty and ill-health and filled with care and drudgery, ended at Goring, just outside Worthing, in 1887.

Jefferies' exploration of the spirit of the place begins with him looking out from the foot of the cliff: 'There is an infinite possibility about the sea. It may do what it has not done before. It is not to be ordered, it may overlap the bounds human observation has fixed for it. It has a potency unfathomable. There is something in it not quite grasped or understood, something still to be discovered.' He manages to express the essence of what so many people find in living by the sea and being in constant communion with it: 'We feel we have wider thoughts than we knew; the soul has been living, as it were, in a nutshell, all unaware of its power and suddenly finds freedom in the sea and the sky.'

Later he ascends and lies on the grass: 'The glory of these glorious downs is the breeze . . . if it comes from the south the waves refine it; if inland the wheat and the flowers distil it. The great headland and the whole rib of the promontory is wind-swept and washed with air; the billows of the atmosphere roll over it.'

This is very beautifully put, but of course the Sussex Downs that Jefferies and his fellow master of nature writing, W. H. Hudson, wandered in the second half of the nineteenth century is beyond recognition now. Where it has not been gobbled up by housing it is annexed by the silent, deserted tracts of arable fields, or domesticated and brought to heel by the National Trust and the warriors of the heritage army. Its native people have gone, their country ways with them.

Between Rottingdean in the west and Eastbourne in the east, sheep kept the turf and wildflowers cropped and springy. The shepherds were the rulers of the Downs. They were grindingly poor and any extra source of income was eagerly seized upon. The arrival in the late summer of a little bird called the wheatear (apparently a corruption of 'white arse') was one such. The wheatears collected on the Downs from all over the country to ready themselves for migration to North Africa. Plucked and roasted on spits, they were consumed in hotels and restaurants and grand houses with the same enthusiasm as aroused by the ortolan in France.

The wheatears' habits made them easy prey. They like to breed in holes and are naturally inclined to take refuge in them to shelter from bad weather or just to rest. To trap them a shepherd dug a shallow, T-shaped trench partially covered with the sod, and placed a snare made of horsehair inside, strong enough to detain the bird without throttling it. So many of these traps were dug that by September the downland looked almost as if it had been ploughed. Enormous numbers of birds were taken – forty or fifty per shepherd per day was standard, with the poulterer in Brighton paying eighteen pence a dozen. A shepherd in Parson Darby's parish of East Dean is recorded as having taken a thousand in a day; so many that, instead of threading them onto crow quills in the normal way, he used his own coat and his wife's petticoat as sacks to take them away.

According to E. V. Lucas in *Highways and Byways in Sussex*, London gourmets travelled down to Brighton to feast on them in the season, in the same way that they migrated to Greenwich for whitebait and Colchester for oysters. For a few years some shepherds were making as much as £50 a year from the trade, but inevitably, given the slaughter, the numbers arriving began to drop steeply. In the 1880s landowners around Rottingdean banned their shepherds from trapping wheatears on the grounds that they were neglecting the sheep. By then many had given up anyway because there weren't enough birds to justify the effort. In 1897 the wheatear was given statutory protection and trapping was banned altogether.

6

STAND UP FOR PEACEHAVEN

Seven Sisters

The ride from Beachy Head was not amusing. The road descends
steeply to Birling Gap, and west from there the clifftop is controlled by the National Trust, which does not welcome cyclists
and installs gates intended to make that clear. I was forced inland
onto the traffic-clogged A259 and as a result I missed the stretch

of coastline including the Seven Sisters, Cuckmere Haven and Seaford Head. I was too cross to appreciate whatever charms Seaford may possess, and I'm afraid the place made no impression of any kind on me. I can, however, report that it does not have a Museum of Sex, despite the singer/songwriter Robyn Hitchcock – characterised by his record label as a 'psychedelic troubadour' – saying it does. But it does have a conventional museum in its Martello Tower, which boasts prehistoric tool fragments, a mock Victorian school-room, a collection of domestic appliances and ancient TVs and radios, plus some history about the 'colourful' Seaford Shags.

You find that colourful is an adjective much favoured by the heritage people to describe activities that in another age would be termed vicious and criminal. The Shags were wreckers, a gang organised to loot ships that came to grief in Seaford Bay and Cuckmere Haven. Their most infamous exploit occurred in December 1809, when a flotilla of merchant ships under the protection of a Royal Navy sloop, the *Harlequin*, were driven into Seaford Bay and onto the beach by a south-westerly gale. Distress guns and rockets were fired and the shore was soon crowded with rescuers, onlookers and the Shags.

The ensuing drama and scandal received national coverage. One report read: 'Most [of those present] were disposed to render every assistance in their power, but among them were some so lost to nature and her charities as to be bent on no other object than plundering the unlucky sufferers.' And not just the sufferers; Mr Hamilton, the Collector of Customs at Newhaven, took off his greatcoat and boots to help in the rescue, and came back to find them filched.

All seven grounded vessels were shattered to pieces. The

passengers and crew on the *Harlequin* were rescued, but thirty-one seamen from the merchant ships were drowned. The Shags fastened on victims dead and alive like vultures, until the local militia were called out to put a stop to their depredations.

Seaford was once a port of some significance as a 'limb' of the Cinque Port of Hastings. It stood at the mouth of the Ouse, which gave access well inland, and had a sheltered harbour to the front. But some time in the sixteenth century it ceased trading after a succession of storms broke through the shingle bar protecting the harbour, and the river found a new exit to the west, near the village of Meeching, later renamed Newhaven. Subsequently the migration of shingle forced the river mouth east again, to the hamlet of Bishopstone. In 1761 three local corn merchants installed a mill there powered by the incoming and ebbing tide.

The mill was taken over in 1803 by a man of lowly birth and remarkable enterprise, William Catt. In Lower's *Worthies of Sussex* Catt is introduced with this fine sonorous sentence: 'If it be desirable to possess a practical belief that under Providence a man is rather the master of the circumstances which surround him than a slave, a small space in the history of Sussex may properly be allotted to the late William Catt, who from a very humble position rose to considerable commercial eminence and whose memory still lives on in the grateful recollection of his children, of his old servants and of his faithful friends.'

Catt greatly expanded the scale of the operation at Bishopstone. He excavated a second millpond and increased the number of millstones powered by the wheels from five pairs to sixteen. They worked whenever there was enough tide flow to drive them, grinding 1500 sacks of flour a week to be transported by barge to Newhaven or up the Ouse. A thriving village grew up around the mills; Catt himself lived in a fine mansion where his one recreation was the cultivation of pears.

He died in 1853, and the business did not survive him for long. It was too exposed to the elements and to competition in the industrialising world. In 1876 a storm flooded the village and badly damaged the mills. Silting and the shifting of shingle made it increasingly difficult for barges to get in and out. The mill was demolished in 1901, although people continued to live in the settlement around it until the outbreak of the Second World War.

The Bishopstone tide mills is now classic edgeland: forsaken, scruffy, random, disorderly, its story obscured beneath a riot of brambles, buddleias and nettles. The pools that were William Catt's pride are still there, choked with mud the colour of mustard from which rise curious relics – wheels, struts of metal, twists of wire. Patches of ruined brickwork are visible through the jungle of vegetation. The openings of the culverts that fed the waterwheels sit on the still grey water like empty eye sockets. Black and greasy remnants of the sluice gates lean against the slope. Sections of walls lie flat as if tanks had smashed their way through and paths without signposts wriggle through the wilderness like animal tracks.

A footbridge over the narrow inland end of the mill creek leads into the eastern fringe of Newhaven, where the railway line serves the harbour. A little way down the line is the mysterious Newhaven Marine Station, which has been closed to passengers since 2006 for 'safety reasons' but continues to make ghostly appearances on timetables. Newhaven has three railway stations (including the spectral Newhaven Marine) but no bank; you feel that without the Dieppe ferry service, which runs at a heavy loss, the town might be in danger of disappearing altogether.

Newhaven and its harbour

It is an odd place, and another of its oddities is its link – real or imaginary – with the Vietnamese revolutionary leader Ho Chi Minh. It is well-known that as a young man Ho travelled widely in Europe and the United States, working in ships' kitchens, a bakery and – allegedly – as a pastry chef in London. It is difficult to know where the story that he worked on the Dieppe–Newhaven ferry service came from – Sophie Quinn-Judge, author of *Ho Chi Minh: The Missing Years* is more than a little sceptical. But to Newhaven's civic leaders any celebrity – even one specialising in war, mass murder and the ruthless elimination of rivals – is better than no celebrity. In February 2013 a bronze statue of Ho – seated, pen in hand, perhaps about to sign a liquidation order – was unveiled at Newhaven Museum. It was donated by the Vietnamese Embassy and the event moved the Mayor of Newhaven to look forward to 'a long and fruitful friendship between Newhaven and Vietnam resulting in exciting business, tourism, educational and cultural opportunities for the town.' Does one detect the whiff of wishful thinking here?

If Ho remembered Newhaven he kept quiet about it. Other nuggets of local history are more firmly based. For instance the Ford Corsair that Lord Lucan bolted in after murdering – or, just conceivably, not murdering – the family nanny was certainly found abandoned in Norman Road. (Lucan's best friend, John Aspinall, always believed that he drowned himself jumping off the ferry to France.) And the last King of France, Louis Philippe, certainly arrived in Newhaven after his abdication and flight from Paris in February 1848. Among those who called on 'Mr Smith' at the Bridge Inn was none other than the Bishopstone tide-mill tycoon William Catt, who in happier times had been summoned by the King to his country mansion, Château d'Eu, to advise on building a mill.

It is entirely likely that Mr Catt – possibly Mr Smith as well – refreshed himself with a pint of Newhaven's most celebrated liquid comforter, Tipper Ale. The brewer of this elixir, Thomas Tipper, is buried in the churchyard with these lines inscribed on his stone:

Honest he was, ingenious, blunt and kind;
And dared do what few dare do, and speak his mind.
Philosophy and history well he knew,

Was versed in physick and in surgery too.
The best old stingo he both brewed and sold
Nor did one knavish act to get his gold.

Tipper's 'best old stingo' was a strong dark ale, admired by – among many others – the Prince Regent, later George IV. Mrs Gamp, in *Martin Chuzzlewit*, took 'a pint of the celebrated staggering ale, old Brighton Tipper' for supper, being 'very punctual and particular' in her drinking.

* * *

Peacehaven

This is Iain Nairn on Peacehaven: 'It has been called a rash on the countryside. It is that, and there is no worse in England. Whose haven is it?'

And Virginia Woolf: 'All that is cheap and greedy and meretricious has here come to the surface and lies like a sore, expressed in gimcrack red houses and raw roads and meaning-less decorations.'

And the writer Geoffrey Morehouse: 'It is a two mile strip of bungaloid horror. It should have been a home for heroes and became a monument for rapacity.'

Peacehaven's problem is that it tells the world what it is so directly. It has no centre, therefore it is easy to conclude that it has no heart. It has no buildings of distinction, no subtleties or surprises. It is constructed on a rigid grid system – roads east to west, avenues north to south – on which stand bungalows, just bungalows. Viewed from above on Google Earth it resembles some kind of electrical circuit box assembled for efficiency and compactness.

It is easy to spend half an hour or ten minutes in Peacehaven and shudder at it, and laugh, and wonder how anyone could bear to live in such a place, and then move swiftly on; which is what journalists and travel writers and self-appointed arbiters of taste and defenders of the English countryside have always done. But I wanted to find someone to stand up for the place, so I put my bike on the train to Brighton intending to go and find that someone.

When I got to Brighton I found the back wheel was slightly buckled. I took it to a bike shop near the station, and while the wheel was being fixed I got chatting with one of the owners and told him where I was heading and why. 'I live in Peace-haven,' he said, looking slightly embarrassed. And? 'People laugh at it but it's a really nice place to live. I mean, a nothing place to look at, but nice, friendly. And it's a great cycle ride along the sea wall to get here.'

He was originally from Leamington. The best thing about

Leamington was catching sight of it in the rear-view mirror. Whereas Peacehaven ... 'Thing is, it knows what it's for. People like me – wife, three kids – can afford to buy there. It's clean and safe, there's the sea. Plus a great ride into Brighton.' He was right: it is a great ride – sea and rocks and shingle one side, soaring white cliffs the other, hard, flat concrete under the wheels, the wind in your face or behind your ears.

I called in on Fred in Cairo Avenue, who happened to be at home with his dog. Fred and his wife had moved from Derbyshire to Hove; she'd always been on at him about living by the sea. They had a flat there and a view of the sea, and they were happy. Then Fred's wife died and he couldn't bear the loneliness and the memories, so he bought the bungalow in Cairo Avenue.

'Saved my life, that did,' Fred said. He extended a hand towards the sea, glittering under blue sky and racing clouds. 'I wake up to that every morning. What could beat that?' He'd done a lot of work on the bungalow over the years. He was good with his hands and in no hurry because he wasn't planning to move anywhere. 'Brighton people look down their noses at Peacehaven. They call it Windy City, but it's just as windy there, plus the people here are a lot friendlier. I love it. Everything I need is here, plus there's the sea, every day just outside the window.'

I pedalled slowly along Peacehaven's roads and avenues, immersing myself in variations on a bungalow theme. There were bungalows in plain red brick, white pebbledash, brown pebbledash, bungalows with timber features, stone cladding, tile cladding, bungalows sideways on, front on, L-shaped, rectangular, with green concrete roof tiles and brown concrete roof tiles. They were all different, all the same. Almost none of the originals – put up less than a hundred years ago – survive in their original form. But the spirit of the bungalow, the spirit of Peacehaven, is entirely intact.

Photographs of Charles Neville, the creator of Peacehaven, suggest a speculator, a showman, a bit of a chancer. His lapels are too wide, his watch-chain too showy, his hat too tilted back for him to be mistaken for a gentleman. As a young man, Neville travelled extensively in America and Australia, making money in real estate. He saw how townships could be made quickly and profitably in the middle of nowhere, given pioneering enterprise and energy and a healthy contempt for rules, regulations and other people's opinions. He brought the idea home with him.

At the beginning of the 1914–18 war Neville and his wife drove west from Newhaven, across a broad tract of downland empty except for the sheep and the odd farmhouse. He started buying up the land at knockdown prices, around £15 an acre, and set up the South Coast Land and Resort Company. In 1916 he announced his plan for a new town on the clifftop and invited the public to enter a competition to name it. With the entry form they received an offer to buy a plot of land. Although the winner, New Anzac-on-Sea, was quickly discarded, the plots were snapped up and the money rolled in.

Because of the war and the subsequent acute shortage of building materials, the first dwellings did not appear until 1920. They were made of sheets of asbestos nailed to wooden frames, with asbestos roof tiles. It was an adventure for those early Arcadians. Many had fought in the war and longed for a simple quiet life in a place of their own. Some brought redundant army huts with them. Others built their own bungalows buying the materials from Neville's company, which offered the use of machinery for free. Neither they nor their landlord needed the permission or help of the local authority. They didn't mind the primitive or non-existent drainage, the lack of street lighting, the unmade roads.

Neville's ambitions went beyond making a buck from selling building plots. He wanted to make Peacehaven into a pleasure resort as well, somewhere to holiday and spend money. He had a swimming pool dug and built the Peacehaven Hotel, complete with sunken Italianate garden, on Phyllis Avenue. In 1922 the Rosemary Tea Rooms opened, with a room for entertainment, inaugurated by Miss Flora Robson reciting 'The Highwayman' and 'The Matinee Hat'. The following year saw the opening night at the Pavilion Theatre, a converted Army canteen imported from France. It was run by two brothers, Felix and George Powell, who had achieved immortality with their 1915 patriotic song 'Pack Up Your Troubles in Your Old Kit Bag'.

As well as staging comedies and musicals and Gilbert and Sullivan, the Powell brothers acted as cheerleaders for the Peacehaven brand. One of their more forgettable compositions went:

Come to Peacehaven,
Come to Peacehaven and build a bungalow
As many have done, you know
Up on the Downland, purple and brown land,
And near enough to townland
If you want to go
And you always find the southern winds

Make you free and fresh
So for rest and recreation, wealth and happiness
Come to Peacehaven by the sea.

The sales slogan was 'Come In On The Rising Tide'. Nor were rest and recreation and sea the only inducements. One advertisement offered 'specially selected sites . . . eminently suitable for Angora wool farming . . . large enough to ensure a profitable business' either from the exotically fluffy Angora rabbits or from more conventional kinds of rabbit fur. 'The tide of a new industry is rising at Peacehaven,' the ad proclaimed. 'Let your barque upon it and ride at the flood to a harbour of happy industry and contentment.'

Few, it seems, chose to sail on Peacehaven's Angora rabbit barque. But many found the harbour of contentment by other means.

Saltdean

Charles Neville's empire expanded steadily westward during the 1920s, and with it the breadth of his vision. Peacehaven grew an extension, Telscombe Cliffs, but there was space beyond for another kind of settlement: classier, more elegant, much more expensive.

It was to be known as Saltdean, and the first radical decision was to jettison the grid system in favour of curves and arcs and ovals and crescents. There were bungalows, but they were smart, spacious bungalows with bathrooms and roofs tiled in diamond patterns. They were mixed in with superior detached residences in various styles: mock Tudor, Hollywood Spanish (stuccoed with green tiles), colonial and several blocks of luxury flats. There were even three uncompromising concrete cubes in Wicklands Avenue designed by the Connell, Ward and Lucas partnership, all fierce disciples of Le Corbusier.

Two buildings summed up the comparative splendour of Saltdean, both the work of the architect R. W. H. Jones. One was the Ocean Hotel: a 400-bedroom extravaganza complete with American bar, ballroom, swimming pool, tennis courts and gardens, with a concave curvilinear frontage overlooking an ornamental pool and fountain. The other was the famous Saltdean Lido, a riot of pavilions and terraces and pillared canopy, inspired by Bexhill's De La Warr Pavilion, but with an exuberance and lightness all its own.

For a short time both these gleaming showpieces trumpeted Charles Neville's vision and magnetised visitors with their glamour and opulence. But that kind of frivolous hedonism was shattered by the outbreak of war, and neither ever recovered its *joie de vivre*. The hotel was requisitioned as a fire station and was subsequently acquired by Billy Butlin and remodelled to fit the Butlin brand. The lido fell victim to a familiar cycle of neglect. It lost some of its most distinctive features, including the three-tiered concrete diving board and the boating pool. It closed, reopened, closed again, while its fabric decayed. It was eventually delivered by Brighton and Hove Council into the hands of a property developer who proposed to get rid of it altogether in favour of a block of one hundred flats. The news was greeted with outrage and the campaign to save the lido was born.

It has now been reprieved from destruction, but remains on the critical list. Several millions need to be spent putting right the injuries of the past; it remains shut and shabby while the great scheme for its eventual resurrection creeps towards fulfilment. Meanwhile the Ocean, having been closed as a hotel in 2005 and having narrowly escaped being turned into a reception centre for asylum seekers, has now been converted into apartments.

Saltdean these days looks and feels like just another coastal suburb. The high ambition of its fast-talking founder faltered, and Charles Neville's spirit is long departed. But in Peacehaven – despite the disappearance of the original dwellings, the quadrupling of the population and the advent of proper drainage, asphalt roads, schools and other facilities – it remains obstinately and rather appealingly alive.

The snobs – Nairn, Virginia Woolf and the rest – miss the point. They sneer at the ordinariness of seaside settlements such as Peacehaven, at the architecture, the absence of high culture and fine dining. They find it hard to forgive the presumption of lower- and middle-class people in intruding their bungalows and rock gardens and suburban attitudes into territory that should, by rights, have been declared off-limits to them.

But the point about the seaside is its cheerful democracy. Very obviously, it is situated at the edge, between land and water. It takes from both but belongs to neither. It is a realm of its own, with a different code, and no one can claim ownership of it. It is open-handed in its welcome. It is a playground for children and their parents and grandparents and uncles and aunts and special friends. It accepts with equal ease the gregarious and the solitary, who wish for nothing more than to watch the waves and feel the unfailing beat of the sea's heart.

The seaside inspires a distinct delight which can be found nowhere else. That is why so many choose to live there, and so many more ensure that the pattern of their lives makes room for regular exposure to it. The snobs do not like the seaside's generosity, the way it spreads its special quality around. So they damn Peacehaven, not that Peacehaven cares.

I learned something valuable there.

7

PRAWNS ANCIENT AND MODERN

Beneath the chalk cliffs the ebbing tide uncovers a marine edge-land of great interest to those who like to delve with nets under curtains of weed or thrust them into dark overhangs. Between Peacehaven and Brighton the chalk platform extending from the shore has been worked by the motions of the sea into a pitted, serrated moonscape, split by miniature canyons, crested by toothy outcrops. This is the realm of the rock pool.

When you are down there, the cliffs shut out the tame upland where Peacehaven gives way to Saltdean, and Saltdean to genteel Rottingdean, and genteel Rottingdean to the stark forbidding institution that is Roedean School. You must take care when you venture out. Much of the rock is blanketed in bladderwrack, which offers a treacherous footing. Beneath the tresses of rubbery weed are jagged rock edges armoured in skin-tearing barnacles and mussels. Limpets and anemones are glued into the cracks and crevasses. There are occasional drifts of sand between the rocks, welcome relief to the feet, where shattered mussel shells gather like some exotic blue ore. Small, sandy-bottomed pools are formed in the bowls in the rocks, where bright-green weed of soap-like slipperiness mingles with another weed, coral in colour, rough and filamentous to the touch.

Such pools are lovely to look at, like miniature aquariums. But these are of no interest to the prawn hunter, who is creeping his way with extreme caution towards the sea, scouring the moonscape for promising refuges. The ideal pool is shut off from the waves and has rock faces that drop vertically – or even better at an inward angle – into at least a foot of water, with bladderwrack or other weed giving shelter along the edge. It may have an island or two, with hidden holes and hiding places beneath the surface. There must be room to manoeuvre the net into the nooks and crannies, and sweep it beneath the weed. These are the places beloved of prawns and those who hunt them.

My mother became headmistress of Roedean School for girls in 1960, when I was nine. We – my three elder brothers and I – were all away at boarding school so we tended to come in the holidays, when the vast institution was echoingly deserted but for a skeleton staff of caretakers and my mother, closeted in her study with a packet of Senior Service and a mountain of paperwork. We had the use of the school gym, which was fun for a while, and the swimming pool, which was fun in fine weather (of which there was very little in the 1960s), and of the cricket nets (Roedean took cricket very seriously). There was Brighton of course: the pier and candyfloss and toffee apples, and Bredons and Beals bookshops in the Lanes. I was too young to take advantage of the town's more exotic attractions.

I loved the rock pools. Roedean had its own tunnel down

through the cliff to the shore with its entrance near the school's main gates. It had been dug sometime in the pre-swimming pool era, as there were sepulchral changing-rooms at the bottom where Roedeanians of old had exchanged uniforms for very respectable bathing costumes before scampering across the rocks to the murky sea. It was dimly lit by feeble bare light bulbs. The air was still, stale, salty and the stairs were covered in a thin layer of sand, ages old, which muffled the slap of our plimsolls. It was more than slightly spooky, and I never went down or up without thinking of being trapped in there with no one to hear my cries.

The tunnel opened onto the sea wall. On sunny days we were blinded by the light off the chalk and the water, standing there in our shorts and Aertex shirts, with our buckets and the nets made for us by the school handyman. We would fan out across the rocks, searching for the deepest pools where the fattest prawns would be found.

The prime time was the hour either side of low tide. After that the incoming sea devoured the pools and we would trudge wearily back up the tunnel steps, swapping the heavy bucket from one hand to the other, slopping the water and an occasional crustacean onto already wet feet. Back home we would run our fingers through the prawns, lifting them and letting them drop back into the bucket, feeling their whiskers and little saws against our skin. Then they would be tipped into a big pan of boiling water and we would marvel again at that instant metamorphosis from translucent life to pink death.

In time we outgrew prawning and rock-pooling. My mother finished at Roedean and we did not go back to the rocks below the cliffs again, although I would occasionally wonder if it had changed much and if the prawns were still there.

In October 2012 we all went back to Roedean to attend the Founders' Day service. My mother had died in January of that year at a great age, and the school wished to commemorate her time there. We had tea with the head teacher and I asked her about the tunnel, assuming that in these Health-and-Safety days it would have been shut up or even filled in. She surprised me by saying it was still in use, and that she would sometimes take senior girls down to the Marina for an ice cream.

By then I was researching this book and a notion took shape. It was time to find out about the prawns.

In August 2013 my eldest brother and I – the others were not available – headed for the south coast. It was a perfect prawning day, warm and sunny, not too breezy. It would have been nice to use the Roedean tunnel but it was the holidays so we parked near St Dunstan's, the startling modernist home for blind service men and women along the clifftop from the school. We had ginger beer and bacon sandwiches at the café at the bottom of the steps there, then made our way west along the sea wall, our nets and buckets drawing some inquiring looks. The sand and shingle beach gives way after a while to rock, much as we remembered except for the encroachment in the distance of Brighton Marina, much talked about in my mother's day although not actually built until some years later.

It was mid-afternoon, an hour or so before low tide. We went separate ways, very cautiously, James towards the tunnel and the Marina, me further east. I proceeded very slowly, fearful of a fall, until I found the kind of pool I was after. It had overhangs on one side draped in weed, and an island of rock in the middle, and when I lowered myself into it the water came up to my shins. I ran my net briskly beneath the bladderwrack and scooped upwards. Among the fronds of weed trapped in the mesh were half a dozen fat prawns and a little fish, a blenny, with flattened face and fan-like pectoral fins. I let out a little whoop of delight.

Further out towards the sea were two lines of brown, barnacle-encrusted blocks of concrete. I did not remember them, although they must have been there in the 1960s as they had originally been put there to carry Magnus Volk's celebrated Seashore Electric Railway, which ran on stilts between Rottingdean and Brighton's Palace Pier at the end of the nineteenth century. Around the base of the blocks the water was knee-deep and the dark holes were well-populated. I scooped back and forth, breaking off to transfer the better prawns to my bucket and release the lesser ones, together with the clods of weed and assorted crabs, gobies, blennies and weevers.

I looked towards the Marina and saw my brother bent at the business, his straw hat inclined low. Time raced by, measured only by the tide retreating to its outer limit then advancing again. It is very absorbing, this rock pooling. You feel very much on your own out on the rocks, detached by a great spiritual distance from the bustle of the Marina and the roar of the coast road.

The tide was halfway back in when we called a halt. The walk back to the car, like the ascent of the tunnel steps, seemed very much longer than it had a few hours before. We had a good haul of prawns, and when I got home that evening I boiled my share for a minute or so then peeled and potted them in butter with mace and cayenne pepper. They were highly unctuous and delicious, the butter and spices veiling but not masking the unmistakable taste of the sea.

* * *

Brighton and the Palace Pier

The gravestone is close to the north wall of the churchyard of St Nicholas, the parish church of Brighton. It stands on a grassy bank, as upright as Brighton folk remembered the old man himself, both in his character and bearing. The name on the stone, Sake Dean Mohammed, is not quite right, but you can hardly blame the monumental mason, for a dark-skinned person from Hindustan was a rare bird in those days and their names were different from ours, and the man himself had spelled his in various ways.

The immense age of 101 recorded on the stone is dubious, too. He died in 1851, which would give a birth year of 1750. But in his own account of his life, *The Travels of Dean Mahomet*, he stated clearly: 'I was born in the year 1759 at Patna, a famous city north of the Ganges ...' But was he? In another book, about the methods for which he became famous, Mahomet wrote: 'I was born in the year 1749 at Patna, the capital of Hindoostan about 290 miles north of Calcutta.'

There are more riddles here. The inscription also records the death of his wife Jane in 1850 at the age of seventy, which would put her birth year at 1780. Yet by his account, he eloped with her in 1784, which is implausible. According to an American historian, Michael Fisher, who has closely studied the records of Mahomet's life, the answer could be that he had two wives, both called Jane.

This much is known. Mahomet trained as a surgeon in Calcutta and was attached to the 27th Regiment of Native Infantry in the Bengal Army. At some point he became the pro-tégé of a Captain Godfrey Baker, an officer of the East India Company from a well-to-do Protestant Anglo-Irish family living in Cork in the west of Ireland. In the 1780s he accompanied Captain Baker from India to Cork, where he formed a strong attachment for an Irish girl, Jane Daly. Against the wishes of her family he married her; they had several children and continued to enjoy the patronage of the Baker family for many years.

In 1807 Dean Mahomet and his family moved to London where he obtained a position working for one of the richest of the Indian nabobs, the Honourable Basil Cochrane. While amassing a vast fortune in India, Cochrane had become interested in the Indian practice of treating various medical conditions in a steam or vapour bath. The version developed by Cochrane consisted of a transparent chamber fed by steam, with a seat on which the patient would have a strange contraption made of flannel, whalebone and metal strapped to the chest to concentrate more steam. Cochrane had one installed in his mansion in Portman Square, and it is likely that Dean Mahomet worked there, possibly even installed it, and that he added to the treatment various methods of massage using exotic oils.

He and Cochrane soon went their separate ways, and Dean Mahomet opened his Hindoostane coffee house in George Street, said to be the first in London to offer authentic Indian cuisine. After running into financial difficulties he moved with his family to Brighton, where he set up a therapeutic bathhouse combining the vapour bath with massages using his 'Indian oils'.

This time he found the right market. In the 1750s Dr Richard Russell had set up his famous practice on Old Steine, prescribing bathing in sea water and drinking it as a treatment for every ailment from gout to heart disease. Dr Russell had thereby established Brighton's reputation as the resort of choice for the well-to-do in search of a cure. Initially the 'original medicated shampooing' offered by the Indian surgeon at Mahomed's Baths was just one more in the portfolio of therapeutic treatments available to Brighton's transient population of invalids and hypochondriacs. But its exoticism and originality, and the suave and soothing manner of its dusky practitioner, soon made it a favourite.

Mahomet's 'shampooing' had little or nothing to do with the

hair or scalp. The patient, having been encouraged to perspire freely in the vapour bath, was placed in a flannel tent. Medicated oils were applied, followed by pummelling of the muscles, ligaments and tendons by strong arms inserted through flaps in the side of the tent.

Extraordinary cures were claimed. Dean Mahomet built up a collection of crutches, spine-stretchers, club-foot reformers, leg-irons and other correctives which his patients had discarded as a result of his treatments. The Prince Regent himself came, and appointed Mahomet Shampooing Surgeon to the Royal Family. Where the Prince led everyone else followed. Testimonials flowed in. Mrs Kent, of Wimpole Street in London, was inspired to verse. She came to Mahomed's Baths

Worn out by anguish and excess of pain
Hope seemed delusive and assistance vain.

But after a good pummelling, she was a new woman –

To thee, Mahomed, let a grateful heart
Its warmest thanks in gratitude impart,
By thy great skill and unremitting care,
One has been saved who might have perished there.
Who while she feels a pulse within her veins
Will bless the name if memory remains.

The Baths prospered, so much so that a sister branch opened in London. Its founder retired in 1843 – aged either eighty-four or ninety-four – handing over to one of his sons, Arthur. According to his obituary in the *Gentleman's Magazine*, Mahomet 'enjoyed uninterrupted good health and retained all his faculties unimpaired almost to the last hour of his life'. The *Brighton Herald* attributed his wellbeing to 'temperate habits and a cheerful and contented mind ... he was highly respected as a man of benevolence, candour and sincerity.'

One of his grandsons subsequently wrote to the paper to clear up the matter of his name – it should have been Deen Mahomed, the 'Sake' being a title which should have been rendered as 'Sheikh', meaning 'elderly respected person'. The family remained in Brighton long after the fashion for medical shampooing had passed and Mahomed's Baths had been pulled down to make way for a hotel. One of the grandsons is recorded as having died in Hove in 1935; he was the Reverend James Deen Kerriman Mahomed, which must be one of the more unusual names on the Church of England's roll.

Brighton in the era of Mahomed's Baths knew its business thoroughly. Its adoption by the Prince Regent in 1783 as his favoured playground added the dimension of pleasure to the round of water treatments advocated by Dr Russell and his followers. Under the Prince's patronage, Brighton rapidly learned to offer a wide range of diversions and facilities. George's notion of amusement encompassed bathing, shooting at chimneys, cards, masques, balls, hunting a stag down the Steine, philandering, gossip-mongering and much besides. Crucially, it also sanctioned the participation of social ranks outside the old aristocracy hitherto considered suitable as royal companions. In Brighton extravagance of dress, behaviour and spending were the norm. Money rubbed shoulders with quality, the flash with the elegant, the seamy with the smart.

In 1827 George IV – as he had become after a long wait – paid his last visit to his Oriental pleasure palace, the Royal Pavilion. His successor, William IV, loved Brighton as well, but he did not last long. Queen Victoria did not share the enthusiasm of her uncles. She and Albert objected to the 'semi-Chinese monstrosities' on display in the Pavilion, and much more strongly to the vulgar curiosity of the hordes of over-dressed and immodest social butterflies flitting along the promenade. 'The people are very indiscreet and troublesome here which makes this place quite a prison,' she complained. They much preferred the understated charms of the Isle of Wight, and once Osborne House was built and fitted out appropriately, they kept away from Brighton altogether.

Brighton did not miss them overmuch. It was too occupied in providing for a clientele much increased and democratised by the opening of the railway line from London in the 1840s. Under challenge from Eastbourne and Bournemouth, its reputation as resort of first choice for the top tier of society declined somewhat. But the start of the winter season in November still witnessed a remarkable influx of titled person-ages, British and foreign, whose comings and goings were faithfully recorded in the 'Local Fashionable Intelligence' column of the *Brighton Gazette*. In 1870 it announced in suc-cessive weeks the presence of, among others, the Duke of Newcastle, Baron Rothschild, Lord and Lady Monson, the Duc de Persigny, the Earl and Countess of Shannon, the Dowager Duchess of Marlborough, the Duke of Rutland, the Duchess of Cambridge, Baroness de Clifford and the Bishop of Chichester.

The routine was leisurely. In fine weather there was a

general saunter along the promenade from noon to one o'clock, followed by lunch. Between three and five in the afternoon came the 'carriage airing', in which an enormous cavalcade of barouches, landaus, broughams, phaetons, wag-gonettes, flys, tandems, and dog-carts processed up and down the seafront, permitting the mob of the quality to take the air, incline their noble brows, doff their hats and exchange titbits of gossip.

In 1866 perhaps the most glorious of the pleasure piers that became an indispensable feature of Victorian seaside resorts was opened opposite Regency Square. The West Pier, with its orna-mental houses, minarets and pinnacles and serpent-entwined gas lamps, was designed by Eugenius Birch to mimic the Oriental extravagance of the Royal Pavilion. It is tempting to see its for-tunes and final fate as a barometer of the fortunes of Brighton itself.

Subsequent additions to the West Pier included a pavilion (later converted into a theatre), a winter gardens and a concert hall. In 1919–20 two million people paid to enjoy its attractions. But within ten years attendances were falling steeply as a result of competition from the Palace Pier and the proliferation of other diversions along the seafront. The days when dukes and duchesses and marquises strolled along the promenade were long gone, and Brighton – like other resorts – was forced down-market. The seedy side of Brighton life, always present but generally kept out of sight, asserted itself.

When Graham Greene's *Brighton Rock* was published in 1938, councillors were appalled by its focus on gangland viciousness and small-time crime at the expense of visitor attractions. The film version of 1946, starring Richard Attenborough as the psychopath Pinkie, was even more dismaying. Its climax saw Pinkie throwing himself off a gaunt, rusted and dismally unloved Palace Pier into a heaving grey sea that no one in his or her right mind would want to swim in. By then both Brighton's piers were in a sad state, as was most of the seafront. The decline of the Palace Pier was halted, but that of the West Pier continued. By the time Richard Attenborough returned to film scenes for his anti-war satire *Oh! What A Lovely War* it was literally on its last legs.

The West Pier's recognition as a Victorian masterpiece came far too late to save it. It was given Grade One status in 1979, but it had closed four years earlier and was derelict and becoming hazardous. Storm and fire eventually completed the job of reducing it to the dismembered, blackened ruin that it remains today.

The challenge of saving the West Pier was beyond the competence of successive Brighton councils of varying political colour. But nothing, it seems, will discourage the elected leaders from embracing grandiose projects to restore the faded glory of Brighton and Hove. There have been many of these, but perhaps the most delightful was the recruitment of the American architect Frank Gehry, the prince of deconstructivism, to design a twin-towered complex of flats and recreational facilities with his trademark wavy walls on the site occupied by the incredibly shabby and dismal King Alfred Leisure Centre in Hove.

The news set off an explosion of excitement, particularly when it was revealed in the media that the Hollywood star and Gehry acolyte Brad Pitt had been 'helping' on the project, and was intending to visit Hove and even occupy one of the 450 luxury apartments himself. Dr Anthony Seldon, at that time the principal of Brighton College, later the biographer of Tony Blair and the extremely publicity-aware head of Wellington College, declared that to reject Gehry's vision 'would be an act of vandalism unparalleled in 200 years'.

Hove

Others – presumably vandals in Dr Seldon's view – dared to question whether Hove, with its terraces and squares of decent, if slightly dull, low-rise Regency houses, really needed a shimmering monster of steel, concrete and glass blocking its view of the sea. Predictably the supposed backers of the plan failed to put their money on the table – another casualty, it was claimed, of the economic downturn.

The project went away, and the dreadful leisure centre still stands. But the appetite of Brighton and Hove Council for headline-stealing regenerative ventures remained very much alive. There was a plan to replace the Brighton Centre with something more architecturally interesting, which would – it was claimed – 'create 380 jobs' and 'bring £865 million into the local economy over 30 years'. The Brighton Centre is still there.

There was a plan to put an £80-million arena and ice rink on the site left derelict since the closure and filling in of the famous Black Rock swimming pool in the 1970s. This, the council announced, would create up to 450 jobs and bring £8 million a year into the local economy. The 'partnership' with the developers foundered, the council began looking for a new partner, and meanwhile the site is given over to a 'temporary sand sculpture theme park', piles of rubble and a riot of graffiti.

Then there was, or is, i360, a futuristic viewing tower waiting to thrust its slender tip 600 feet into the air from where the stem of the wrecked West Pier meets the seafront. This, the consultants confidently predicted, would create 500 jobs and draw an extra 800,000 visitors to the town each year. So anxious was the council to have something to show for the latest product of its dream factory that it offered £14 million from its severely squeezed reserves towards the overall cost of £38 million. After the company behind the project reported a 'slippage in time scales' for the rest of the money to be forthcoming, the council upped its contribution – in the form of a loan – to £36 million.

A local builder quoted in the *Brighton Argus* assessed the chances of the tower being built as slightly less than that of Nelson getting his eye back, but work on it is in progress and – barring disasters – it is due to open in 2016.

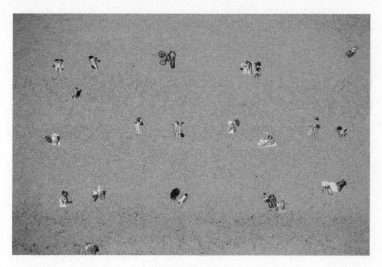

Brighton Beach

Brighton remains a curiously beguiling amalgam of the flashy, the trashy, the bizarre, the ugly and the lovely. Lord knows how much public money has been blown on drawing up, consulting on and discarding various 'big projects'. Meanwhile the budget for the boring, basic maintenance of the surviving fabric of the resort is slashed. The Big Wheel, no different from all the other Big Wheels elsewhere, makes its tedious revolutions. Underneath, the glorious latticed ironwork and cast-iron pillars of Madeira Terrace are left to rust and discolour, and the paving slabs to crack and list.

Brighton has its nude bathers and now nude cyclists, but you can still buy rubbery whelks and cockles in vinegar from the stall on the Palace Pier, with a little fork to stab them with. Anglers hoping for a plaice or a dab lob their lugworms from the platform at the end of the pier. Elderly couples nod in their deckchairs and recall the days when Tommy Trinder topped the bill at the theatre.

The aquarium is still the aquarium, even if it's called the Sea Life Centre. Candy-floss machines still occasionally whirr into sugary life. Along the Madeira Drive promenade, bolted to the grimy concrete wall, is a 'public artpiece' consisting of big steel letters stating that 'I Have Great Desire My Desire Is Great'. Its purpose, according to its creator, Naoimh Looney, is to remind those who pause in front of it of their own desires, and that desire is a great force. Brighton, Ms Looney asserts, is defined by a diverse set of desires.

Quite.

8

BUGGER BOGNOR?

Southwick used to be a proper village, close to but distinct from the western edge of Hove. It lost that distinction a long time ago, gobbled up by the coastal conurbation that now stretches almost unbroken from Brighton to Littlehampton. But its village green and its cricket club survive as reminders of a quieter age.

In 1932 Southwick Urban District Council banned cricket from the green on the grounds that it constituted a danger to passers-by and the increasing volume of traffic using the roads along the boundary. But the council had not bargained for the fighting spirit of Southwick CC and its president, the writer, broadcaster and all-round champion of England and things English, S. P. B. Mais.

Mais – the initials stood for Stuart Petre Brodie, but he was usually known as SPB – lived in The Hall, an imposing brick-and-flint residence with fine upstanding chimneys overlooking the cricket square from the angle of wide mid-wicket (or deep third man, depending on which end is bowling). He wrote books celebrating the countryside, walking, pubs, churches, local salt-of-the-earth characters, morris dancing and folk singing, with titles like *This Unknown Island* and *England's Pleasance*.

Permanently beset by financial pressures, forever veering between prosperity and indigence, SPB produced books at an amazing pace – around 300 in all, sometimes as many as eight in a single year. In addition to travelogues, he churned out novels, undemanding studies of English literature, meditations on English history and character, a history of a steel company and another of pneumatic tools, and a torrent of newspaper and magazine articles – anything, in fact, that helped pay the bills. His vast output is now pretty much forgotten, all except five words – he is credited by the *Dictionary of Slang* with having coined the insult 'dead from the neck up'.

The edict from Southwick Urban District Council roused SPB to bulldog stance. To him an Englishman's right to play cricket on his village green was as sacred as a vicar's to preach in church. He orchestrated a clamorous publicity campaign that culminated in the police solemnly recording the names of the Southwick eleven and their opponents as they stood in their whites beside the pitch. SPB announced that he would take the case to the House of Lords if need be. He also refused to pay his rates, which gave the council the chance to prosecute him and have him evicted from The Hall.

A new council elected the following year had the sense to rescind the ban. By then, though, SPB and his family had moved from Southwick down the road to Shoreham. But he always considered Southwick to have been his true home, and in his autobiography wrote that if he ever came back as a ghost he would be found hovering over the oak seat given to the cricket club by his daughters.

The Hall is still standing, looking across the green to the Cricketers, a singularly nasty 1960s rebuild of the old pub where SPB once quaffed good Sussex ale and swapped tales with Sussex men of gallant deeds with willow and leather. There is a blue plaque on the front of the house remembering the man 'who fought for cricket on the Green' which would surely have pleased SPB greatly. A notice on the front of the club's modest wooden pavilion appeals for colts, players, umpires and scorers to step forward. 'There is magic on this Green,' SPB wrote in an article for the *Sussex County Magazine*. There still is, just about.

Shoreham

Shoreham is harbour and housing. The harbour, scooped out of the eastern spur of the elongated mouth of the river Adur, is edged by wharves, cranes, warehouses, chemical tanks, stacks of timber and pre-stressed concrete and steel girders, heaps of sand and gravel, lines of containers and lorries. On the western side of the harbour entrance stands Shoreham Fort, a mid-nineteenth-century coastal battery. Extending west from the fort like a thumb stuck horizontally between the sea and the Adur is Shoreham Beach, now a prime residential area filled by the usual mishmash of mediocre gated mansions with swimming pools, tarted-up villas, derivative new-builds and shiny glass and steel apartment blocks.

Shoreham Beach's past, not that distant in time, has been pretty thoroughly wiped from the map. But, far from being forgotten, the genesis and short life of the old beach community are celebrated with love and loving attention to detail by a splendid website, www.shorehambysea.com. One of the first colonists was a popular Edwardian music-hall star, Marie Loftus, who happened to visit on a day off from performing in Brighton. She was smitten by this out-of-the-way stretch of shingle and built a bungalow to which she invited her many friends in the vaudeville and theatre business. Some were as beguiled as she was by the peace and remoteness of the location, and acquired their own bungalows along Old Fort Road.

Over the years the bungalows and chalets multiplied and spread west. A number were constructed of carriages purchased from the London, Brighton and South Coast Railway Company for £10 each and dragged by carthorse across the estuary to the beach. Others were built more conventionally of wood, but with towers, pinnacles, castellations and carved gables to proclaim their individuality. There was no electric lighting or mains drainage; paraffin lamps were the norm, and waste was taken away by night in a horse-drawn tank and dumped at sea by a barge.

By 1938 the spit of land between the sea and the estuary was home to around 700 dwellings. Many were let as holiday homes and many had become somewhat shabby as a result of neglect and battering by storms. Two years later the Army gave residents forty-eight hours' notice to leave, then cleared away most of the bungalows to prepare for the expected German invasion.

Hostilities over, some of the plotholders returned to reclaim their patches of beach and personal freedom. But government, local and national, had other ideas. The 1947 Town and Country Planning Act enshrined in law the principle that owning land conferred no right to build on it. Henceforth planning permission was required; and furthermore the local authority had the power to compel owners to sell land for approved development to take place.

That is what Sussex County Council did in the case of Shoreham Beach. The notion of allowing the reappearance of what, in effect, had been a shanty town was horrible to a new generation of town planners trained to know exactly what was best for everyone. In the words of Dennis Hardy and Colin Ward, in *Arcadia for All*, at Shoreham 'order and geometry replaced spontaneity'.

But not entirely. Along the inner side of the beach the old spirit is alive and kicking. Around forty redundant vessels, including a German minesweeper and a Royal Navy ammunition barge, have been hauled into positions at right angles to the bank of the Adur estuary and converted into individual – and in some cases downright bizarre – residences. The beach is close, there are no cars, there is a view over an RSPB bird reserve, and freedom reigns.

* * *

Worthing Pier

Worthing has a pier, not the best but not abandoned to wrack and ruin either. It has a first-rate cycle path along the seafront, and the shingle beach parcelled out by the groynes is as appealing as anywhere else's along this shingly shore. Almost all its outstanding buildings have been demolished, but quite a number of pleasant Regency terraces and squares survive, as do many rows of nice, neat brick cottages.

It has some bits and bobs of history. George III's fifteenth and last child, Princess Amelia, was sent to Worthing in the hope that a course of sea-bathing would help her tubercular knee. It was celebrated for its glasshouse tomatoes in the late nineteenth century. Oscar Wilde stayed there with his family and wrote *The Importance of Being Earnest* when not consorting with a newspaper delivery boy called Alphonse Conway, a dalliance which was picked over in excruciating detail at his trial. Harold

Pinter lived in Worthing for a time in the 1960s and wrote *Homecoming* there.

My own particular reason for lingering there was to visit Broadwater Cemetery, a magnificently characteristic Victorian burial ground spread over many acres on the inland side of town. It has been nursed back to something like decent order by a gallant band of volunteers after decades of neglect and vandalism. Twenty-five thousand of Worthing's finest are buried there. Two of them – though not strictly speaking Worthing men – were incomparable observers and chroniclers of the wonders and beauties of the English south country, and of the ways of the country people.

They lie almost side by side, Richard Jefferies and W. H. Hudson. It was Hudson's wish to be near Jefferies, whom he loved and hero-worshipped. Sharing Hudson's grave is his wife Emily, to whom he was married for forty-five years – 'I was never in love with my wife nor she with me,' he wrote after her death. She was a martyr to ill-health and lived in a boarding-house in Worthing for the last eight years of her life. Hudson visited her regularly, but Worthing's charms were lost on him: 'I hate the place and have never met anyone there who was the slightest use to me. It is talk, talk, talk but never a gleam of an original or fresh remark or view of anything that does not come out of a book or a newspaper.'

Hudson was, I think, the better writer, certainly the more approachable. His once famous South American romance, *Green Mansions*, has dated beyond hope of retrieval, but his memoir of his boyhood in Argentina, *Far Away and Long Ago*, is a masterpiece, and there are many passages in his books about nature and country life in his adopted England which still hold the attention.

There is a beautiful account in his *Nature in Downland* of visiting the cottage in Goring where Richard Jefferies died, and of going down to the beach and watching a group of dotterel feeding on a patch of sand enclosed by shingle. He meets an old man, a carter, who feeds his horses bunches of ribbon seaweed. The carter explains to Hudson that not all horses like it, but those that do are the stronger and healthier for it. 'I was happy and I laughed with the old carter as we talked,' Hudson wrote. 'But the thought of Jefferies, slain before his time by hateful destiny, still haunted me, and deep down beneath my happiness was an ineffable sadness.'

Passing through Goring myself, I got talking – not to an old carter about feeding seaweed to horses, but to an elderly lady about her beach hut. Hers, like all the others, was made of wooden planks painted white, with a symmetrical pitched roof and a rectangle of concrete slabs in front on which to sit and soak up the sun. She had bought it for £300 in 1980; now they were going for £10,000 each.

Beach huts are integral to the English seaside scene. Media attention invariably focusses on stories about huts selling for fabulous and ludicrous prices. Travel writers tend to be condescending or downright disdainful about them and the people who love them. Paul Theroux, in *Kingdom by the Sea*, dubbed them 'shallys' and mocked them for their furnishings and prints of dogs, cats and sailboats, and for having names like Sunny Hours and Bide-a-Wee. He asserts that the shallys, although very close together, are very private, their occupants unwilling or unable to engage with neighbours. This is nonsense. They can be private, if that's what the beach-hut person wants, but if you bother to talk to them, you find that the easy, informal sociability of the settlement is a huge attraction. Friendships are forged here, and marriages – good, solid ones.

To the lady at Goring her beach hut had been one of the blessings of her life – for her and her husband, for their children, and now for their grandchildren. She liked the fact that you had to make your own fun; there was no amusement park or fun-fair, not even a chippie, just an old-fashioned café where you could get a cup of tea and an ice cream. She liked there always being someone to chat to. There were 130 owners, all with something to say about dogs on the beach or ever-increasing council charges or the weather. Always the weather.

She had one sadness. To shore up the beach and restrain the eastward drift of shingle, the groynes had been reinforced by ramparts of granite boulders. One incidental effect had been to make the slope of the shingle into the water steeper – too steep for her to get out unaided any more. So she had had to give up her daily swim, which was a shame.

She offered me a mug of tea brewed on her little stove. But time was pressing, so I politely refused and pedalled off in a westerly direction.

I passed through Ferring, Angmering-on-Sea and Rustington – and quite possibly East and West Preston as well – without having any idea which one I was in at any particular time. The sameness of these coastal settlements is reinforced by the presence along much of the shoreline of a thick barrier of the salt-tolerant shrub *Elaeagnus*, separating the beach from an extended band of communal greensward.

Cycling is not encouraged on the greensward, but I kept to it where I could. The alternatives were to drag my bike over the shingle, which is very tiring and annoying, or detour far inland. I asked a bloke walking his dog how much the mansions backing onto the greensward went for. Three million, some of them, he said. I said that if I had three million, I didn't think I would choose to live there, wherever there was. Nice and quiet, though, he said, which was true. And there was the beach, very wide and empty at low tide. I watched a couple walking along the sea's edge, where the shingle gave way to wet, grey sand and the lines of waves queued for their turn to break and lose themselves. I envied them their closeness to the water.

There is an imposing convalescent home on the sea road at Rustington described in Nikolaus Pevsner and Iain Nairn's *Buildings of England: Sussex* as 'the best kind of seaside building'. There was an elderly man going turn and turn about along one of the gravel walks, visibly striving to impose his will on his dodgy pins. It struck me that there must be many worse places to recover your strength after injury or illness.

Rustington gives way to Littlehampton's rather meagre sliver of seafront, the main part of the town being to the north, arranged around a baffling one-way system along the side of the Arun estuary. E. V. Lucas, in his *Highways and Byways in Sussex*, records an anecdote of the poet Coleridge encountering the celebrated translator of Dante, Henry Francis Cary, on Littlehampton Beach. Cary was accompanied by his thirteen-year-old son and was quoting passages from Homer's *Iliad* to the lad, which is not something you would be likely to come across today. A feature of the beach that would have astonished poet and scholar alike is the celebrated East Beach Café, made of misshapen layers or ribbons of rusted steel wrapped around a glass frontage, so that from a distance it looks like an outsize piece of wreckage or flotsam.

* * *

As a small boy my brothers and I and our first cousins were taken on holiday to Middleton by my grandmother. Two nannies came as well, as did Gladys and Ern – Gladys an intimidating dragon who had been my granny's parlourmaid or some such in a long-departed era of prosperity, and Ern her exceedingly henpecked husband. We stayed in a largish house called Château Vert, although I can remember nothing green about it. The beach was greyish, the stones sharp beneath tender feet, the sea very cold. We had more fun crawling around the foundations of the house, which for some reason had been built above ground and left exposed. We paid out lengths of string to enable us to find our way back, and pretended we were being pursued along secret tunnels by enemy agents.

Returning well over half a century later, I had a sentimental notion of trying to find Château Vert. Middleton disdains straight roads leading anywhere, comprising instead a maze of crescents and circles and dead-end closes in which I quickly lost my bearings. I thought I remembered Château Vert being much bigger than most of the other houses, but now I found that they were nearly all big; and furthermore that most of them were clearly less than fifty years old. It was clear to me that the chances of the château having retained its name and escaped demolition were nil, so I gave up.

The beach had not changed at all: shingle, patches of wet sand, water in several shades of grey, streaks of reddish mud and reddish weed, dark groynes poking sharp lines at the sea. Getting to Bognor along the shore was theoretically possible, but there was no path and all manner of obstacles to lug the bike over. I wondered irritably why there was no sea wall with a smooth cycle path on top of it. The answer, of course, is that Middleton is very attentive to its 'a sought-after location' status. It is also very close to humble Bognor while wishing it wasn't, and Middleton does not want the riffraff infringing on its expensive seclusion.

So I went around via Felpham, and approached Bognor along Sea Road, the skyline gradually filling with the white canopies and cones of Butlins, like an immense pudding pavilioned in meringue.

Butlins and Bognor

I'm afraid that Bognor seafront looks as if it has been overtaken by some slow-burning tragedy. The pier is a disgrace, a ramshackle stain on the face of the town. Many, too many, of the prime positions along the front have been annexed by dreary blocks of retirement flats, and if the local council gets its way, there are plenty more of the same to come. The one decently turned-out hotel left, the Royal Norfolk, looks entirely incongruous among the general tattiness, as if it had landed by accident in Bognor instead of Eastbourne or Torquay.

For several years the great minds of Arun District Council have been trying in vain to address the wretched condition of what should be, and always was, Bognor's greatest asset. Naturally enough, they have a Seafront Strategy, a document bloated with references to hubs, flagship projects, big pictures, landmark developments, branding challenges, public-realm guidance and all the other familiar stale jargon of planning pipe dreams. Its one substantive proposal is for a multiplex cinema and more flats on the one remaining sizeable seafront site – a masterstroke which has reduced the Bognor Civic Society to gnashing its teeth in impotent rage.

It's a great shame. Although Bognor was never counted among the elite watering holes, it had its moments and its admirers. The greatest of those moments, of course, occurred in 1929 when Buckingham Palace announced that George V would be convalescing from his recent illness at the seaside – more specifically at 'Craigwell House, Bognor'.

In the words of Bognor's admirable historian, Gerard Young, 'a sense of incredulity swept through the council chambers.' Bognor, for goodness sake – the place only recently described by the writer Beverley Nichols as 'the most agonisingly hideous creation of Man on earth.' The fact that Craigwell House – the home of the president of Dunlop rubber, Sir Arthur Du Cros –

was not in Bognor at all but the neighbouring parish of Ald-wick did not deter the town from taking the King to their hearts and claiming him for their own.

At 12.30 p.m. on Saturday 9 February an ambulance carrying the monarch, recumbent on white pillows, made its way to the gates of Craigwell House, which stood overlooking the beach and had its own private promenade. A large crowd looked on. Hats were respectfully removed and handkerchiefs waved. Then, in the affecting words of the *Bognor Post*'s reporter, 'a thing happened that unlocked the floodgates of the crowd's emotions – the King waved back a greeting and the cheers would not be denied.'

For the next thirteen weeks his presence and that of Queen Mary kept Bognor and its journalists in a state of high alert. The Queen popped into town to shop at Woolworths and look for thrillers for the King. He was fond of light music and at Easter the Kneller Hall Band played a selection of favourites in the grounds of Craigwell, with hundreds of local people standing at a decent distance on the sand to share his pleasure. By then he was well enough to receive the Prime Minister, Stanley Baldwin, and was back on the cigarettes that seven years later would precipitate his final illness.

The weather was mostly pretty vile, but by May George was pronounced fit enough to resume his duties. The official car taking him back to London stopped long enough in Bognor for him to receive good wishes from the chairman of the council, and to raise his hat to cheering crowds. The following month civic pride swelled to unprecedented volume with the announcement that the King had bestowed upon Bognor 'the very greatest honour that, as a southern watering place, it could hope to attain'. From henceforth it would be Bognor Regis.

Did George ever actually say 'Bugger Bognor'? If he did, it was when his private secretary, Lord Stamfordham, presented the humble petition from the town's worthies (it is recounted that when Stamfordham returned to the delegation he said: 'The King has been graciously pleased to grant your request.'). How the myth that they were his dying words took hold is a mystery – in fact his last utterance before the morphine administered by Lord Dawson took fatal effect was 'God damn you' and was addressed to a nurse who was giving him a sedative.

One of the most touching glimpses of the King's stay at the seaside was a photograph showing him sitting on a bench watching his six-year-old granddaughter Princess Elizabeth at work on a grand and elaborate sandcastle. The picture is a subtle illustration of the liberating and levelling influence of the beach. The immensely remote, whiskered patriarchal monarch is at a stroke humanised, while the child who herself will one day be Queen appears just like any other little girl moved by the urge to shape sand into structure.

Bognor's most notable literary connection is wonderfully improbable. A blue plaque on the outside wall of a nondescript semi in Clarence Road records that James and Nora Joyce stayed in the Alexandra Guest House – as it was then – in July and August 1923. While there Joyce wrote his comical treatments of the legends of St Kevin and St Patrick and the Druid, which were later incorporated into the immortal opacities of *Finnegans Wake*.

Joyce liked it in Bognor, particularly lying on the beach and listening to the sea and the seagulls. His friend and great supporter, T. S. Eliot, arrived one day and took him off by car for a tour of the countryside inland. One of the stops was in the village of Sidlesham, in whose churchyard Joyce noticed the name Earwicker on several gravestones and borrowed it for the hero of *Finnegans Wake*, Humphrey Chimpden Earwicker.

For a time in the 1930s Bognor had hopes of being admitted to the top tier of seaside resorts. Royal patronage and the acquisition of the extra handle to its name persuaded the council that first-class status beckoned. The one amenity the town clearly lacked – that would enable it to match Bournemouth, Eastbourne, Scarborough and the rest – was an elegant and comfortable venue for refined entertainment all year round. In short, a winter gardens.

But Bognor's worthies were intimidated by the cost, and while they dithered, property developers were busy making money and lowering the tone. The land that had been attached to Craigwell House was parcelled out and the house itself was demolished. Lady Diana Cooper, who with her husband Duff Cooper, owned a house in Aldwick, lamented that 'the cornfields gave way to villadom.' The arrival in Bognor of an eager and resourceful young entrepreneur called Billy Butlin can be seen, with hindsight, to have been the final nail in the coffin of Bognor's pretensions.

Butlin began with a funfair on the esplanade, which he followed by building a zoo. On the morning it was due to open, the London *News Chronicle* carried a report that its lion had escaped and was roaming the Sussex countryside. This sensation was followed by another: a sheep had been savaged near Pagham. In fact Butlin's zoo was not due to have a lion at all, but he could see a publicity coup in the offing and swiftly arranged to buy one from a circus in Maidstone. Butlin and Bognor were on every front page, and the blaze of publicity was maintained when a local freelance journalist – coincidentally the son of a *News Chronicle* staff man – was convicted of the offence of 'putting the public in fear by circulating false statements about an escaped lion and arranging for a sheep to appear as if it had been mauled by a predator.'

In 1960 Butlin opened his famous holiday camp on a forty-acre site linking Bognor with its extremely status-conscious neighbour to the east, Felpham. Felpham was appalled; one resident referred to the horror of 'hundreds of people walking around with fish-and-chips'. But the council, intimidated by Butlin's financial muscle and disarmed by his boundless personal charm, opened its arms to the legions of campers, the redcoats, the chalets, the fluttering flags and neon signs and floodlights, the boom of the conga. One dissenting voice was heard in the council chamber. Councillor Norman Lewis forecast that if the holiday camp were permitted, Bognor would become identified with Butlin's. 'Is it money we should be after,' he demanded, 'or a town to live in?'

Half a century on Butlins has dropped the apostrophe and changed considerably in other ways. Chalets have made way for hotels, the outside pool has become an indoor pool; there is even a conference centre to go with the spa. But it remains a looming presence in the town, separate and self-contained but economically dominant. The Faustian pact alluded to by Councillor Lewis still stands, and his prophecy – that Butlins and Bognor would be perceived as one – hangs over the town like a curse that no one knows how to have lifted.

9

DID JESUS COME TO HAYLING ISLAND?

Pagham Harbour

West of Bognor and Aldwick is Pagham Harbour. A thousand years ago this natural inlet was much bigger, and deep enough for navigation. But silting and the action of the sea reduced it over time to a lonely, bird-haunted expanse of salt marsh, mud-flats and tidal creeks.

The coastal strip peters out beside the entrance to the harbour. It was an obvious place for plotlanders to head for, with the road going nowhere. Shacks and chalets sprouted above the beach, joined by railway carriages, and another remote, peaceful, self-contained and harmless little community grew. It survived the 1939–45 war but thereafter soon fell foul of the men in suits. According to Gerard Young 'at County Hall they offer prayers that Pagham may be destroyed by a tidal wave . . . the very thought of it numbs the planners' minds.'

They need not have worried. Pagham, like everywhere else, was tamed. A handful of the old carriages may still be spotted, subsumed into respectable whitewashed bungalows, their origins recalled by names like The Buffers and Pagham Halt. The last houses look across the neck of the harbour which is narrow enough to chuck a cricket ball across. Alas the tide dashes in and out with tremendous energy between the settlement and the long tongue of sand curled around from the other side, and there was no crossing it; so in order to get to Selsey I had to loop far inland, via Sidlesham, stronghold of the Earwickers.

When Pagham Harbour really was a harbour, Selsey Bill was almost an island. It extended far further out to sea than it does now, a broad foreland shaped like the head of a hammer. In 681 AD Saint Wilfrith landed somewhere along that shore, converted the Saxons to Christianity and – almost as important – showed them how to catch fish at sea.

The abbey he founded has long since vanished. Although the story that its ruins lie somewhere out under the waves is generally discounted these days, the depredations of the hungry sea have always been and remain a constant element in the lives of those who live along this stretch of coast. Selsey has long been in retreat, as has West Wittering four miles further on. Between the two, efforts to keep the sea at bay have finally been abandoned. Over the past few years the Environment Agency has spent nearly £30 million on building a new system of flood defences well inland, and in the winter of 2013 the barrier along the beach was deliberately breached to allow the sea to colonise 180 hectares of low-lying land and turn it into salt marsh.

Selsey Bill

Selsey Bill in the 1930s was unspoilt and almost unknown. In summer the sun shone and the breezes blew across the empty beaches. It was an ideal location for men and women keen on the outdoors, vigorous exercise and organised games to come for a camping holiday – particularly if they also shared a

contempt for luxury, soft sofas, nightclubs, aesthetes and homo-
sexuals, and a hatred of left-wingers and Jews.

Oswald Mosley's Blackshirts had held small-scale summer
camps at Pagham, Aldwick and West Wittering between 1933
and 1936. In 1937 the leadership decided to organise a much
bigger and more splendid camp on the western edge of Selsey,
beside a familiar local landmark, the Medmerry Windmill.
Stirring appeals were issued for donations so that cadets and
poorer Blackshirt families could attend. In the event more than
a thousand campers converged on Selsey, and the fields by the
sea were covered in white tents. The August weather was fine
and the days were filled with swimming, sandcastle building,
games and races, rallies and the singing of rousing patriotic
songs around the campfires.

The highlight was the attendance of the Leader himself over
the Bank Holiday. Newsreel footage shows a slim and smiling
Mosley, black short-sleeved Aertex shirt tucked into tightly
belted trousers, shaking hands with followers, waving to
campers, lifting a little girl and patting her leg. He watched a
boxing match and a demonstration of Diabolo, joined in the
singing of the British Union of Fascists' anthem 'Britain Awake'
and gave a speech exhorting his Blackshirts to join him in
building 'the England of our dreams'.

Among the welcoming committee of prominent local
fascists was one outstandingly odd oddball. Although Sir Archibald Hamilton was long resident in Selsey – had indeed been
president of the Selsey Conservatives – he was immensely
proud of his Scottish ancestry. He dressed in a kilt and was
attended on formal occasions by his own Rob Roy Pipers,
whose showpiece was Sir Archibald's favourite song, 'Cock o'

the North'. He smoked eucalyptus leaves in his pipe and was a devout convert to Islam, becoming Sir Archibald Abdullah Hamilton.

He died in 1939, the year before the British Union of Fascists was proscribed and Mosley himself was interned. His best friend in Selsey, Edward Heron-Allen – the historian of Selsey, translator of the *Rubaiyat of Omar Khayyam* and a world authority on minute marine organisms – wrote a touching obituary in the *Chichester Observer* which ended by quoting Phao's tribute to Akela in the *Jungle Book*: 'Howl, dogs! For a wolf has died tonight!'

Despite the undoubted underlying nastiness of the movement, there was a kind of innocence about the Sussex summer camps. In his book *Blackshirts-on-Sea* Jeremy Booker quotes the happy memories of a number of rank-and-file BUF members of the holiday at Selsey. One recalled veterans of vicious street battles building enormous sandcastles: 'Instead of the grim, clenched-jaw faces you saw at rallies and marches when you could be slashed with a razor at any time, everyone was smiling and relaxed and happy. I thought, this is what it's going to be like when Mosley wins power.'

In his rallying speech Mosley looked forward to the day when 'the young manhood and womanhood of Britain will gather in great camps the same as this.' In a way he was right. The fields where the Blackshirt tents were pitched and the standards raised are now covered by Bunn Leisure's West Sands Holiday Park; although whether the massed ranks of mobile homes bristling with satellite dishes correspond with Mosley's vision of the 'great comradeship of the Fascist future' is open to doubt.

Not far away, down a lane off the High Street, is Selsey Cricket Club's ground. For many years this was a spiritual home of the astronomer Sir Patrick Moore, a Selsey institution and a worthy successor to Sir Archibald Abdullah Hamilton in the role of local eccentric. Well into his seventies Moore was still turning out for a Selsey XI; by his own admission he was a useless batsman and worse fielder, but his apparently guileless looping leg-breaks bamboozled many a hapless victim over his long career. Oddly enough, Moore's political views were not dissimilar to Mosley's. But with Moore, rampant racism, sexism and Little Englandism were somehow rendered innocuous and even lovable by his shambling presence and wide range of peculiar mannerisms.

In East Wittering I met Neil, who was about to mow someone else's lawn. He had long grey hair gathered into a ponytail,

West Wittering

which made him look like an old rocker. It turned out that he was an old rocker, who had worked for many years as a roadie setting up gigs for the likes of Joan Armatrading and The Kinks. He had seen some wild stuff, had Neil, you could tell from his seamed face and knowing eyes and the slow way he nodded his head. Then he had met a local girl and settled down. Now he looked after peoples' gardens for them.

East Wittering, Neil said, was not as classy as West Wittering. Keith Richards had a house at West Wittering, as did Richard Branson's mother. Keith had given thirty grand for the village hall's new roof. And he came in the pub when he was around, which admittedly was not often. A real regular guy, Keith.

Classier maybe, but East Wittering has the flood defences. West Wittering just has its beach, which at low tide is enormous. I watched a windsurfer plodding over the sand towards a distant pale sea, the sails of his board flapping like the wings of a huge blue injured bird.

Behind the beach is a line of very smart, neat beach huts painted blue and green and red and white, with little verandahs and an immensity of sand in front. Keith Richards had one of them; paid £60,000 for it, according to the newspapers. They don't come up very often and those on the waiting list are invited to submit sealed bids.

The road ends abruptly, and the beach runs out, and you are at the mouth of Chichester Harbour and no longer on the Channel shore. Sussex is finished. Across the water are Hampshire and the riddles of Hayling Island.

* * *

Hayling Island

There was an elderly man standing on the shingle staring peacefully at the shallow sea. It was mid-April, blowy and a bit chilly, the water choppy under a broken sky. He wore a black overcoat and black gloves and one of those hats worn by Russian leaders of the Brezhnev era. He told me he could not be happy unless he was near the sea. He had been born at Whitley Bay near Newcastle and had lived in Poole for thirty years before retiring to Hayling Island.

'I like it here,' he said. 'I can hear the sea from my bedroom. It sends me to sleep. What is it about the seaside? I don't know, I just know I can't be without it.'

The middle-aged lady working in the library was fourth-generation Hayling Island. She had seen the whole of the southern end of the island built over and suburbanised. It was a shame, she said, but that was the way of things. You couldn't expect it to stay as it was. No, she had no desire to get away. 'If

I'm inland for any length of time I start getting breathless. I have to be somewhere on the edge.' She walked on the beach every day, on the shingle. 'It doesn't matter what the weather is, your feet stay clean. I love that.'

Below the band of shingle, low tide exposes a great expanse of pale sand. John Betjeman wrote fondly of 'the ripple and suck of a smooth tide flooding over silvery mud, and the salt, sand-coated vegetation of the marsh.' Betjeman was there in time to enjoy the old Hayling Island, before the village became a shapeless holiday resort and the prime sites along the seafront were filled with modern villas and anonymous blocks of flats. Towards the western end is Norfolk Crescent, an incongruously gracious Georgian relic of a short-lived attempt in the 1820s to create a smart seaside resort, which has been permitted to slide into a sad state of decay.

Hayling Island's one undisputed claim to fame, or at least notice, is that windsurfing was invented there by a local lad, Peter Chilvers, whose invention has conquered the world and brought him honour wherever the wind whips across waves. More contentious is the story that the Holy Grail is buried somewhere on the island; and more contentious still the theory that Jesus Christ himself spent time there.

First, the Grail. It hasn't been found on Hayling Island yet, nor – unless I have missed something – in any of the other locations proposed by Grail enthusiasts between Ethiopia and Nova Scotia. There is, however, a Knights Templar cross on the floor of the chancel of St Mary's Church, which some like to see as a clue. It was enough, apparently, to persuade the novelist Nevil Shute that it should be investigated by unorthodox means.

Shute's full name was Nevil Shute Norway. Born in 1899, he

was a brilliantly original aeronautical engineer and designer who founded a highly successful aircraft company in Portsmouth and became a millionaire, and who wrote fiction to relax. In 1940 Shute Norway joined a highly hush-hush unit called the Department of Miscellaneous Weapons, known colloquially as the Wheezers and Dodgers, where he designed or helped design a variety of death-dealing contraptions. The best-known of these was the Great Panjandrum, a cylinder suspended between two Catherine wheels bristling with rockets which was intended to carry 4000 pounds of high explosives at 60 m.p.h. up and through Rommel's concrete defence wall along the Normandy beaches, although the project was abandoned after trials at Westward Ho! ended prematurely amid a storm of errant exploding rockets.

Shute Norway had a briskly uncomplicated view of novel-writing in wartime: 'I have no respect for the writer of any age or sex who thinks he or she can serve the country best by sitting still and writing.' Nevertheless he did sit still and write in the evenings after work, and right at the end of the war produced the book which became one of his greatest successes.

No Highway is an extraordinary novel, extraordinary in its ordinariness. The story, such as it is, revolves around a new airliner which is rushed prematurely into commercial use with disastrous results. The setting is mainly suburban; the protagonist is a dull, socially inept nonentity; there is some love but no sex; not much action, no violence. The prose is flat and functional, the dialogue wooden, the characterisation perfunctory, the denouement more than somewhat absurd. Yet it sold in mounds, and was made into a Hollywood picture with James Stewart and Marlene Dietrich. Did I miss something?

The climax of *No Highway* sees the designer of the airliner put his daughter into a trance and prompt her, by means of a planchette, to identify the location in the Canadian wilderness of the tailpiece of the crashed plane. Like other hard-nosed boffins, Shute Norway had a strong mystical streak, which apparently led him to try to make contact with those Knights Templar (or possibly French monks) who may or may not have brought the Grail to Hayling Island.

Shute Norway and his family lived in Pond Head House, a large, secluded residence close to Mengeham Rythe, a creek on the south-eastern side of the island giving access to Chichester Harbour. His neighbour and fellow sailing-club stalwart was Rear-Admiral Ralph Fisher. The story goes that Fisher had a barn or Wendy house on his property, very hidden away, and that seances were conducted there to try to ascertain the whereabouts of the chalice from which Jesus drank at the Last Supper. Details are sketchy – actually, more like non-existent – but I think we can safely assume that firm information about the Grail's whereabouts was not forthcoming.

By the time *No Highway* was published, Nevil Shute Norway had had enough of Hayling Island, and indeed of England. He was much upset by a row at the sailing club, which led to him being rebuked by the Commodore for the unspeakable offence of untying a boat that had used his mooring without permission and letting it float out to sea. He was also a deep-dyed Conservative and meritocrat who loathed the idea of a welfare state, and regarded the election of the Labour government with horror. He emigrated to Australia, where he wrote more bestsellers including *A Town Like Alice*, and his famous vision of post-nuclear dystopia, *On The Beach*. Incidentally,

Shute Norway much disliked the Hollywood version of this, his last completed book, because it depicted the love between Gregory Peck and Ava Gardner being consummated, whereas the point in the novel was that the two protagonists were too decent to give way to coarse fleshly urges.

So, did Jesus come to Hayling Island?

To my uninformed eye, the case looks rather thin; in fact it makes the Holy Grail story seem as solid as rock. The main evidence adduced by the authors of a recent guide to the island is a reference in a letter from St Augustine to the Pope of the time to a 'Royal Island' with a church 'built by no human act but by the hands of Christ himself.' This Royal Island, the authors of the guide assert, can be none other than Hayling Island, its royal status derived from a connection with Commius, leader of the Atrebates tribe in Gaul. They claim it was given special protected status by Julius Caesar, which would have made it a safe haven for the Jewish tin merchant Joseph of Arimathea when he came to Britain with his young charge – Jesus of Nazareth.

'It is exciting to think that the young Jesus could have enjoyed life on this island,' the guide says. 'We could easily imagine him teaching and healing people near the church.' Indeed. But then again . . .

10

WIGHT

I feel I owe the Isle of Wight an apology for leaving it out of this book, although I am confident it will survive the blow. I have also omitted the Channel Islands, but am not inclined to apologise to them, as my subject is the Channel shore and the Channel Islands clearly do not belong to it.

For the same reason I have left out the major Channel ports except where – as in the case of Dover, Folkestone and Newhaven – they face directly onto the open sea. I do not think I need to say sorry to Chichester, Portsmouth, Gosport, Southampton, Lymington, Poole, Dartmouth, Plymouth, Fowey or Falmouth. The point about them is that, strictly speaking, they are NOT on the Channel. They had good, deep anchorages and protected, defensible access to the open sea, which is why they became what they became. That was their good fortune, and England's good fortune.

So I need not feel I have let these historic ports down. But I am troubled by the Isle of Wight. It clearly does have a Channel shore, between Bembridge and the Needles, and indeed was part of the mainland until a mere seven thousand years ago. All I can say in my defence is that I decided on a mainland journey and I stuck to that. I hope the Isle will forgive me, for I think highly of it and its people and have had happy seaside days there both as boy and man.

The Isle of Wight became detached from what is now Hampshire as a result of the enormous rise in sea levels that followed the end of the last Ice Age. Very broadly speaking, the Channel as we know it took shape as part of that process. At the eastern end, between Dover and Calais, a final break with mainland Europe was effected. West was open sea, leading to the Atlantic.

Sonar imaging of the Channel bed has revealed the existence of a submerged valley miles wide and up to fifty metres deep which the scientists believe was scoured from the chalk bedrock by a flood of cataclysmic violence around 450,000 years ago. Their hypothesis is that it was caused when the southern wall holding in a giant lake extending from East Anglia across the southern North Sea to Germany gave way, or was breached – possibly as a result of an earthquake. It is likely that there was a second cataclysm, 200,000 years or so after the first, which left the chalk cliffs along the Kent coast near Dover and along the north French coast as relics of the ridge as it had been, with a shelf between that would have been periodically submerged by rises in sea levels, and finally submerged for good.

Although that process left the proto-Channel familiar to us now, the eastern section – roughly from the Isle of Wight to Dover – was vulnerable to further significant reshaping. It was low-lying and composed of softish rock, easily eroded. Over time that stretch of coastline collapsed into marsh and shallow sea – the old cliff line is discernible as an arc between Hastings and Hythe – although it was subsequently reclaimed as dry or dryish land.

West of the Solent the line of the coast has been altered much less, partly because the rock is generally harder, partly because the lie of the hinterland is higher. Cliff faces have been pushed back and continue to be pushed back, those of sandstone much more obviously than those of granite. What were once river valleys have been invaded by the sea and turned into estuaries or permanent inlets, such as the one between Salcombe and Kingsbridge in Devon. But overall the line has been modified rather than radically redrawn, in contrast to the eastern section.

The character of the beaches changes with the coastline itself. The typical West Country beach is of fine sand overlaying a substratum of rock. The sand is the pulverised fragments of the rocks and stones and clays caught between the headlands and pounded and beaten by the waves. Further east, where the coast is less fractured by headlands and therefore more open, shingle predominates. The prevailing west and south-west winds compel an incessant eastward shifting of stones great and small. East of the Isle of Wight most of the beaches are of shingle down to the half-tide mark. The shingle gives way to sand, which then slopes more gently down to the sea's edge, and on below the water. Actually sand is present all the way up to high-tide level, but overlaid by the stones.

This shift of the shingle is an inexorable process. The waves break at an angle against the beach (although the backwash is perpendicular). One small pebble can be shunted several feet to the east by one wave of modest force. But it is only the top layer of stones that is exposed to the force of the waves. The remainder stay where they are until they are exposed. Then it is their turn. In cycles the whole enormous mass of stones migrates along the shore, an implacable, relentless march. The positioning of groynes along the beaches checks the march; the shingle piles up to the west of these obstructions, forming steep drops in the eastern side. Left to their own devices the groynes are eventually buried.

Hurst Castle

After the break that is the Solent, the Channel shore resumes at Hurst Point, the low spit of land on which Hurst Castle was built on the orders of Henry VIII to guard the western approach to Southampton. The first significant settlement to the west is Milford-on-Sea (or Milford On Sea, no one seems entirely sure of the hyphens) which is bunched above low, rapidly eroding sandstone and gravel cliffs a couple of miles west of Hurst Point. It is a pleasant, unremarkable place, the old village centre enclosed by the usual sprawl of modern housing. There is not much sign now of what it might have been.

In the 1880s the local bigwig, William Cornwallis-West, decided to emulate what his friend the Duke of Devonshire had done in Eastbourne, and turn Milford into a classy seaside resort. The plans were ambitious. There would be a pier, a railway station, warm-water baths, elegant hotels, a fine esplanade. The first step was to amplify Milford's name by adding the 'On Sea', and the second was to lay out spacious pleasure gardens on the clifftop. There was no third step; the funds available from Cornwallis-West were swiftly exhausted, and his hopes of attracting investors were apparently stymied by an outbreak of typhoid.

In time the Milford estate – centred on Newlands Manor, a Gothic pile to the north of the village – was inherited by William's only son, George. Unloved and ignored by his mother, he was a profligate young man with a penchant for unsuitable and short-lived marriages – first to Winston Churchill's mother (he was about the same age as Winston), and then to the actress Mrs Patrick Campbell. With Newlands Manor he also inherited the family's other estate, Ruthin Castle in Denbighshire, but both were by then saddled by crushing debt. He sold the Welsh castle and estate in 1919 and Newlands Manor the following year. Poor chap, he continued to be plagued by money worries for the rest of his life, which ended abruptly in 1951 in his suicide.

I have a soft spot for him because he had a soft spot for fish and fishing. In addition to a very popular volume of memoirs, *Edwardian Heydays*, George put together a charming medley of fishing tales which he called *Edwardians Go Fishing*. As a boy he caught roach in the lake at Newlands, dace and trout in the little stream that ran out of the New Forest into the Solent at

Keyhaven and some decent sea trout in its estuary. But most of the book consists of a string of anecdotes peppered with the names of the blue bloods, the rich, the idle and the highly privileged. A typical Cornwallis-West paragraph begins thus:

'Many years ago I found myself at a weekend party at Keele Hall, where the late King Edward was also a guest. At the bottom of the garden was a large clear pond fed by springs, and in it innumerable trout had been placed by Colonel Ralph Sneyd, the owner of the place which at that time was let to Grand Duke Michael of Russia . . .'

The coastline between Hurst Point and Christchurch Harbour has been in steady retreat for centuries. Late sixteenth-century maps show Milford well inland and the village of Hordle and its church just to the west and close to the sea. Two centuries later the church was crumbling on the cliff edge and the houses nearby were abandoned. The Earl of Bute was thoroughly irritated by the reduction in his estate at Highcliffe, and when his cliff path disappeared over the edge his workmen dug a new one in the hope that he would not notice the difference. Examination of the first Ordnance Survey map of 1810 suggests that the cliff edge has retreated around 200 yards since then.

This stretch of Channel shore took a tremendous battering in the storms of late winter 2014. The worst, on St Valentine's Day, destroyed many of Milford's distinctive concrete beach huts and sent huge waves laced with stones bursting over the back of the beach, the sea wall and the road. The windows of the Marine Restaurant on Hurst Road were shattered and its ground floor was engulfed by sea water; couples who'd arrived intent on romance found themselves being rescued by the Army.

The next settlement to the west, Barton, finds itself contemplating ever closer communion with the advancing sea. Many of the older cottages built near the edge were gobbled up by major landslips in 1953 and in the winter of 1974–5, and since then there have been many more, less spectacular slippages. A wide buffer of greensward was left between the cliffs and the bungalows and villas and blocks of flats that spread across what was previously open farmland from the 1930s onwards. At the time it must have seemed ample protection against the sea, but little by little it is being nibbled away.

Between Milford and Barton are the rolling fairways and emerald greens of Barton Golf Club. There are probably a few club stalwarts who would elect to have their mortal remains interred there if they could, but thus far the only memorial is not to a golfer at all, but to a horse – or, to be more precise, a pony.

Remember the 1968 Mexico Olympics? Bob Beamon's immortal leap. The Fosbury Flop. The Black Power salute. David Hemery's gold in the 400m hurdles. Wonderful Lillian Board's silver. And Stroller, the only pony ever to showjump at Olympic level.

Showjumping was very big on the BBC in those distant days. The music from Mozart via Waldo de los Rios, commentary from Dorian Williams and Raymond Brooks-Ward, men and women in hats and tight jackets and breeches circumnavigating Hickstead knocking poles down. My grandmother – who lived next door to us and had a TV when we did not – loved it with a passion. I detested it as a non-sport, but the Olympics was different. It would have required a heart of stone not to have been stirred and moved by the gallantry and delicacy of this little horse and the fresh-faced farmer's daughter who rode him, wholesome Marion Coakes.

How we booed her great rival, the German Alwin Schocke-möhle on his Teutonic beast. But it was the American Bill Steinkraus and Snowbound who thwarted Coakes and Stroller in the individual jumping. She had two down in the final round, he had one. But never mind – in that innocent, pre-professional era we loved our brave losers as much as our rare winners, and none lost more bravely than little Stroller.

He was already almost eighteen when winning silver in Mexico, and he went on competing into his twenties before retiring to graze honourably at the farm owned by Marion's parents. Stroller lived to thirty-six, by which time part of the farm had been sold to be incorporated into Barton golf course. And I went back to detesting showjumping.

Barton-on-Sea

On the greensward at Barton two old naval salts were walking their schnauzers. They had both served at HMS *Ganges*, the training establishment in Suffolk, but at different times, so hadn't known each other until retirement to Barton brought them together. Now both their wives were dead, and they met twice a day in fine weather to stroll a little creakily in one direction and then back while the little dogs snuffled and scampered about.

I asked about Barton. 'Wind and widows,' the one in the woolly hat said. 'Or in our case widowers.' He'd been there ten years — 'it'll be a pine box job,' he replied when I asked him if he ever thought of moving. 'Best view in England,' his friend said. And on a morning like that morning, the sky blue, the sea blue and flecked with white wave crests, the Needles gleaming to the east and Old Harry to the west, I could not argue.

* * *

I had to wait a while at Mudeford for the ferry across to Hengistbury Head. The incoming tide was racing through the narrow entrance into Christchurch Harbour, forcing the navigation buoys back at an angle against their taut chains, boiling and gurgling around the boats at anchor. I watched a fisherman tidying up the ropes and pots in his vessel. I asked him how the fishing was. 'Bloody awful,' he snarled. He'd been at it for fifty years, couldn't remember a worse three months: the wind in the east, the sole and plaice somewhere, but not in Christchurch Bay where they should have been. 'Bloody hopeless waste of time,' he grunted, then stalked off to the pub.

Beach huts at Hengistbury Head

The most costly beach huts in the country are those arranged in two snaking lines along the tongue of sand and scrubby grass licking across the mouth of Christchurch Harbour from the west. One line looks out to sea, the other across the harbour, and it is these that are the most select: £200,000 plus is the going rate, which at £1000 a square foot puts them up with a flat in Mayfair.

They are bigger than normal beach huts – big enough to accommodate a minute mezzanine – and the regulations allow overnight use for eight months of the year. I accosted an elderly chap doing good work with a dustpan and brush. He said his was owned by his son, who'd done nicely in property. There was a wooden ladder leading up to where the mattresses were laid out under the pitched roof. He told me Christchurch Council charged £3000 ground rent for each property and

£30,000 in fees when one changed hands, which made Mudeford Spit a nice little milch cow.

I wheeled my bike past the clutter of dinghies and kayaks and surfboards. Wetsuits encrusted with sand had been slung over every verandah rail. Where the huts end and the slopes of Hengistbury Head begin there is a pond with a notice beside it appealing for its colony of natterjack toads to be left in peace. A million people a year come to Hengistbury Head to tramp around the network of paths, gaze over the water and study other noticeboards about the sea knotgrass, carnivorous heath-land flowers, green hairstreak butterflies, rare beetles, skylarks, Dartford warblers and other flora and fauna to be found there.

It is the last significant stretch of coastland in East Dorset that has not been covered in houses. It is a Nature Reserve, a Site of Special Scientific Interest (SSSI), a Special Area of Conservation, a Special Protection Area, an Environmentally Sensitive Area and a Site of Nature Conservation Interest. (I may have missed out one or two other designations.) In a world ideal for natterjack toads and Dartford warblers no one would go near the place. But they are not the point, they are merely the advertised – though infrequently spotted – attractions. The point is that the Head is an asset, and to emphasise the point, a spanking-new and tremendously eco (grass roof, straw-bale walls, solar heating, etc.) £1.25 million visitor centre has been opened.

It is close to the Double Dykes, a visually uninteresting for-tification of some kind raised by Iron Age people. A particularly lavish display board nearby informs the eager visitor that Hengistbury Head was then the most important port in Britain, which makes you wonder about its rivals. Olives, wine, glass and assorted luxuries are said to have been imported. Exports included precious metals, slaves and hunting dogs. Hunting dogs? Where did they get that from?

Everything would have been very different around here if Gordon Selfridge, of Selfridges in Oxford Street, had got his way – as he usually did. At the end of the 1914–18 war Selfridge was the tenant of Highcliffe Castle, from whose battlements he cast hungry eyes across Christchurch Bay to Hengistbury Head. Having built the biggest department store in London, it must have seemed the obvious next step for this epitome of the American money-crazed vulgarian to build the biggest castle in the world.

He bought the Head from Sir George Meyrick, who owned a goodly chunk of Anglesey and of the most valuable land in Bournemouth. Selfridge summoned the fashionable architect of the day, Philip Tilden, and instructed him to think bigger than he had ever have dreamed of.

Tilden's design, expressed in hundreds of drawings, envisaged encircling the high ground of Hengistbury Head with four miles of walls punctuated by towers. There would be a lesser castle sheer to the sea and a greater castle within. A dual drive would sweep up on the inland side, and divide to pass through two gateways in the bastioned walls. Two hundred and fifty guest suites, each with bedroom, bathroom, dressing room and sitting room, would be accommodated within a tower 300 feet high. There would a dome with a diameter only ten feet less than that of St Paul's, a theatre, art galleries, tennis courts, winter gardens, a hall of mirrors to match the one at Versailles, a covered lake and a Gothic hall complete with organ.

The cost of this exercise in gigantism was put at a modest £2.5 million (at least £100 million in today's money). But as Tilden's portfolio of designs grew, Selfridge's fortune diminished. The Wall Street crash dealt a mortal blow to any lingering hopes that Hengistbury Castle might ever take physical form. In 1930 Selfridge sold the land to Bournemouth Borough Council for a little over £25,000. A few years later he was virtually penniless, cleaned out by his addiction to high living, gambling and the company of parasitic female hangers-on.

11

PEACE AND LOVE

'Very pleasant is this winter residence which retains its ever-green beauty and aromatic odours through all the severity of winter.' These words, from one of the innumerable Victorian and Edwardian guides to the genteel charms of Bournemouth, echoed somewhat hollowly on a boisterous late January day. The south-west gale drove flying sand into the eyes rather than distributing aromatic odours. Evergreens there certainly were, wind-blasted and sombre, lining the Pine Walk (disappointingly no longer known as the Invalids' Walk). The grey heaving sea dispatched line after line of white waves to beat against the criss-cross supports of the pier. A flotilla of surfers bobbed on the water, craning black-hooded heads to identify the standout crest that would lift them and drive them to the beach.

I had a wander through the town centre, which seemed to me rather meagre for such an enormous conurbation. There were no pubs of the kind that would draw me through the doors, not a restaurant where I would willingly have eaten, no fishing tackle or secondhand bookshops or interesting junk shops; just flash bars and Tex-Mex and the usual chains. The

wind, laced with rain, muscled down Avenue Road and whipped around the deserted space of The Square, buffeting the
circular glass café at the centre where fugitives from the weather
huddled over their *lattes*.

I had a room at the Royal Bath Hotel, attracted partly by
Oscar Wilde's recommendation – he congratulated the propri-
etors for creating 'a palace of the greatest beauty and elegance'
and filling it with 'gems of art' – and also by the offer of dinner,
bed and breakfast for £62. The dinner, however, was a serious
disappointment. The restaurant, inevitably called Oscar's, was
virtually empty, which did not stop the head waiter scolding me
for not booking a table. The choices for the set menu were
wretched: I paid a £7 surcharge for an exiguous ribeye steak.
Having demolished my slice of strawberry gâteau in three
mouthfuls I asked the waiter if it might be possible to have a
little cheese to help fill up a hungry traveller. He looked at me
as if I'd asked him to procure a tart, shook his head and went off
to rattle some more cutlery.

In the morning workmen were busy demolishing the IMAX
cinema on the seafront. The one distinction in the very short
life of this glass-and-steel crime against architecture was to have
won a national poll to identify the most hated building in
Britain, and it has now been replaced by an 'open-air multi-use
events space'. The council justified getting rid of it on the
grounds that it was ugly, which it certainly was. It occurred to
me that, were the removal of ugly buildings to be adopted as a
council priority, a long list of Bournemouth's more recent
constructions would be at risk, starting with the town's International Centre.

The hideous and brutal BIC squats like a monstrous dark-red

toad opposite the IMAX site. One cannot even revile the designers of this enormity by name – the plaque inside the entrance recording the official opening in 1984 identifies the architects as Module 2 Bridgend. As far as I can ascertain, this company no longer exists. When it did, it advertised itself as specialising in 'low-cost recreation and sports centre facilities'; it was chosen by the Conservative council because its estimate was lower than anyone else's.

I crossed the road to another building, starkly angular with soaring redbrick walls, a square tower and a needle of a spire. The Punshon Memorial Methodist Church may not be easy on the eye – it isn't – but at least it articulates an idea of what a public building should be. It was built in the 1950s when the Methodists must have been going strong in Bournemouth, which they no longer are. Worship ceased there a few years ago and the church was bought by a well-known Bournemouth property developer, Philip Oram.

I wandered inside and immediately encountered a man who looked like a beardless version of the former Liverpool football manager, Rafael Benítez. He introduced himself as Derek Stuart and said he was an associate of Mr Oram. Encouraged by my interest, he embarked upon an account of the ups and downs of his business career – including how he came to own two E-Type Jags at seventeen and a Rolls-Royce at eighteen. From that Mr Stuart moved seamlessly into a complex narrative concerning the negotiations with Bournemouth Council over the church's future, which I found somewhat difficult to follow. The upshot, however, was clear: it was to be transformed into the John Lennon Hotel of Peace and Love under the control of a charity which planned to fund the £4 million asking price by selling the four million bricks used to build it at £1 each to four million children in the 196 countries of the world.

Even though the details of Derek Stuart's business plan seemed a little imprecise, I thought Lennon would have liked the notion. He was famously keen on peace and love, which seemed to be exactly what Bournemouth needed a lot more of.

I took refuge from the wind and rain in the light and airy public library. Upstairs there is a splendid local studies and history section, where dedicated staff guard and cherish Bournemouth's rich literary heritage. Considering that two hundred years ago it was no more than a scattering of fishermen's hovels, and even fifty years later had a population of just two thousand, it is extraordinary how many writers and other notables have associations with the town. It is speckled with blue plaques; I was told that they had run out of money for any more.

Shelley's heart, famously – and possibly apocryphally – snatched by Trelawny from the funeral fire on the beach near Viareggio, is interred at St Peter's Church. The last time Gladstone appeared in public was at Bournemouth Station, on his way home to die – in response to the cheers he delivered his last public utterance: 'God bless you all and this place and the land you love.' Robert Louis Stevenson spent three years at various addresses along the seafront where he wrote *Kidnapped* and *The Strange Case of Doctor Jekyll and Mr Hyde*. Rupert Brooke stayed with his grandfather in Dean Park Road – the plaque states proudly 'here Rupert Brooke discovered poetry'. Galsworthy went to school in Bournemouth and D. H. Lawrence wrote his story *The Trespasser* while staying at a boarding house in St Peter's Road.

It is pleasing to think of the French symbolist Paul Verlaine – absinthe addict and scandalous bisexual – teaching the sons of Bournemouth worthies at St Aloysius's School in Surrey Road. Apart from trying to drum into their heads the essentials of his own mother tongue and what he called 'the dead languages', Verlaine took the boys bathing most days and spent a lot of time staring at the sea. He wrote a poem, called *Bournemouth*:

> *Le long bois de sapins se tord jusqu'au rivage,*
> *L'étroit bois de sapins, de lauriers et de pins,*
> *Avec la ville autour déguisée en village:*
> *Chalets éparpillés rouges dans le feuillage*
> *Et les blanches villas des stations de bains . . .*

Other associations are perhaps less elevated. Dorothy L. Sayers gave birth in secret to her only child at a discreet maternity home in Tuckton, the eastern outpost of Bournemouth. J. R. R. Tolkien spent many holidays in Room 37 of the Hotel Miramar between Grove Road and East Overcliff Drive, and eventually retired to a bungalow in Lakeside Road, Branksome. Bill Bryson spent two years as a sub-editor on the *Bournemouth Echo* and wrote affectionately about the town in *Notes from a Small Island*. That phenomenon of verbal fecundity, John Creasey, lived in Bournemouth for twenty years and tried in vain to become the town's Liberal MP; he wrote 7000 words every day, published more than 600 books under twenty-eight different names, twenty-nine of them in a single year, and is now utterly forgotten.

*

Tolstoy did not come to Bournemouth, but his spirit was very strongly present. For ten years his most fervent disciple – his lover, according to Tolstoy's crazily jealous wife, Sonya – was resident in the quiet and respectable suburb of Tuckton. Count Vladimir Tcherkov has not, on the whole, received favourable notices. In the film dramatisation of Tolstoy's old age, *The Last Station*, he was portrayed by the American actor Paul Giamatti as sleek, devious, tyrannical and ruthless in his determination to shut Tolstoy's wife and most of their children out of what was left of his life. Henri Troyat's epic biography of the writer presents Tcherkov in a very similar light, and Tolstoy as being torn and buffeted between competing claims of spiritual ownership.

Certainly Tcherkov did – for better or worse – devote himself with singular energy to supporting and encouraging Tolstoy and promoting his work. Born into an immensely wealthy family, he met the writer for the first time in 1883 and succumbed immediately to Tolstoy's magnetism. Spreading the Tolstoyan message became his single mission, one that inevitably attracted unfavourable attention from the Tsarist censors. Tcherkov left for England in 1897 and graduated in time to Tuckton, where his mother had settled. There was an established community of exiled Russians at Tuckton House, which Tcherkov quickly took control of and converted to Tolstoyan principles. They wore smocks and lived the simple life: hard beds, upright wooden chairs, plenty of hard work outdoors, modest portions of vegetarian food, no alcohol, no indulgence in the vices of the flesh.

Tcherkov acquired a pumping station from Bournemouth Gas and Water Company and converted it into a branch of the Free Age Press, devoted to publishing Tolstoy's religious and ethical works in English and other European languages. Tcherkov had the building fitted with a steel-lined strong room, in which were stored all the original manuscripts, and to which only he had the key.

Eventually the Russian authorities relented and allowed Tcherkov to return and renew his collaboration with the master. After Tolstoy's death in 1910, he exploited his position as literary executor to tighten his control over the legacy. The Bolsheviks seem to have taken the view that, in spirit anyway, Tolstoy was one of them, and Lenin commissioned Tcherkov to oversee a new edition of the complete works. He was clearly a survivor – his father was executed and his mother returned to Bournemouth as an exile, but he remained in Moscow and in favour until his death in 1937.

Among the exiles who found sanctuary at Tuckton House was Alexander Sirnis, half-Latvian, half-Russian, wholly revolutionary. He had been recruited by Tcherkov to help translate Tolstoy's diaries into English, and while living at the commune met and married a middle-class English woman of advanced political views, Gertrude Stedman. Sirnis later became the first translator of Lenin's works into English, but his contribution to the Communist cause was to be far eclipsed by that of his daughter Melita, whom he called Letty. In 1999 she was revealed – to general astonishment – to have been a long-term spy for the Russians. As Melita Norwood she had passed vital secrets about the Anglo-American atomic bomb project to Moscow, and had been regarded by the KGB as a more precious asset than Philby, Burgess and Maclean.

I came across a curious footnote to the story of the Russians of Tuckton in the form of a letter published in the *Bournemouth*

Echo on 4 February 1962. It came from Vladimir V. Tcherkov, a resident of Moscow, and recalled his happy days playing at left-back for Tuckton Football Club when his father was the president (and, incidentally, Alexander Sirnis was playing on the left-wing). The letter says that the writer has been distressed to hear from his friend, Mr Potter, that the team were having a hard time of it in the local league. 'I hope that the boys will play better in the second half of the season,' Mr Tcherkov wrote.

There is a plaque on the wall of the old pumping station in Tuckton in memory of its Tolstoy connection. No novelist secured greater fame in his lifetime and retained it thereafter than Tolstoy. Few, if any, can have subsided into deeper obscurity than a former resident of 4 Amira Court, a modestly proportioned whitewashed block of apartments across Bourne Avenue from the Bournemouth Tennis Club.

Yet there was a time when the latest offering from Rupert Croft-Cooke – a novel, a detective story, a volume of memoirs – was, if not eagerly awaited by a large and avid readership, at least guaranteed to receive some respectful notices and respectable sales. Croft-Cooke covered a wide range. There was his policeman, Sergeant Beef, and his gentleman schoolmaster detective, Carolus Deene (*A Louse for the Hangman*, *A Bone and a Hank of Hair* and more than twenty others). There were books about cooking, darts, the circus, Buffalo Bill. There were novels, thirty or so of them. Above all there was the autobiography, under the umbrella title *The Sensual World*: twenty-four volumes of it (with three supplementaries), surely the most extended such exercise ever published.

Such concentration on the life lived would suggest an ego to match. But to judge from the last in the series, *The Green, Green Grass* – written in Bournemouth and a lot of it about his life there – Croft-Cooke was actually rather modest. Like Nevil Shute's *No Highway*, its distinction is in its ordinariness. He writes like the regular at the bar in the Three Horseshoes, pint of bitter to hand, in cardigan and old corduroys, holding forth gently, but not insistently or disputatiously, about the little things that make up daily life.

In *The Green, Green Grass* Croft-Cooke explains that he has come to live in Bournemouth after many years abroad because his parents, his brother and a favourite nephew all spent their honeymoons at the Royal Bath Hotel (Croft-Cooke himself was a homosexual who did six months in Wormwood Scrubs in 1953 after being convicted on highly dubious evidence of illicit sex with two Navy cooks). He is not worried by the sky-high rates of income tax – this is 1973 – 'since I do not earn enough to make it payable'. He likes his cheerful flat and the view it gives him of the tennis courts where 'tanned and handsome young men stripped to the waist disport themselves'. He finds the town endlessly diverting – 'discreetly plutocratic in its residents, Midlands in its holidaymakers, swinging and cosmopolitan in its youth.'

As a result of a stroke, Croft-Cooke is confined indoors and discovers the joys of television. He relishes Morecambe and Wise and Joyce Grenfell, enjoys The Goodies (who 'so cleverly exploit the unexpected'), adores *It Ain't Half Hot Mum* for its 'nostalgic reality, truth of detail and verisimilitude … I find it sublimely funny.' He considers breakfast cereals, wondering if the Force Flakes and Grape Nuts of his youth were any better than the Weetabix and Corn Flakes of today. He muses on the pleasures of bloaters and kedgeree and pickled pork, and is delighted by the antics of grey squirrels outside the window. Of his writing he says: 'Looking back . . . I recognise that there is far too much of it, but I am not sure that if I had written less I would have written better.'

The Green, Green Grass was published in 1977, two years before Rupert Croft-Cooke's death. I have no idea how many copies it sold, but I do not think it can have been many. There is no blue plaque at Amira Court to recall his time there. The tenant when I knocked on the door turned out to be a Zimbabwean. He showed a polite interest in the story of the flat's previous occupant, but I did not get the impression that he would be hastening to the library to seek out Croft-Cooke's work. I doubt if I will either, although a handful are available in ebook form from Bloomsbury, which suggests that someone somewhere is interested.

The last of my trio of Bournemouth literary lights is a poet – not Shelley nor Brooke nor Verlaine, but a less familiar name. Here are some characteristic lines about Cumberland Clark's home town:

> *The climate mild the best is styled*
> *For those who're seeking health.*
> *The tonic air they meet with there*
> *Is better far than wealth.*
> *So, if you're feeling rather down*
> *Just take a trip to Bournemouth town.*

Clark was born in 1862 and in his youth travelled the world, earning his living as a Congregational minister, farming sheep and cattle, and even mining for gold. He wrote a host of books about Shakespeare and Dickens, as well as a series of tracts exposing the wickedness of communism. But his particular talent was for a rhyme, the more banal the better. Among his many volumes of verse was his *Bournemouth Song Book* which contained such gems as 'Bournemouth's Milk Supply' and 'The Soil and Water Supply'. Clark's one big hit was a song called 'The Ogo-Pogo', with music by a popular tunesmith of the day, Mark Strong. It begins thus:

One fine day in Hindustan,
I met a funny little man.
With googly eyes and lantern jaws,
A new silk hat and some old plus fours.

The abundant flow of his muse was abruptly halted by a German incendiary bomb that landed on his flat in St Stephen's Road in 1941. By chance one of his final offerings contained these lines:

Let the bombs bounce round above us
And the shells come whizzing by
Down in our air-raid shelter
We'll be cosy, you and I.

* * *

Malcolm Muggeridge wrote in the 1930s that Bournemouth 'is for men and women who like their pleasures to be as steady as their bank accounts . . . people move along the promenade with more dignity than hilarity ... there are no slums or proletariat in Bournemouth.' Muggeridge quoted from a pompous town guide: 'In catering for patrons who desire recreation and restored mental and physical energy, its exemption from the ravages of the lower class of tripper is assured.'

This was the Bournemouth brand from the start. From the mid-1840s onwards, the slopes and heights and dells of what had previously been deserted heathland were gradually covered in Gardenesque developments of villas, and houses and cottages of Elizabethan, Gothic and mock rustic design with spacious gardens shut off by luxuriant hedges. They were occupied by a representative sample of the well-to-do and the made-good: bankers, industrialists, Army officers, clergymen, doctors, merchants, whose common characteristic was that their days of toil or service to their country were over.

Some rented for the summer or winter seasons; many – attracted by the real or imagined salubrity of the climate and the company, not too close, of those of the same class – settled permanently. In the seasons the smart hotels and seafront mansions were taken by a more elevated class of patron; earls and countesses were common, princes and princesses not unknown.

Bournemouth's reputation for elegance and intense respectability proved remarkably enduring; indeed elements of it persist today as a kind of popular myth, long after the town was forced to embrace new and often uncomfortable realities. In 1946 Sir Patrick Abercrombie, the great high priest of post-war urban redevelopment, presented his plan for the future of Christchurch, Bournemouth and Poole. Among other things, it envisaged the complete rebuilding of Bournemouth town centre, the provision of a network of new through roads, an imposing new civic centre on East Cliff and the replacement of many of the clusters of villas by blocks of flats.

Although some of Abercrombie's proposals were followed through, most were not. Instead, the council – bewildered by changing circumstances and incapable of drawing up its own strategy – left the task of expanding the town and changing its face to speculators and developers. High-rise blocks of flats sprouted to fracture the skyline, and many of the spacious older houses previously let to genteel persons on fixed incomes were converted into flats or demolished to make way for more blocks.

The era of unrestrained building gave way, in the 1970s, to the era of the grand scheme with its intoxicating visions of conference facilities and gleaming luxury hotels and sports centres and shopping centres and multi-storey car parks and soaring palaces of high-rent flats. One followed another, different in detail and location, but all sharing the characteristics of inflated ambition and disdain for the existing townscape. The International Centre did manage to get built, but one by one the other ventures fell by the wayside. Slowly the council learned the painful lesson that sometimes it might be better to hold on to what you had rather than cash it in in return for a sheaf of fancy drawings.

However, the expensive farce of the IMAX cinema suggests that there is still learning to be done. The council pushed through the demolition of the Winter Gardens in 2006, without having anything to put in its place, and the site is still a car park. A £50 million proposal to cover the gardens next to the Pavilion with a nine-screen cinema, multiple restaurants and flats went belly-up early in 2014 when the funding failed to materialise. The best one can find to say about Bournemouth is that the worst may be over.

Bournemouth Pier

But winter does Bournemouth no favours. Like other seaside resorts – but perhaps more so than some – it needs to be seen in summer sunshine. It is redeemed by blue sky and blue sea and the full exposure of its magnificent golden beach. I returned on my bike on such a day, at the start of what was to prove the generally fine summer of 2013. It was too early to be in the sea, but – considering it was a working day – half the town seemed to be on the beach, or strolling along the promenade or spread out in the municipal gardens. A large proportion were young – students, perhaps, or benefit scroungers or bar staff kept in work by Bournemouth's £12-million-a-year alcohol economy. But young and old and middle-aged, everyone seemed content, everyone hoping the sun would keep shining.

Not everyone. I talked to a lady of a certain age who was taking the air on a bench beside the West Cliff zigzag path. Bournemouth, she said, had gone irretrievably downhill in the thirty-five years she had lived there. Too many foreigners, too many old people, too many rubbishy shops. It was 4.10 in the afternoon and she said she was looking forward to her first drink of the day. 'Bournemouth is boring,' she grumbled. I happened to mention to her that I had been in Barton-on-Sea earlier. She looked at me incredulously. 'Christ, Barton's worse than Bournemouth.'

Sandbanks

But neither Bournemouth nor Barton can, in my view, compare with Sandbanks as a place to be avoided if possible. Those who wish to sell real estate there have set it up as some kind of paradise on earth. It is not. It is horrible.

I leant my bicycle against the window of one of the estate

agents and went in. They looked at me briefly – one glance was enough to know that I did not have the £2 million needed for the average Sandbanks property. Everything they had, however trashy, was stunning, unique, iconic or luxury. Some required all these adjectives to do them justice.

Twenty years ago the Sandbanks style was just big and brash. But more recently it has been refined into something very white and angular and curvy, with a pastel roof, a great deal of tinted glass, a great deal of shiny tubular steel and invariably with a pair of huge, remote-controlled gates. Many of the newest and most ridiculously costly properties in Sandbanks and nearby Branksome are the work of a company called Seven Developments, owned by a local businessman. For those with strong stomachs or revolutionary inclinations, I recommend having a peek at some of the company's prize offerings on its website: the *Moonraker* ('even the garage doors have curvature'), the *Bowie* ('sleek, ageless'), the *Utopia* ('epitomises luxury lifestyle'), the *Gladiator* ('a modern architectural masterpiece').

On the ferry mercifully removing me across the mouth of Poole Harbour to Studland, I confided my impressions of Sandbanks to a fellow cyclist. 'We used to live there,' he said. 'It was nice once.' He and his wife had moved to Swanage. Wise people.

12

SAVAGE COAST

Exchanging Sandbanks for the Isle of Purbeck is like getting away from the moneychangers in the temple and reaching the hills of Canaan. Beyond the mouth of Poole Harbour the landgrabbers and speculators and developers who have conspired over the years to cover the coastline west of Hengistbury Head with bricks, mortar and concrete have been held back by the virtuous hand of the National Trust. The road west from the ferry landing cuts through a landscape of heathland, past shallow, reed-fringed acid ponds, thickets of gorse and gatherings of ragged, stunted pines. There is hardly a dwelling to be seen.

To the east, out of sight, is Studland Bay, a long curve of gritty sand backed by low dunes spotted with clumps of marram grass. It takes an hour or so of leisurely cycling to reach Studland itself, although you would hardly know you were there, as the village has no beginning, middle or end. The church is as randomly situated as the rest of it but is worth searching out. On a triangle of grass near the door is a memorial to Sergeant William Lawrence of the 40th Regiment of Foot, whose long career took him to South America, where he fought the Spanish, to Spain itself for the Peninsular War and to Waterloo.

After Napoleon's final defeat, Sergeant Lawrence went to Paris with the army of occupation where he fell for a French girl whose father had a stall outside the barracks gates. He married her and brought her back to England and finally to Studland, where they took over the New Inn and renamed it the Wellington Arms. In old age he dictated his memories of his fighting days. They are simply told, as much concerned with comradeship and the humble detail of camp life as the blood and thunder of battle, and they give a vivid notion of what it was like for an ordinary soldier under Wellington's generalship.

The Wellington Arms stood across the lane from what is now the Bankes Arms, a fine old creeper-clad stone-built hostelry with an enormous choice of beers, hearty food and a bed for me. I warmed to Studland.

Old Harry's Rocks

At seven o'clock the next morning I was sitting as close as I dared to Old Harry's Rock and Old Harry's Wife – she being the smaller of the two famous columns of chalk that rear up from the clear sea south of Studland.

The sea and the sky, both devoid of colour, met and mingled beyond the great expanse of Christchurch Bay. It was flat calm, the surface of the sea minutely disturbed here and there by soft breaths of breeze. A fishing boat chugged out of Poole Harbour, spreading its wake in enormous Vs. In the far distance was the Isle of Wight, although I wasn't sure if I was looking at it or an island of cloud resting on the horizon. Through the binoculars other islands of vapour took shape and dissolved. The diffuseness of the light made it impossible to make out anything of the great Bournemouth conurbation stretched along the distant coastline.

Peering over the edge, I watched tiny waves spend their feeble force against the foot of the cliffs. They made a gentle whispering, just audible when the gulls shut up for a moment.

I thought about the enormous part played in the life of the nation by the National Trust. Now that the Church of England has rather fallen from favour, the National Trust has replaced it in public esteem and in the hierarchy of great institutions – below the monarchy, probably above the judiciary and certainly above the civil service. A certain kind of person who used to go to church regular as clockwork but doesn't any more has become a National Trust volunteer. He or she is entirely white, entirely middle-class, buys organic, cycles where possible, walks a lot, watches BBC Four and listens to Radio 4, helps out willingly with the grandchildren and reads Arthur Ransome and *Wind in the Willlows* to them, is unfailingly polite to visitors however tiresome they may be, but can be firm with people who drop litter or park their 4x4s across the pavement.

The National Trust is a force for good and its people are the backbone of Britain. We are very fortunate to have it, and them. It has done precious work in keeping our most beautiful buildings and countryside out of the clutches of the sharks and barbarians who would despoil everything if they had the chance. It is almost impossible to find anything unkind to say about this most virtuous body.

Yet sometimes, I am ashamed to say, the urge comes over me. On the whole the Trust governs with a light touch, but there are still plenty of rules. Don't cycle on the footpaths, don't let your dog off the lead, put litter in bins, don't pick wildflowers or fungi, don't light a fire on the beach, don't use a lasso, don't carve your initials on a rock or tree, don't rollerskate, don't sleep overnight in the car park, don't camp, don't touch furniture, don't swear. And so on.

The Trust has its scoutmaster side, the one that urges everyone to get up and get outside whatever the weather and join together in defeating the forces of couch-potatoism and the evil seductive lure of computer games and iPads. This voice is heard with grating heartiness in such initiatives as their 50 Things To Do Before You Are Eleven-and-three-quarters: collect frogspawn, hold a scary beast, catch a crab, climb a tree, etc. I am afraid that with some people of depraved character, it is a function of the book of rules and the list of healthy outdoor activities that they incite a yearning to behave badly.

As I sat alone by Old Harry's Rock, I wondered what I could do that would most offend the righteousness of the National Trust. I could light a barbecue. I could play pop music on a portable radio very loudly. I could roar along the footpaths on a motorbike. My favourite thought was to acquire a hotdog van and bring it to this peaceful spot and dispense disgusting tubes of mechanically recovered pork in powdery rolls to the accompaniment of poorly amplified tunes by One Direction.

Naturally I did nothing of the kind, just headed for Swanage.

Swanage

Swanage is a modest seaside resort, both in size and character, but full of eccentricity. Its growth and transformation towards the end of the nineteenth century was bemoaned by some of those who had known it of old. Among them was a remarkable and appealing Dorset man, Frederick Treves, best known today as the surgeon who treated and befriended the Elephant Man, Joseph Merrick. Treves made his medical reputation through his pioneering treatment of appendicitis, a condition which at the time – the turn of the nineteenth century – was more often than not fatal. In 1902 he was called in to examine the infected appendix of the new King, Edward VII. The coronation was due; Treves said it must be postponed. When Edward argued, the surgeon told him that if he didn't have an operation with a period for recovery there would be a funeral instead of a coronation. The King submitted, the appendix was drained and Treves was made a baronet for his deft work with the knife.

Frederick Treves' contribution to the incomparable Highways and Byways series of guidebooks published by Macmillan between 1899 and 1939 is one of the best. It is stuffed with curious tales and recondite information, and imbued with the vigour and energy that its author displayed as he tramped, cycled, swam and sailed in and around his beloved home county. Treves was a lifelong friend of Thomas Hardy, and when he died suddenly in 1923 of an infected gallbladder, it was the ancient Hardy who arranged the funeral in Dorchester, chose the hymns and wrote a brief epitaph.

Treves had known Swanage when it was a 'queer little town with a rambling High Street and a jumble of picturesque cottages of Purbeck stone'. He objected to what he termed 'the feverish struggle' between rival developers to turn it into something else and prophesied that in a few years it would become indistinguishable from any other seaside resort. He was wrong, as prophets of doom tend to be. The rows of redbrick villas that he disliked so much have mellowed into the townscape, and most of Swanage's architectural oddities – which Treves viewed with a kindly puzzlement – have survived, as does a good deal of the charm of the place.

These oddities were the gifts of two local lads made extremely good. John Mowlem began his working life lugging stone in a local quarry, before migrating to London and founding what would become a great building firm (the name of Mowlem Construction lives on). He recruited his very smart young nephew, George Burt, to work with him, and in time both men retired back to Swanage and set about exalting the town according to their idiosyncratic taste.

Mowlem built a pier and a reading room known as the Mowlem Institute 'for the benefit and mutual improvement of the working classes'. Much stirred by an account – entirely apocryphal – of a great naval victory won in Swanage Bay by Alfred the Great over the invading Danes, he installed a memorial column to the great English King on the seafront and had placed on top of it four cannonballs retrieved from ships recently returned from the Crimean War, which give it a whimsical air.

His nephew was considerably more ambitious. George Burt was a great recycler of materials and features from elsewhere. He built himself a mansion in Swanage High Street in the Scottish baronial style, much of which – the Portland stone, the iron columns, the panelling and even the gilded weather vane – came from the recently demolished Billingsgate Market in London. The bizarre clock-less clock tower standing on the shore near the lifeboat station began life as part of a planned memorial to the Duke of Wellington at the southern end of London Bridge. It was declared surplus to requirements after the clock kept going wrong, so George Burt snapped it up and shipped it down to Swanage (although for some reason the clock did not make the trip).

He decided the town should have a proper town hall, so he built one of plain red brick and grafted onto it the seventeenth-century frontage of the Mercers' Hall from Cheapside, discarded by its owners because it was so blackened by soot. Having finished with Swanage itself, he then built an absurdly small castle above it at Durlston Head and installed on the steep slope below it his most outlandish fancy. Burt's Great Globe is exactly that, a great globe ten feet wide and weighing forty-six tons, composed of fifteen sections of Portland stone held together by granite dowels, on which are carved the continents and oceans of the world.

Charles Harper, whom we met previously singing the praises of St Margaret's Bay in Kent, celebrated the legacy of George Burt in his companion volume about the Dorset coast. He hit the right note when he wrote of 'the amazing Burt, in whose nature eccentricity and business capacity and the instincts of the pedagogue, the philanthropist and the money-maker seem to have been strangely mixed.' It was all too much for a later resident of Swanage, the painter Paul Nash, who lived for a few years in the 1930s in a cottage overlooking the harbour and painted many scenes of Swanage Bay. Nash damned the clock tower as 'repulsive Victorian Gothic', the Mowlem Institute as 'the most dismal building in Dorset' and the Great Globe and Durlston Castle as 'ludicrous ... they have to be seen to be believed'. Nash alleged that the people of Swanage preferred to avert their eyes from 'its extreme ugliness' and look out to sea. But he also conceded that it had a 'strange fascination, like all places which combine beauty, ugliness and the power to disquiet.'

Purbeck stone was the mainstay of the Swanage economy before the trippers and holidaymakers started coming, and it is still quarried in various parts of the Isle. A hard and durable form of limestone, it was used for Salisbury Cathedral and Westminster Abbey and was shipped up the east coast to distant Durham for its cathedral. Until the arrival of the railway in Swanage in 1885, the stone was stacked in carts which were dragged by horses into the sea to be transferred to lighters which were then rowed to the waiting ketches for loading. The quarries were modest affairs, often just a single shaft dug by the holder of the quarrying rights, from which the slabs were lifted on trolleys by chains attached to a wooden capstan turned by a mule or donkey.

The beasts were much valued. On a bridle path inland from Swanage is a stone inscribed thus:

> *Beneath this stone lie our mule*
> *She was a faithful creature*
> *Drawing up the stone from this*
> *Quarry for 32 years. Died aged 34.*
> > *Also*
> *Our little cat named Too-too*
> *Who followed her master from*
> *This quarry to his home and back for 20 years*
> > *RIP.*

Old Harry and his missus rise from the sea where the whale-back hump of Ballard Down is cut off as if by a cleaver. You need to be at sea on a sunny day to grasp properly the abrupt-ness of the drop and the resulting brilliant clash of white chalk and blue sea. Fortunately the next best thing to a boat trip is available on a wondrous website, the *Geology of the*

Wessex Coast, created and maintained by Dr Ian West of South-ampton University and various of his colleagues, students and friends.

This amazing treasury of information and photographs covers pretty much every inch of the coastline between the Solent and Torquay. Its scale and attention to detail are extraordinary. I have never met or spoken to Dr West, but I feel I know him a little through the energy of his prose and through his appearance in many of the pictures; gangling, bespectacled, windblown, his face alight with his geological passion. He and his website have been great assets to me, and it is a pleasure to acknowledge here the debt I owe to him and his team and his university for their great gift to the rest of us.

Despite the grandeur of the seascape, Swanage Bay is a gentle stretch of shore, protected by the mainland from the worst of the westerly storms and to the east by the bulwark of the Isle of Wight. But west of Durlston Head the character of the bound-ary between land and sea changes dramatically. Exposed to the storms from whatever direction they may come, this is a rugged, battered, savage stretch of coast. The rock faces, of Purbeck or Portland stone, are stern and lowering, fissured by the onslaught of seas and gales. The clifftops are pockmarked with the shafts dug by the quarrymen. The few bays are rough and rocky and inaccessible. Tidal races surge menacingly around and over half-hidden ledges. There are mighty boulders and beetling drops, rocks in twisted arches, caverns where the thunder of the waves echoes and moans.

Over the centuries this has been a prodigious graveyard of ships. One celebrated victim was the *Halsewell*, an East India-man bound for Bengal on what was to be the last round trip for her captain, Richard Pierce, before his retirement. She was carrying 242 passengers and crew, among them two of Captain Pierce's daughters and two of his nieces. The ship put out from Gravesend on 1 January 1786 into a bitter north-easterly gale. Snow and ice coated the sails and clogged the rigging and she began to take in water. Pierce ordered the mainmast to be cut away to avoid foundering in the heavy seas. She was driven down the Channel as far west as Lyme Bay, then the gale turned into the south-west, pushing her back east.

Pierce's intention was to make shelter at Portsmouth. He managed to avoid Portland Bill but the *Halsewell* – by now missing her mizenmast, mainmast and most of her sails – was helpless. On the night of the 5th of January the sky cleared without warning to reveal the black bulk of St Aldhelm's Head a mile and a half to leeward. Pierce ordered the anchor to be released. The ship rode the storm for an hour before the anchor hold gave way. The wind was now in the south, thrusting her towards the cliffs. At 2 a.m. she struck the rocks between Winspit and Seacombe, was turned side on and immediately began to break in two against the mouth of a cavern.

There was one hope of escape: to get from the stricken ship into the cave. Crewmen began scrambling from the raised poop deck onto the rocks. Captain Pierce asked his second mate, Henry Meriton, if he thought there was any hope of saving the girls. Meriton replied that the ship was disintegrating. Pierce went to the roundhouse to comfort his daughters and nieces and the other female passengers. Meriton crawled along a broken spar towards the rocks, was swept from it by a wave, then picked up by another wave and deposited in the back of the cave, where he was helped onto a ledge out of reach of the sea. The roundhouse gave way under the pounding of the sea and Captain Pierce and the girls were seen no more.

When dawn broke there was nothing left of the *Halsewell* but floating wreckage. Distress cannon had been fired before she struck, but the spot was remote and no one on land heard the sound. Eighty or so survivors were huddled in the cave, unseen from shore and unreachable from the sea. A group edged out and along the foot of the cliff and began to climb. Two managed to reach the top and made their way to the nearest house, where the steward of the several nearby quarries lived. Alerted by him, quarrymen made their way to the clifftop with ropes.

All that day men were lifted to safety, or themselves scrambled up to the top. An unknown number, enfeebled by their ordeal, were either washed off the rocks at the bottom and drowned, or fell to their deaths from the ropes. Henry Meriton had almost reached the top by his own efforts when he lost his handhold on the rock. As he fell he seized a rope and was hauled up to the waiting arms of the quarrymen.

In all seventy-four of the passengers and crew who had set sail from Gravesend four days earlier survived. The disaster – made more poignant than others by the deaths of the young women and the conduct of Captain Pierce – created a media sensation and prompted an outpouring of public horror and grief. Within fifteen days an account provided by Henry Meriton and the third mate, John Rogers, had been rushed into print and went into numerous editions. George III was taken to the scene, and his court composer, Augustus Kollman, put together a symphony lamenting the loss. Thomas Stothard painted an affecting scene showing Pierce with his face raised towards a swaying lamp, his daughters in their bonnets whimpering against his chest.

Although the ship was smashed to pieces, objects from her have been yielded up by the sea over the years, and are still occasionally found by divers. There were three pieces from a chess set – a pawn, a bishop and a castle – carved from bone. A cupboard door came ashore, and a mirror wrapped in seaweed. A four-hour glass sand timer was also delivered intact, wrapped in weed. Most of the bodies were never found; those that were recovered were mangled and battered to the point of being unrecognisable.

13

BLACK OIL, WHITE NOTHE

The clifftop between the site of the *Halsewell* disaster and St Aldhelm's Head is riddled with shafts and galleries and holes and ledges left by the quarrymen of long ago. The last quarry along the cliff edge closed in the 1950s, leaving a legacy of fractured rock and ruined storehouses and sheds through which the walkers on the South-West Coast Path pick their way.

The Head itself stands 350 feet above the sea. In Treves' words: 'There is a sense of defiance about this strong cape, a suggestion of a clenched fist outstretched in the tideway to challenge the elements.' A fierce tidal race surges this way and that over a hidden ledge extending well out to sea from the base of the cliff, creating short, choppy seas which sailors are strongly advised to avoid. Even on the calmest days, the surface is stirred by tensions and stresses. There is a coastguard station at the top where volunteers watch out for vessels in trouble. Nearby is a tiny Norman chapel with a low doorway pitted by the excavated refuges of countless generations of bees.

A track strikes inland through bare, windswept fields to an isolated farm, where the lane leading to the excellent pub in

Worth Matravers can be picked up. A little to the west is the vale of Encombe with its long, low, stone mansion, the country retreat of John Scott, the first Earl of Eldon and a long-serving Lord Chancellor in successive administrations under George III. There was once a public road down to the sea through the estate, but it was closed by a later Earl. His action incensed Charles Harper but Frederick Treves applauded him and denounced 'the atrocious conduct of the trippers' who had abused his hospitality.

Encombe, now owned by an airline tycoon of Gibraltarian origin, remains secluded and I only saw it from a distance. But I did have a glorious ride along the bridleway which runs inland from Encombe and behind Swyre Head to the village of Kimmeridge. Below me on one side was the vale enclosing Smedmore House, with green fields rising steeply on the far side towards the edge of the hidden sea. On the other side the chalk downs of the Purbeck Hills rolled away, dabbed with gorse and woodland, the fields sharply defined by hedgerows. Beyond the hills, gleaming like some great inland lake, was Poole Harbour, with the dark smudge of Brownsea Island at its mouth. As I pedalled slowly and happily west, Kimmeridge Bay revealed itself, and in the far distance the teardrop shape of Portland Bill.

The cliffs around Kimmeridge Bay are a sombre dark grey, composed of clay and shale, the shale being imbued with black, sticky, viscous bitumen, a form of petroleum. As far back as the Neolithic period the bituminous shale was cut and polished into ornaments rather like jet. It was used in Roman times and for centuries after by local people as fuel; it burns hot, although giving off sulphurous fumes which stink to high heaven. In the sixteenth century the estate containing the bay and its surroundings came into the possession of an old Dorset family, the Clavells. In the reign of James I, Sir William Clavell embarked upon an ambitious project to turn Kimmeridge into an industrial centre, based on shale power.

His first venture was the production of alum, a salt mined locally which, when heat treated, was used extensively in dyeing and tanning and as a medical treatment. But Sir William fell foul of a monopoly in alum granted by the Crown to someone else, so he switched to boiling sea water to make salt, only to encounter more opposition from patent holders. Finally he diversified into glass, and built a pier for small ships to transport his glassware. But the succession of setbacks had stretched his finances beyond breaking point; having served time in the Marshalsea debtors' prison he abandoned his attempts to become an industrial magnate.

In the second half of the nineteenth century a succession of enterprises tried to make money out of the Kimmeridge shale. One involved a group of French entrepreneurs who converted it into lamp oil. The problem was the same as had persuaded Sir William Clavell to build his home upwind of his factory, and caused distress to his downwind neighbours: the stink of hydrogen sulphide. In the 1870s the Kimmeridge Oil and Carbon Company dug new shafts and a mile of tunnels fitted with metal tracks for its waggons to run on. A series of remarkable photographs on Dr Ian West's website shows rails dangling down the cliff face, and the rusted side of one of the waggons revealed by erosion.

Mining petered out by 1900, and since then no one has bothered with the shale. However, since 1961 the associated deposits of petroleum below sea level have been extracted through what is the oldest oil well in Britain. It still produces sixty barrels or so a day, although on the day of my visit the nodding donkey in the ledge above the bay was refusing to incline its head, having been shut down for repairs.

Kimmeridge Bay is far from picturesque in the conventional way, but is oddly fascinating. Because of the influence of Portland Bill – please don't ask me to explain – it has extended low tides and abbreviated high tides. A big low tide reveals the ledges of shale extending from the shore; apparently it is then possible to walk across the mouth of the bay, although the rock is extremely slippery and the tide comes in fast.

Overlooking the bay from the east is Hen Cliff, on the top of which is perched a comical colonnaded folly known as Clavell Tower. This was the fanciful notion of a later owner of the estate, the Reverend John Richards Clavell. Unfortunately he neglected to take due account of the effects of erosion, so it has had to be moved inland at enormous expense by the Landmark Trust, which has turned it into one of their dinky holiday lets.

There is a little row of coastguard cottages tucked into the lee of Hen Cliff, enclosed by trees and nicely protected from the gales. I found a retired GP at home in one of them who turned out to be a classic case of seaside recruitment. He had come to Kimmeridge for summer holidays with his parents for years; then many more years had passed, but the memories of rock-pooling and swimming and wandering the cliffs did not fade. One day he came with his mother, now elderly, just to revisit old scenes. He found one of the coastguard cottages was for sale, so he and his wife came to live there.

So many south-coast villages are afflicted by the second-home curse, so that out of season they are reduced spiritually to ghost settlements. But according to the doctor, Kimmeridge is different. There are plenty of holiday lets but the Smedmore Estate – which owns most of the village and its surroundings – operates positive discrimination in favour of full-time residents. There are enough young families with children to require a school bus, which may not sound much but in a place like this is an important factor. There is no pub, but Clavell's Café – which, with its associated farm shop, is run by a family who also farm in the area – makes a first-rate substitute.

The doctor told me he felt utterly at home. The fascination exercised by the dark cliffs, the rock pools and ledges, the glorious sweep of countryside behind, had not dimmed. He was evidently a man of energy: morris dancer, accordionist, director of the local choir and now – with his wife – involved in a tremendous new enterprise for the village.

The Kimmeridge Project seeks to provide a home worthy of one of the most important collections of fossils in the country. It has been assembled over decades of ferreting and fossicking around rocks by a central-heating engineer, Steve Etches, who lives in the village. Mr Etches' speciality is uncovering the secrets hidden in the Jurassic Kimmeridge Clay – which is named after the Dorset village but is a major source of oil in various parts of Europe. His finds range in size from a minute barnacle to the jawbone of a gigantic pliosaur, and include lobsters, squid – one with its ink sac intact – parts of sharks and turtles, the wings of a ray and a host of ammonites and bivalves.

The significance of the collection is internationally recognised but it has never been fully displayed to the public. A lottery fund has set the project on its way, and a new hall being built opposite the café will see it realised, providing the village with an attraction likely to guarantee its viability as a community into the foreseeable future.

Unlike Tyneham.

It is a sad story.

West from Kimmeridge Bay are, in sequence, Hobarrow Bay, Brandy Bay and Worbarrow Bay, which Treves considered the most beautiful in Dorset. A path leads inland from its eastern side beside a little stream, the Gwyle. After a mile it reaches a cluster of ruins: roofless cottages of Purbeck stone, the walls smothered by vegetation, the derelict old schoolhouse and post office, further on the shattered remains of the Elizabethan manor house. Only the church is intact, although no one has taken the sacrament there for seventy years.

This is, or was, Tyneham, and its story is well enough known. When war came in 1939, Tyneham was trapped in a semi-feudal time warp. Every house and all the land around belonged to the Bond family, who had lived at the manor house for centuries. Just before Christmas 1943 the villagers and their overlords received a letter from the War Office telling them that Worbarrow Bay and the entire estate were needed to train troops for what would be the Normandy landings. They had six days to leave their homes, the only homes they had ever known. They were told – or thought they were told – that they could return when it was all over. A notice was pinned to the church door asking the military to look after the buildings and treat the village kindly. The War Office did neither, and in 1948 annexed Tyneham and the estate for good by means of compulsory purchase. The houses fell into ruin and the villagers never came back.

Belatedly its fate has been to become a visitor attraction. Most weekends the Army allows people in to stare at the ghost of the village and walk down to the sea where the fishermen used to wait for the coming of the mackerel shoals. But on the day I cycled past, the gates were locked and the warning signs were up. The best I could do was look down into the valley where the grey shells of the houses peeped through the trees, and across to the forbidden heights of Flower's Barrow. It was silent, incredibly tranquil: not a gun, not a vehicle, not a voice. The paradox – as the good doctor in Kimmeridge had explained to me – is that by annexing Tyneham, the Army had, in all probability, actually saved this unreal peace and idyllic beauty from being blighted by some kind of holiday development.

Not that the Army cared.

The valley of Tyneham is part of the Lulworth Ranges, seven thousand acres of uninhabited coastal wilderness, virgin and unspoiled but for the tank tracks, targets and blasted earth and rocks. Lulworth Camp itself – the home of the Armoured Fighting Vehicle School of Gunnery – proclaims the usual military contempt for notions of pleasant design or harmony with the landscape. Blocks of functional semis face the road from behind the wire and the high-voltage lights. There are no gardens or screens of trees – the only decoration is provided by the ornamental tanks. Inland, looking towards Wareham, is another Danger Area, of heathland scarred by tank tracks and artillery fire. Like Tyneham it was entirely silent when I passed by. I watched a group of fallow deer moving through the gorse at their leisure. Nearby, the rusted corpses of two tanks lay clasped in the embrace of the under-growth.

The Army finally surrenders control just east of the per-fection of Lulworth Cove. Geologists love this exquisite pale bowl in the cliffs, and the stretch of coastline beyond, almost as much as the visitors who swamp it in summer and the walkers who look down into its clear, aquamarine waters from the coastal path. The sea has made wonders here, scooping out the bedrock to form the cove itself, creating caves and arches and stacks and sheer cliffs either side. There are layers of chalk, limestone, sandstone, oil sand, lignite, pebble beds, clays, marls, quartz, grits, ancient soil and tree remains, and within them fossils, stromatolites, ostracods and a host of other exciting treasures promiscuously laid down over the aeons.

Lulworth Cove is overwhelmingly lovely in the evening light when the crowds have gone and the car park is empty and even the geologists have packed away their tools. The enclosing cliff faces, the blue water darkening as the light fades, the pale pebble beach, the wide sea beyond, the boats shifting at anchor together form an extraordinary composition. But you are aware of its impermanence, that you are there at a moment in an immense history of erosion, the sea eating away at what the sea itself has made. And should you forget, there are signs every-where: DANGER. KEEP AWAY. ROCKFALLS. UNSTABLE CLIFFS.

Frederick Treves had a singular experience here. On 7

September 1892 an eleven-year-old girl, Edith Leckie, fell 380 feet from the clifftop onto the beach. Treves was staying in a cottage nearby and was summoned to the coast-guards' boathouse to attend her. Amazingly she was not merely alive, but had suffered no disabling injuries, which Treves attributed to the fact that she had fallen with her back to the cliff so that her clothes caught on its rough face, slowing her descent.

Nothing so interesting happened to me, but I did watch a crabbing boat come in to the shore. I wanted to see if there were any crabs and maybe chat to the fisherman, so I went and offered to help drag her up the shingle. My offer was refused; rather brusquely, I thought.

Inland from the cove is West Lulworth where there is a very handsome late Victorian church of Purbeck stone. Treves was old enough to remember its tiny and dilapidated predecessor which served the village before the red-brick villas and lodging houses appeared. The choir was accompanied by violin, bass viol, flute and an early version of the tuba which Treves refers to as a serpent, otherwise known as the ophicleide.

A bridle path cuts away from the road behind West Lulworth, close to the Durdle Door holiday park. It is a lovely cycle ride. Inland a patchwork of cultivated fields reaches into the Downs. Towards the sea, grassland rolls like breakers between Durdle Door and White Nothe, each trough opening a view of the sea itself. At White Nothe a huge landslide of chalk ends the sequence of sheer cliff drops. The undercliff is a rough tangle of blackthorn, hawthorn and privet overlaid by honeysuckle and ivy. There are patches of reedy bog created by seeping groundwater, and grassy clearings where various shy orchids flower.

The ancestors of the foxes that roam through this wilderness were much admired for their boldness and cunning by the writer Llewelyn Powys, who for several years in the 1920s lived in one of the row of gaunt coastguard cottages on top of the Nothe. He knew it as White Nose, invoking the authority of Thomas Hardy who declared that it had always been White Nose because it was shaped like a nose, the nose in question being that of the Duke of Wellington. Nothe or Nose, for isolation and wind-blasted discomfort there can have been few places to beat it. Powys related how windows were sometimes blown in by the force of the wind, and clumps of seaweed flew over the clifftop to join the slates plucked from the roof and dispatched inland 'as though they were sycamore leaves'. At other times sea mists would roll in, smothering everything, and the foghorn on the Shambles lighthouse across Weymouth Bay would boom.

They were an odd literary brood, the Powys brothers, John Cowper, Theodore and Llewelyn. They all wrote voluminously in their own, intensely individual ways, disdaining popularity and inspiring small, loyal bands of readers who regarded them – and still regard them – as touched by genius. John Cowper Powys is perhaps the best-known of them today, although there cannot be many with the stamina and dedication to survive *Wolf Solent* or *A Glastonbury Romance*, let alone the 1600 pages of his Welsh bardic fantasy *Porius*, which true devotees – including Powys himself – considered his masterpiece.

Weymouth

In childhood they spent happy holidays with their grandparents in Weymouth, which they loved and which John Cowper Powys repaid with a novel he called *Weymouth Sands*. The sands were looking a picture when I pedalled past, the sunshine infused with the warmth of the south, enough to suggest that a proper summer might not be far off. I found myself being surprised again by how many people of school and working age managed to get to the beach on school and working days. Weymouth's esplanade was thronged and the beach was well-populated with the usual loungers, scroungers, sunbathers, dog-walkers and philosophers.

I watched an elderly gent coming out of the sea. He wore Union Jack trunks repaired in a couple of places with sticky tape. He got a towel from his beach hut and rubbed himself vigorously. He was in amazing shape for someone of his age, which was over seventy: lean, muscled, tanned from summers past, the skin a little loose. He told me the water was between nine and ten degrees Celsius. I shuddered at the thought. He said it had been between four and five in February, and I shuddered some more.

He swam most days, then ran to the eastern end of the esplanade and back. He liked Weymouth well enough. I said it must have been a proud moment when the Olympics came to the town. His face darkened and he embarked on a lengthy tirade against the council for having got rid of the seafront's well-loved Victorian fairy lights and replacing them with a laser display called Veils of Lights. 'They called it regeneration,' he said derisively. 'I call it degeneration.' He laced his trainers and pounded off, leaving me feeling distinctly slothful.

Weymouth is still a delight. Its sand is golden and its seafront retains much of its original Georgian elegance and jauntiness. The beach huts are outstandingly attractive, the esplanade is wide and welcoming and cheerful in the slightly vulgar way esplanades need to be. The harbour, with its quays and old brick warehouses, offers an agreeable diversion, and there are little streets all around which are a pleasure to wander. Weymouth has an excellent old-fashioned sweet shop, a fishing tackle shop and a decent secondhand bookshop, all reliable indicators of a place that has not entirely lost its soul.

Of course Weymouth, in common with other seaside towns, suffers from having its economy so heavily skewed to tourism and being therefore at the mercy of factors over which it has little control, principally the weather. It has too much traffic in the wrong places, a railway station at the end of the line, plenty of boarded-up shops and struggling hotels, an abundance of drunks and oafs, and a stack of intractable social problems.

Nevertheless it has charm, even beauty, and an enviable capacity to provide a jolly day out at the seaside, which is a great asset.

George III liked it very much, even in the throes of the porphyria that darkened his life and robbed him of his dignity. The diarist Fanny Burney, a member of the royal entourage, left a deliciously vivid picture of that first, famous royal visit of 1789.

At a welcoming reception the Mayor advanced to be introduced to Queen Charlotte and astonished all and sundry by taking her hand and kissing it but failing to kneel. 'You should have knelt, sir,' hissed one of the equerries, to which the Mayor answered that he could not on account of his wooden leg. Regrettably the other, two-legged Weymouth worthies took their cue from the Mayor and treated the Queen in the same grossly familiar manner.

Despite this *faux pas* royal approval was bestowed on Weymouth, and the town did very well out of it. The King bathed daily from a specially constructed bathing machine; an illustration shows him entirely naked, without even his wig on, closely attended by the Royal 'dippers'. According to Fanny Burney this ritual was accompanied by renditions of 'God Save the King' by musicians concealed in a neighbouring bathing machine. She was much struck by the displays of popular enthusiasm. Patriotic labels were stuck in shop windows, in children's bonnets and labourers' hats and loud huzzahs greeted the Royal family wherever they went.

The King and the itinerant court returned to Weymouth most summers over the next decade. Apart from the prescribed sea-bathing, George liked outings: watching the pony racing on the beach, going to the theatre, visiting the sites of shipwrecks (including the *Halsewell*), dining on the celebrated Portland mutton at the Portland Arms. One excursion was to Maiden Castle to watch rural sports, which included 'a Contest of cricket for a Round of Beef ... a Pound of Tobacco to be Grinned for, a good Hat to be cudgelled for, a handsome Hat for the Boy most expert in catching a Roll dipped in Treacle and suspended by a string ... a Pig to whoever catches him by the Tail.'

The King's health collapsed again in 1801. His last visits to Weymouth were in the summers of 1804 and 1805. The mood of the nation was adversely affected by hysteria over the threat of French invasion. George wore a green eye shade and was clearly in a poor way. In 1806 a local newspaper lamented: 'It is with much concern we now generally believe that his Majesty and the Royal Family will not honour us with their presence this season.'

They never came again. But the town consoled itself as best it could with a permanent and prominent reminder of royal favour in the shape of a painted statue of the King in his robes and Order of the Garter next to 'an antique table' with his crown on it, a pile of books, a 'very bold cornucopia' and his sword and sceptre. This peculiar composition has aroused much derision over the years – Betjeman called its colouring ridiculous and Treves described it as 'an object of ridicule to the easily amused ... only of interest as a sign of the times.' But Weymouth has stuck by it, and standing where it does on the seafront – now accompanied by a replica of the royal bathing machine – it enhances the general cheeriness of the scene no end.

14

HALF-COCK

The tidal race off Portland Bill is one of the most notorious navigational hazards along the Channel shore (so I've read – I wouldn't go near it myself). The Bill thrusts south from the mainland in the shape of a tear about to drop, provoking a whirl of eddies along its eastern and western sides which collide off the southern tip and meet the flow of the tide over an extended submerged ledge. The resulting mêlée is made worse by the influence of the Shambles, an evil sandbank to the south-east of the Bill.

At spring tides the speed of the tidal race can reach seven knots, sometimes even more, and if the wind is head on, the sea is lacerated into steep and fearsome waves. There is a passage about all this in Jonathan Raban's seafaring memoir *Coasting*, which made me feel uneasy sitting by the fire in the living room. Seven knots, Raban points out, may sound comfortable on a bicycle but is a 'wild and dangerous speed for a body of ocean water ... the water stands on end in foamy pillars ... it seethes and hisses and growls ... it can reach out and grab any boat ass enough to be in sight of it.' And plenty have been so grabbed, hence the name for the curve of sea between the Bill and Chesil Beach: Deadman's Bay.

The fortunes of the Bill itself have always been bound up intimately in its stone and its harbour. Frederick Treves characterised it as 'ever windswept, barren and sour, treeless and ill-equipped' and its natives 'recluses of unpleasant habits ... exceedingly jealous of strangers ... they married only with their own folk and possessed curious laws and still more curious morals.' The virtues of Portland stone – a species of limestone that is both durable and workable – were exploited by James I's chief architect, Inigo Jones, who used it for the banqueting hall at Whitehall Palace and on the old St Paul's. When London was rebuilt after the Great Fire, Portland stone was the material of first choice for public buildings and has remained so, its strength and grandeur displayed by such buildings as Somerset House, the British Museum and County Hall.

So much was shipped to London that it was said there was more of it in the capital than left on the Bill. Nevertheless, the supply remains healthy; new quarries are still being opened up as the old ones are worked out and turned over to the heritage business.

High above Portland Bill is All Saints Church, Wyke Regis, whose graveyards have swallowed many of those destroyed and spat out by the murderous seas below. Scores of ships came to grief on one side of Portland Bill or the other, events that tended to be regarded by local people more as economic opportunities than tragedies. To the so-called wreckers, appropriating valuables came before offering help to the hapless victims, particularly when so many of them were dark-skinned foreigners without a word of English. One of the most notorious displays of callousness followed the wreck of a Dutch merchant ship, the *Hope of Amsterdam*, at the eastern end of Chesil Beach in January 1749.

She was carrying a fortune in gold and jewels, and word of her fate soon spread. The men of Portland, Wyke and Weymouth were first on the scene, followed in the course of the day by treasure-hunters from all over Dorset. The wreckers organised themselves into groups of twenty or so to scour the wreckage, ignoring the plight of the crew of the ship, seventy of whom managed to save themselves by their own efforts. Over the next ten days the crowd swelled to several thousand, and they defied all attempts by customs men to remove them. Some got away rich men, others died of exposure in the extreme cold.

The spectacle provoked a wave of national revulsion. But only two of those involved were ever brought to trial, and they were acquitted on the curious grounds that the Dutch were no more than pirates who had plundered the gold from the Spanish, and it must be lawful to plunder pirates.

Among those commemorated in the church is Captain John Wordsworth, brother of the poet, who – with more than 250 others – was drowned in February 1805 when the *Earl of Abergavenny* was steered onto the Shambles at the direction of an incompetent local pilot. But the majority of those buried in the two graveyards by Wyke Church were never identified. They were nameless, storyless nobodies, often picked up as hands in some faraway port and discarded, mangled and lifeless, on a storm-battered Dorset shore. But even where the names were known and recorded, the lettering on their gravestones has generally been eaten away by time, assisted by the salt spray blown on the wind; unless by chance their stone was arranged to face inland, away from the sea.

Chesil Beach

In preparation for visiting Chesil Beach, I thought I would read Ian McEwan's short novel *On Chesil Beach*. I hoped it might mention interesting aspects of the longest shingle beach in the United Kingdom, such as its geomorphological profile or the unusual composition and distribution of the pebbles, or the eel fishing in the Fleet, the shallow, brackish lagoon behind the beach, or the quality of the angling for pollack and ling from the steep-shelving outer bank.

I was disappointed. It turned out to be the story of a young man driven half-mad by sexual frustration, who marries a young woman half-mad with sexual repression and ruins both their lives by prematurely ejaculating onto her on their wedding night –

which happens to take place in a hotel near Chesil Beach. I may have missed something – I must have missed something – but I have rarely come across a short book that seemed longer, and the description of his unruly emission 'filling her navel, coating her belly, thighs and even a portion of her breasts in tepid, viscous fluid' is enough to put you off your breakfast.

Fortunately other sources – among them Dr Ian West's geological website – are more informative. For example, you may not have known that the Chesil is an unusual kind of tombolo, which means a ridge or spit connecting an island (Portland Bill) to the mainland. This particular tombolo is eighteen miles long, extending from Portland to West Bay (or possibly fifteen miles long, extending to Cogden Beach – there is dispute on the matter). It is forty-five feet high at its highest point. The pebbles are mainly chert and flint of local origin, pale in colour. But mixed in are some startling red and purple quartzite stones washed over from Budleigh Salterton in Devon, and a very few examples of jasper, a form of silica. The pebbles are pea-sized at the eastern end, swelling gradually to the proportions of cobbles as you go west, and are harder than steel.

The Fleet is the largest tidal lagoon in the country, 200 acres in extent, eight miles long, varying between 100 and 900 yards in width. It hosts a wealth of interesting aquatic flora, including the great beds of eel grass on which the famous swans of Abbotsbury feed. There are oysters there, and bass, and plenty of freshwater eels which the Environment Agency issues licences to trap. The beach itself is a major draw for sea anglers, although it is not a good place to fall in, as a powerful undertow is likely to seize you and drown you.

*

A little less than halfway along the Chesil, set back from the Fleet, is the very small village of Langton Herring. It is one of the thirteen 'doubly thankful' villages in England and Wales, in that all those it sent to both world wars came back safely. Treves called it dismal but it seemed perfectly pleasant to me, and it has a pub called the Elm Tree with decent beer and some interesting history.

It's a spy story of the old kind, the flavour of le Carré all over it. Two lowly clerks at the Admiralty Underwater Weapons Establishment at Portland – Harry Houghton, an alcoholic in a failed marriage spending beyond his means, and Ethel Gee, a spinster in her forties weighed down by the burden of caring for elderly relatives – began an affair. They were approached and charmed by a handsome flatterer who told them that his name was Alex Johnson, and that he was a US naval commander interested in seeing what the British were up to with their nuclear submarines.

In fact he was a KGB prize asset, born Konstantin or Konon Molodiy in Moscow, better known both in London and North America as Gordon Lonsdale. Houghton and Gee began passing him drawings and specifications; they often had a drink or two in the Elm Tree in Langton Herring before catching a train to Waterloo to hand the packages to their benefactor. He would take the packages to a seemingly innocuous pair of antiquarian book dealers, Helen and Peter Kroger, who lived in a bungalow in Ruislip, 45 Cranley Drive. Mr and Mrs Kroger were actually the American Communist spies Morris and Lona Cohen, whose real interest was not in leather-bound volumes but transmitting the deepest secrets of Britain's nuclear weapons programme back to Moscow.

The so-called Portland Spy Ring was rounded up on 7 January 1961. Superintendent George Smith of Special Branch arrested Houghton, Gee and Lonsdale/Johnson/Molodiy near the Old Vic in London. Inside Ethel Gee's shopping bag was a sheaf of documents setting out the lethal potential of Britain's first nuclear submarine, HMS *Dreadnought*. A co-ordinated search of the bungalow in Ruislip yielded a pile of the latest espionage gear including a radio transmitter, a microdot reader and cypher codes, as well as secret documents and false passports.

The trial at the Old Bailey was a sensation of sorts. Lonsdale said nothing. The Krogers also refused to testify. Ethel Gee maintained she had no idea the information was going to the Russians; she had acted out of love for Houghton, her first love. He gallantly attempted to minimise her part, saying he had been blackmailed. They got fifteen years, the Krogers twenty years and Lonsdale twenty-five. Within a few years the Russian had been exchanged for the British spy Greville Wynne; Molodiy died mysteriously some years later on what the Moscow authorities said was a 'mushroom-picking expedition'. The Krogers also ended up in Moscow in a spy exchange deal.

But no one was interested in negotiating freedom for the couple who had canoodled in the pub in Langton Herring. After their release in 1970 an enterprising freelance journalist spotted Houghton at Poole railway station, chased him into a building nearby and cornered him in a cupboard. Asked if he was intending to marry Ethel Gee, Houghton replied that if he hadn't been on parole he would have punched the reporter's head off. But he did the decent thing, and together they ran a guesthouse in Bournemouth for a while before fading into total obscurity.

* * *

A lane leads down from Langton Herring through fields to the edge of the Fleet. It was a glorious morning and the warmth had brought out a great cloud of hawthorn flies, which were hovering and darting between the hedges searching for mates. The Fleet was as flat as glass, the pale wall of stones on its far side perfectly reflected. Beyond the Chesil the blue sea was fretted with gentle waves.

There is a row of cottages originally intended for coastguards, now much smartened up into holiday lets and seaside hideaways. One was being renovated for an amiable former naval officer turned estate agent who had evidently done very nicely from specialising in seaside properties. He gave me a cup of coffee and told me that he had homes in Brighton and Antigua, but who could resist this? He waved languidly towards the Chesil and I had to agree. We watched a low, flat-bottomed punt-like boat creep across the surface of the Fleet. The two blokes in it were eel fishermen, on their way to lift their fyke nets. I wished quite acutely that I was with them, but they were in no hurry and for me time, as ever, was pressing.

Abbotsbury is famous for its swans. Personally I do not share the general fondness for swans. They have spoiled too many promising fishing moments with their hissing and slurping and pointless wing-flapping and tearing at weed with their horrible black bills and churning up the water and disturbing the fish. But I admit that they did look quite charming as they sailed across the Fleet in stately squadrons. If there must be swans, better here than on a precious stretch of trouty chalkstream.

Chesil Beach and Abbotsbury Swannery

The swannery was established 700 years ago to provide food for Abbotsbury's Benedictine Abbey. Charles Harper quotes a droll piece of doggerel about preparing swans for the table:

> *To a gravy of beef, good and strong, I opine*
> *You'll be right if you add half a pint of port wine;*
> *Pour this through the swan – yes, quite through the belly*
> *Then serve the whole up with some hot currant jelly.*

Of the abbey nothing survives except a gatehouse, an archway and some stubs of pillars. The rest was plundered by Sir Giles Strangways, who supervised the abbey's dissolution on behalf of Henry VIII and Thomas Cromwell. As well as the abbey estates, Sir Giles took possession of the swannery and within living memory it was still the custom for a plump cygnet to be sent over to the family seat at Melbury Sampford for dinner when required.

St Catherine's Chapel

Abbotsbury is highly picturesque even without its abbey. There is a huge medieval barn with mighty buttresses and a fine arched gateway, a good fifteenth- and sixteenth-century parish church, an ancient chapel dedicated to St Catherine which is perched on top of a smooth green hill between the village and the Chesil, and a long, meandering main street fronted by old stone cottages, some thatched, some roofed in rough tiles. There is an excellent pub, the Ilchester Arms, useful shops (including Abbotsbury Fishing Tackle!) and a picture-postcard village cricket ground.

It all looks idyllic, but the man at my B & B was full of resentment against 'the estate', which still owns most of the village. As a result of a series of inopportune deaths, this has come down from the Strangways (later the Earls of Ilchester) to Mrs Charlotte Townshend, the richest woman in Dorset. My landlord was embroiled in a long-running dispute with those he referred to as her 'clueless minions', something to do with the blocking or unblocking of a watercourse through his garden, I couldn't follow all the ins and outs. His grievances included the stealing of part of his view by the new property next door, the greed of 'the estate' in starting up various commercial offshoots in competition with village businesses, the ending of a long-standing concession allowing locals to help themselves to firewood and some others I don't remember.

After supper, as the light faded, I pedalled down a bridle path to the Chesil. I left my bike propped up against a bush and crunched up the enormous rampart of stones. The sun was going down in an apricot sky behind the Golden Cap far to the west. The sea shimmered like a silken cloak streaked by gold. Little waves slapped against the pebbles, hissing in their retreat.

At intervals along the downward slope anglers had fixed their rods on tripods. Latecomers were lugging their gear in trolleys along the crest of the beach searching for a pitch. I watched one fisherman leap from his seat to seize his rod. The tip bent briefly, but there was little fight in the fish – a bass, a codling, I couldn't tell in the light – and it was soon hauled across the stones to be unhooked.

Towards the western end of the Chesil is Cogden Beach, where an unusual event occurred in June 1757 and was recorded thus in the *History and Antiquities of the County of Dorset*, compiled by the Rector of Wareham, the Reverend John Hutchins:

'A mermaid was thrown up by the sea, thirteen feet long, the upper part of it had some resemblance to a human form, the lower was like that of a fish: the head was partly like that of a man and partly like that of a hog. Its fins resembled hands: it had forty-eight large teeth in each jaw not unlike those in the jawbone of a man.'

That is all – nothing about the circumstances or what happened to the mermaid subsequently, which is most frustrating. Frederick Treves scoffs at the account of 'this romantic individual' but elsewhere in his monumental *History*, Hutchins does not come over as an especially credulous chronicler. Although there do not seem to be any other contemporary references to the Cogden Beach mermaid, there have been sightings of other exotic sea creatures along the Dorset coast. Hollinshed's *Chronicles* mentions that in November 1457, at Portland, 'was seen a cocke coming out of the sea having a great crest upon its head and a red beard having legs half-a-yard long'. It crowed four times, turning and nodding its head, 'then vanished away'.

A contemporary historian of Weymouth, Martin Ball, has alleged that civic leaders there deliberately covered up the story of the Cogden Beach mermaid because they feared it would deter potential visitors to the resort. In 1995 Mr Ball himself saw an enormous creature off Chesil Beach which he described in a magazine article as being twelve feet tall, 'half fish and half giant sea horse'. He identified it as the Veasta, the Dorset word for sea monster, and speculated that its home was off Portland where 'tides from the east and the west converge, drawing upon the forces of the sun and the moon to reflect raw energies to the ocean depths.'

The mermaid is a familiar figure in the sea lore of many nations. There is an extensive body of stories in many languages recording sightings and exploring the peculiar physiology of mermaids, particularly that of their vaginas, which are said to be constructed so as not to permit sexual intercourse with humans. Unfortunately it is the nature of such mysteries that they attract the attention of lunatics and cranks, making it difficult to disentangle hard fact from fantasy. Who knows what was washed up on Cogden Beach in the far-off summer of 1757? Reason suggests that it was not a mermaid, but since when has reason covered every eventuality? I cannot help thinking about the forty-eight teeth, on each jaw. Someone counted them.

These days Cogden Beach is overlooked by a caravan park, so if a mermaid were to show herself again, someone would surely capture the event on a mobile-phone camera. Caravan parks arouse conflicting views. The self-appointed guardians of the purity of the coastline and the countryside – generally members of the National Trust – tend to regard them with distaste. And it is true that rows of rectangular metal boxes each with a car beside it inevitably diminish the charm of a place when viewed from a distance.

On the other hand they are loved and cherished by those who own or rent them. I chatted for a while to a couple from Pershore in Worcestershire who were sitting on their verandah looking out over the sea. He had a camera on a tripod, lens pointing in the direction of the mermaid's emergence. They came down whenever the weather was fine and had made good friends among the other caravanners. They felt the sea did them a power of good.

There is another much bigger and brasher caravan park to the west of Burton Bradstock. Freshwater Beach, as it calls itself, offers the full holiday experience: Jurassic Fun Park, cabaret nights, fun 'n' frolic nights, 70s weekends, all sorts. Its rows of boxes spill right down to the beach and far back into the hinterland, thoroughly defacing the coastline between the little river Bride and the fairways of the Bridport and West Dorset golf course to the west. As I approached, I briefly mistook the glare of the sun off the roofs of the caravans for an interesting coastal lagoon. I would not want to stay in such a place myself, but there are many that do, and if we lose the odd stretch of coastline to give them pleasure, is that such a bad thing?

Treves called Burton Bradstock 'exceedingly pretty', which the old part certainly is. But he also noted its discovery by 'the diligent holidaymaker' to whose ranks have been added, much later, the legions of the retired. He would doubtless groan with dismay if he could see the accretions of dull modern housing all around it today.

On the beach I came upon an angler scaling a plump bass for supper. He was a refugee from Hertfordshire where, he said, he had burned himself out running a restaurant. 'Now I go fishing and listen to the sea as I go to sleep,' he said. 'It's very calming.'

The cliffs between Burton Bradstock and West Bay are a sheer, biscuit-coloured drop composed of layers of friable sandstone between shelves of much harder, cemented sandstone, to give the appearance of a cross-section of some complex work of bakery. They are also inclined to release chunks of rock without warning, so beach users are warned to keep well away from the foot.

The beach is familiar to lovers of vintage British television as the backdrop of the opening of the immortal *The Fall and Rise of Reginald Perrin*, in which Reginald Iolanthe Perrin, in the form of Leonard Rossiter, flings off his clothes and skips down the fine shingle beach into the sea to swim towards his presumed extinction. More recently it figured in the ITV police drama *Broadchurch*, bringing the glow of celebrity to the otherwise rather uninteresting resort of West Bay. For a time the question 'Who killed Danny?' was being asked across the land (it was the lady copper's husband, as predicted by me halfway through), and the cliff from which he might have fallen/been pushed (he wasn't) became a familiar landmark.

So great was the sensation created by this series that, according to local newspaper reports, the organiser of the long-standing Jane Austen tour of nearby Lyme Regis had decided to branch out into Who Killed Danny? tours of West Bay, concentrating on the cliff and beach, the newsagent's where Jack Marshall (chief suspect owing to dodgy past) endured angry insults (he eventually topped himself) and the private estate up the hill where all the passions brewed and stewed and boiled over.

The skyline to the west is commanded by the great headland known as the Golden Cap, at 620 feet the highest point anywhere along the Channel. The gold – and it is gold – is a layer of sandstone standing out above the dark, crumbly Jurassic clays below. It has always been a prized landmark for mariners, although the creeping encroachment of vegetation has made it less gold, and therefore less visible from afar, than it used to be.

Seatown, Dorset

The Golden Cap was acquired in 1978 by the National Trust, which now controls a five-mile stretch of coastline and hinterland between Eype and Charmouth, broken only by the little resort of Seaton. The coastal path winds along the clifftops and into the vales. The land is divided between small farms according to ancient boundaries. The fields are small and irregular, the hedges and fences are well maintained and rules forbidding the use of chemical fertilisers and sprays are rigorously enforced. It is working countryside, accessible in a discreet way, and the manner in which it ends, with sheep and cattle munching at the land's edge, is a source of wonder.

There is a track behind the Golden Cap that leads through what was once the village of Stanton St Gabriel until they moved the coast road inland to what is now the route of the A35, and the settlement mouldered into ruin. It passes the shell of the village church, clasped in bramble and wild rose.

A little way further on I happened upon a stable where a tall, good-looking woman was tending a large, good-looking horse with affectionate murmurs while several dogs romped around.

She told me in her soft Dorset voice that she had been brought up at Upcott Farm which stood where five fields and a copse met on the hillside nearby. It had been her father's and now her brother was the tenant: 480 acres of grazing (though erosion nibbled away a little every year), no chemicals, just honest manure laboriously transported to improve the yield, and year-round toil to make a living from it. 'But it's in the blood, isn't it?' she said. She was working as a carer in Bridport but it was clear where her heart was. 'I've lived all my life with the sound of the sea,' she said.

* * *

Lyme Regis

I really like Lyme Regis and have had very happy times there. I like the obvious things about it – the harbour and the Cobb, the museum, the crooked old cottages along the front, the beach of imported sand, the cheery Marine Parade, the narrow twisting streets and well-tended municipal gardens.

I like it for having a proper secondhand bookshop, a cinema, a splendid bakery in the old mill where the breakfasts are a marvel. There are a couple of decent pubs and, of late, a classy fish restaurant up the hill. There are some proper shops, including an old-fashioned hardware store where I was able to get a set of Allen keys to adjust my handlebars; and a lot of shops of the kind you don't mind looking through the window of even if you never actually buy anything. One thing Lyme Regis lacks is a butcher's, which is odd, considering the kind of place it is.

I like the fact that if you wander of an evening around to the end of the Cobb you are quite likely to come across the trawler *New Seeker* unloading her catch in fading light: polystyrene boxes of squid, ray, gurnard, black bream, the odd turbot and monkfish. This is real fishing, day in, day out, all weathers, the year round; a very far cry from the sedate routines of the town. There is an eccentric aquarium by the quay whose principal attraction is a tank of tame mullet trained to nibble fish food from your fingers.

There is little for me to say about Lyme. It is so conscious of its rich history and heritage – fossils, Jane Austen, Monmouth's rebellion, *The French Lieutenant's Woman*, storms and shipwrecks, Mary Anning, civil war and so on – and markets them with such well-mannered assiduousness that there seem to be no obscure corners to be explored or dark deeds to be unearthed. Somehow it would be improper to say anything unkind about Lyme Regis, and I wouldn't wish to.

Instead I will address myself to the one burning question about Lyme: did Jane Austen swim naked there?

The novelist's visits in 1803 and 1804 have been documented to the point of tedium, as has her use of the location in crucial scenes in *Persuasion*. She certainly bathed in the sea there, as did her sisters. But what, if anything, was she wearing?

The first thing to understand is that they bathed. They did not swim. Very few people could swim in those days. The purpose was therapeutic, not to take exercise. Bathers like the Austen sisters would immerse themselves in the water inside or close to their bathing machines. An illustration of one of the royal visits to Weymouth shows three princesses inside their machine, two in dresses at the side, the third in the water unashamedly nude.

By the time the Austens came to Lyme for their holidays, sea bathing had become a favourite diversion at all resorts for people of all classes. Where bathing machines were not available or were too expensive, males and females went in where and how they pleased. At Liverpool in 1795 both sexes went naked. In Kent and Sussex girls and women generally wore flannel gowns, although some – generally those of the working class – were naked. An observer in Scarborough noted 'charming maids in kindly clinging garments'. Men were always naked; it was generally believed that wearing anything lessened the benign effects of sea water.

The indiscriminate mixing of naked men and maids in kindly clinging garments aroused unease. In 1800 the *Observer* reported that 'the indecency of numerous naked men bathing in the sea close to the ladies' bathing machines and under the windows of the principal houses at most of the watering places has long been complained of but in general has not been redressed.' A guide to Worthing complained that the appearance of many bathers was 'indecent and inconsistent with the rules of propriety and morality'. The great caricaturist Gillray's depiction of a summer day at Margate showed naked men frolicking between the bathing machines while being watched from the esplanade by young women with telescopes.

Little by little local authorities introduced regulations to enforce public decency. As swimming became more popular (as distinct from bathing), women covered themselves up. But the effectiveness of the covering was sometimes questionable. A correspondent for the *Observer* – which seems to have taken a particularly close interest in the matter – reported that at Margate 'females lay on their backs waiting for the coming waves in the most *degagée* style . . . the waves carry their dresses up to their necks so that as far as decency is concerned they might as well be without dresses at all.' The same newspaper – possibly the same outraged correspondent – groused about men gambolling around 'in a complete state of nature' and women disporting themselves 'in questionable costumes', the spectacle watched by crowds 'of all ages and both sexes'.

Such scenes were an affront to Victorian notions of propriety. Councils in seaside towns found themselves under pressure from the Church and other guardians of morality to segregate men and women and force them to cover their objectionable parts. In 1866 the local authority in

Scarborough received two petitions, one from the clergy and the other from a group of residents, claiming that the indecent behaviour of bathers was keeping people away from the resort. The main problem was with naked men, but when the council proposed a bylaw requiring them to wear bathing costumes, the operators of the bathing machines objected that 'first-class visitors' who 'have hitherto come here to bathe according to ancient useage' would take their nakedness elsewhere. The eventual compromise was that men were required to cover up on the main beach between 7 a.m. and 9 p.m., but were allowed to go as nature intended at other times and on other beaches.

The diarist and clergyman Francis Kilvert spoke for many dedicated followers of nudity when he wrote of the 'delicious feeling of freedom in stripping in the open air and running naked to the sea.' He objected strongly to being required to wear drawers at Shanklin on the Isle of Wight in the 1870s. 'If ladies don't like to see men naked why don't they keep away from the sight?' he demanded. There is an arresting passage in his diary of 1874 in which he lingers over the appearance of a girl at Shanklin – 'a supple, slender waist, the gentle dawn and tender swell of the bosom and budding breasts, the graceful rounding of the delicately beautiful limbs and above all the soft exquisite curves of the rosy dimpled bottom and broad white thighs.' Phew!

By then most councils had introduced broadly similar by-laws to outlaw such exhibitions. But as John Travis – a former hotelier turned academic – has shown in his research, many of them preferred to do little or nothing to enforce them. Brighton ordered bathers to be segregated and men to wear costumes but the *Observer* found 'men in a state of nature and women with apologies of covering, exposed to the stares and remarks of the crowds'. In Margate 'ladies outraged decorum' by fixing opera glasses on the antics of nude men, while the council did nothing.

Dr Travis reveals that the general covering up of the nude swimmer came about more through market forces than flaky public morality. As family seaside holidays grew in popularity towards the end of the nineteenth century, so did the pressure for mixed bathing. It is often stated that Bexhill in Sussex was the first resort to license mixed bathing, in 1902. In fact Paignton introduced it in 1896, Dawlish in 1897, Worthing and Bognor in 1899 and Torquay in 1900. The bathing machine, designed for concealment, was becoming redundant, and with families spread indiscriminately across the sand and shingle, no one wanted naked men around any more, for understandable reasons.

Although the 'fearless old fashion', as *Cosmopolitan* magazine called it, survived on the margins, from roughly 1900 onwards costumes became the general rule. That remains the case, with allowance for minority topless display and the provision of some discreet nudist beaches (interestingly the one in Brighton, opened in 1980, is still the only one in a major resort). But the business of changing into swimming gear caused, and still causes, awkwardness.

In 1927 the Labour MP for Southwark Central, Harry Day, asked the Home Secretary, William Joynson-Hicks, to consider legislation to ban undressing on beaches 'for bathing purposes' in view of the many complaints on the subject. Mr Day asked the Home Secretary if he was aware that in many cases 'large groups of people undress on the beach without any covering at all.' 'In any case of that kind,' Joynson-Hicks replied drolly, 'I am quite sure the Honourable Member would not be present.'

So did Jane Austen bathe naked at Lyme Regis? Maybe she did.

15

KEEPING THE RIFFRAFF OUT

Although I am fond of Lyme, I am not sure I would want to live there and I definitely would not want to become infirm there. The cliffs to the west are dark and crumbly and the beaches too are dark, and when a stiff onshore breeze persists, the sea along the edge becomes ashy grey and murky and unappealing.

So it can be dour at times, and is very steep at all times. I met an elderly man walking briskly at the western extremity of the town, where it peters out in a huddle of beach huts and mobile homes. He and his wife had migrated from inland Sussex. He had wanted to stay closer to London but she had her heart set on Lyme Regis. Now she had had a heart attack and couldn't get around as she did before. 'It's too bloody steep,' he said angrily. 'We didn't think of that. We're going to have to move to Torquay.'

The cliffs and clifftops west of Lyme are famously fossiliferous and notoriously unstable. Landslips are and have always been a hazard, the most celebrated of which brought natural disaster enthusiasts, fossil hunters and whiskered amateur geologists hurrying down in the winter of 1839–40. It had been an

Cliffs near Pinhay Bay, Devon

exceptionally wet and miserable summer and autumn, and in early December cracks appeared and widened along the cliff edge between Lyme and Seaton.

On 23 December William Critchard noticed that the front door of his cottage was reluctant to open. The following night, Christmas Eve, the path to the cottage had sunk by a foot, and by the morning of Christmas Day it had risen seven feet. Something was evidently up, and Critchard set off to alert his employer at Bindon Farm, a mile or so inland.

His wife and their neighbours set about gathering up their possessions and getting out. The ground shook and groaned, the sound likened to the tearing of cloth. A party out shooting rabbits narrowly avoided being swallowed up by one of the fissures appearing along the clifftop. In the course of that Christmas Day a section broke away and sank, creating a ravine half a mile long, up to 400 yards wide and between 130 and 200 feet deep. The outward thrust of the subsidence caused an upheaval of the sea bottom and the temporary appearance off-shore of a considerable reef. Most of the cottages were wrecked and the unfortunate Critchard's disappeared entirely.

The undercliff settled over time. What had previously been fields of wheat became a wilderness, densely overgrown and fractured by deep gulleys. The path through it is not accessible to a man with a bike, so I missed it and instead took the very smart bridle path into the Rousdon estate and past a great pile bristling with high chimneys and sporting a timbered gable and arcade, a rectangular tower with pyramidal roof, a multitude of mullioned windows and much else. Rousdon was built in the 1870s at the behest of Sir Henry Peek, who made a great deal of money from biscuits (Peek Frean) and selling spices and groceries.

He was a philanthropist of the old, semi-feudal kind. In addition to his mansion, Sir Henry commissioned a new church, a model estate farm, workers' cottages, a blacksmith's forge, slaughterhouse, barns, kennels, stables – a small, self-contained community able to feed and look after itself. It was a high-minded project, but such projects have a habit of becoming unstuck once the great wealth that made them possible runs out or the intense personal interest lapses with death or a change of circumstances.

Like many other excessively large and draughty houses, Rousdon eventually became a school, Allhallows, which itself outlived its usefulness in time and closed. Now it has all been converted for twenty-first-century easy living: apartments and holiday lets and new houses built to imitate the old imitative style. It is a great place for DFLs – Down From Londons – two of whom I met pushing their buggies along the smoothly mown fringe of the estate road. The husband of one worked at home in their conversion, the other's spouse was in London Monday to Friday – 'so basically every weekend is a holiday which is cool. Yah, it works really well. It's so lovely here.'

Beyond and below Rousdon, the river Axe glides discreetly into the sea. There is a concrete bridge over it which was built in 1877, making it the oldest such construction in the country. These days it serves as a footbridge; next to it there is a modern boring bridge of the modern boring bridge type which takes the road traffic.

At twenty-two miles long, the Axe is hardly a major river. Yet size is not everything, with rivers as with much else, and the Axe is rich in history and association – so rich, in fact, that when George Pulman came to write its story he ended up producing a book running to more than 900 pages. Pulman was born in Axminster, became a printer and bookseller, edited the *Yeovil Times* and founded Crewkerne's first newspaper. He was a dedicated local journalist and historian, and a fly-fisherman of great distinction, a fine combination. In fishing history, Pulman is credited with being the first angler systematically to use a floating (dry) fly to catch trout instead of a sunken (wet) fly, which may not sound much to non-anglers but was a mighty revolution in its day. He wrote a little book full of wisdom and sound advice called *The Vade Mecum of Fly-Fishing for Trout*. But his great labour was his *The Book of the Axe*, which is not so much a guidebook as a love offering to the little river on which he spent so much of his time, and which gave him such delight.

Pulman gives a very full account of the melancholy fate that overtook the once thriving port of Axmouth. In 1346 it was important enough to supply two ships and twenty-five men for the expedition to seize Calais, and it remained a major regional centre for shipping for a long time after that. But it was cursed by the inexorable eastward drift of shingle across the mouth of the river. The celebrated antiquarian William Stukeley recorded in 1724 that 'it has been a great haven and excellent port of which they still keep up the memory' but that the mouth was filled up with 'coggles, gravel, sand, shells and such matter as is thrown up by the rowl of the ocean.'

As at Rye and Winchelsea far to the east, laborious, extremely expensive and ultimately unavailing efforts were periodically made to clear the harbour. At one stage there was a very grand plan for a canal across to Bristol which would have saved ships coming around by Land's End, but it came to nothing. The arrival of the railway finished the job of consigning Axmouth port to oblivion. Nowadays there is a basin below the concrete footbridge where small boats are tied up. Below it the river curves east then west around a spit of shingle, narrowing like the neck of a wine flask.

I watched a silver-haired man in a baseball cap steer his boat out past the gravel bar. He went slowly and steadily, his engine a throaty chug, his fishing rod at an angle in the bow. It was a delicious morning, for fishing or anything else. I thought: that's what I would do if I lived by the sea, get a boat and take it out on gentle days like this and catch some bass and mackerel. And what could be better than that?

Another elderly bloke, in shorts and trainers, with a stick and a rucksack over his bony shoulders, was heading off purposefully along the beach towards Lyme Regis. His feet scrunched audibly on the clean-washed salty stones. He stopped, stared at the water for some time, carried on. He gave the impression of having all the time in the world to get to wherever he was going.

Seaton Cliffs

Seaton is set back behind its own stony beach across the mouth of the Axe. The railway that killed off the port was the making of Seaton for a time. It became quite a classy resort, boasting fourteen hotels and a theatre, but its charms have, I fear, faded a good deal since that heyday. The seafront, which makes or breaks a resort, is too much taken up with mediocre blocks of holiday and residential flats. Seaton does, however, boast a turf labyrinth on the edge of town, although the reasons for it being there are not readily apparent to the casual visitor. Those entering are urged to 'look deeply, bravely and sincerely at whatever circumstances are trying to teach you.' I found that circumstances were trying to teach me to go to the nearby Seaton Hole café for a bacon bap and a slab of cold bread pudding.

There was one other customer there, eating a healthy salad sandwich. She was somewhat glum about Seaton, which she had known for a long time. 'It's become a rather sad place,' she said. 'Nothing ever seems to happen here.'

One thing that did happen was the collapse in summer 2012 of part of the clifftop carrying the old road to Beer, which has now been abandoned for good. Beer is a sweet little holiday place, much perkier than Seaton. It makes much of its history as a centre of smuggling, and of the adventures of a local lad, Jack Rattenbury, who spent half a lifetime dodging the excise men and wrote a book about his adventures which is invariably referred to as 'colourful'.

Beer Head

But the main interest of Beer is geological and belongs to the headland to the south, Beer Head. Here the theme that has recurred at intervals from St Margaret's Bay in Kent takes its final bow, for Beer Head is the last chalk cliff on the Channel. It is a fine one, surmounted by craggy pinnacles, dropping steeply into clear aquamarine water, its face pitted with holes and scarred by rockfalls. The sudden reappearance of the white chalk to the east and west of Beer is all the more striking because either side – at Seaton and Branscombe – a new theme has been introduced in the form of the deep terracotta of the Triassic Mercia Mudstone. Variations on this tone – sometimes as dark as uncooked liver, more often lighter but always strikingly maroon – dominate the coast as far as Torquay, giving rise to the label Red Devon.

Devon is often too lovely for its own good. At Branscombe three wooded vales come together in a straggling village of low, ancient stone dwellings with creepers and roses around their doors and little walled cottage gardens outside. A tiny stream twists through it and finds the sea through a gently shelving beach with a thatched café beside it. With the sea on one side, and green fields broken by woods to the other, Branscombe is perfect.

It is difficult not to dream of having a bolthole in such a place, and for those with a stack of spare cash it is not a great leap to obtaining one. So Branscombe, like so many sweet and lovely villages in south-west England, has become a settlement of second homes: full of life and noise and fun in the holiday season, quiet as night outside it. It has a school and two pubs, a post office and a forge with a real blacksmith, and even a little brewery producing fine ale, so the life has not been extinguished altogether. But its familiar blight is that its young people cannot afford to stay.

Branscombe's dead rest in the graveyards either side of its exceptionally lovely church. An elderly couple were at work keeping the graves and the paths tidy. She was one of a tiny handful of Branscombe born and bred – there were four others left, she told me. She pointed out to me a pair of cottages set back from the lane, intended for living in, bought by someone from outside, converted, hardly used. 'It's a curse,' her husband said bitterly. 'There's nowhere for the children to live.'

Branscombe made the national headlines once, in 2007, although it was an episode the village would probably prefer to forget. It began with the grounding offshore and breaking up of a container ship, the *Napoli*, and the arrival on Branscombe beach of forty or so of its giant metal boxes which the sea conveniently smashed open. A global treasure trove was revealed which included BMW motorbikes, casks of brandy, morphine, Nintendo and Xbox games, vast mountains of disposable nappies, quantities of anti-wrinkle cream and frozen Peking duck, pet food, a consignment of Bibles in the Xhosa language, seven cigarette cards featuring pigeons and a single Iraqi 50 dinar note.

The event set off a wild rebirth of the bad old practice of wreck plundering. Locals soon made off with the choicest items, but word spread and within a couple of days the roads leading to Branscombe were jammed with bargain hunters from all over Britain, and even some from abroad. The looting of the cargo of the *Napoli* became a national scandal. The impotence of the authorities, the use of mobile phones to spread the news, the reckless greed and oafishness of the looters, the chaotic and revolting nature of the spectacle shown on TV, all seemed to come together in a paradigm of society's abdication of moral standards. The editorial columns hummed with expressions of outrage, ministers spluttered with indignation; inevitably, an official inquiry was set up (conclusion: leadership failure).

Then the story died. The salvage teams disposed of the *Napoli* and what was left of its load, and Branscombe was left battered and dazed. The trauma of those lawless days and nights is recalled by the presence next to the beach of the mighty anchor from the ship, which was presented to the village by her owners.

The road inland passes Weston and its donkey sanctuary, where the air is filled with the contented braying of its pampered inmates. I got back to the sea along a dip in the landscape leading to Southcombe Farm. The loveliness of the place was almost unreal; green fields overlaying red earth speckled by grazing beasts, hedges and copses in between, at the edge the red cliffs and the blue sea. I cycled down the track very happily, then hauled the bike up the appallingly steep slope of Salcombe Hill. At the top is a stone memorial to the man whose generosity of spirit ensured that this glorious spot has remained undefiled and free to anyone with sound legs and wind to enjoy.

The Cornishes were an old Devon family, widely dispersed. I knew the name of C. J. Cornish through an enchanting book, *A Naturalist on the Thames*, which is full of good stuff about chub and eel traps and the like. But I had never heard of his younger brother, Vaughan, a distinguished geographer specialising in wave forms who later developed a theory of what he called 'aesthetic geography', the power of natural scenery to promote spiritual wellbeing. Cornish campaigned energetically on behalf of the Council for the Preservation of Rural England, focussing on the protection of the coast and clifftops.

He claimed for cliff scenery a superiority over the inland landscape that he likened to that of a sculpture over a bas-relief. He wanted to see an open strip five chains wide (110 yards) that would remain inaccessible to cars, free from seats, shelters, litter bins and noticeboards. And he put his fields where his mouth was. On inheriting Southcombe Farm, he made an agreement with the local council that it should be preserved as open space with public access in perpetuity. The South-West Coast Path now threads its way between the fields and the drop to the sea – not five chains wide, but wide enough. Vaughan Cornish deserves his stone.

Breathing heavily I heaved my bike over a gate at the top of Salcombe Hill. On the other side was a lady sitting on a bench facing east where the afternoon sun struck against the dark-red cliffs. She had walked up from Sidmouth with her golden retriever, which was slumped on the ground beside her. She had been a GP in Sidmouth for many years and had stayed there after retirement. She liked it and always had, but said it was not what it once was. Tesco were trying to get in, and Morrisons. 'We've always been perfectly happy with Waitrose,' she said.

Sidmouth

In 1933 Sidmouth Urban District Council rejected a proposal to build a holiday camp at Salcombe Regis on the grounds that holiday camps and Sidmouth did not go together. Until 1945 changing on the beach was banned at Sidmouth, as were ice-cream stalls, whelk stands and photographers. It had a new esplanade and the Connaught Pleasure Gardens, but none of the vulgar attractions – pavilions, piers, amusement arcades and the like – adopted by other seaside resorts. It had bowls, croquet, tennis and a putting green.

In 1952 the council decided to form a committee to promote the town, but voted against allowing hoteliers or retailers to be on it. Ten years later the committee came up with a slogan defining Sidmouth's image of itself: Sidmouth Caters for the Discriminating. In pursuit of the mission 'to preserve old-world graciousness', a bylaw was passed in the 1970s prohibiting 'wirelesses in public places'.

Sidmouth was the first proper Devon seaside resort. Throughout its long history it has prospered by attracting a flow of well-heeled patrons to its expensive and intensely respectable hotels. It has pursued a strategy of discreet exclusion of the lower orders, by the simple expedient of refusing to provide any of the amenities and amusements that the lower orders expect. As a result Sidmouth has always had a particular flavour, derided by its critics but savoured by its admirers. John Betjeman was one:

Mansions for admirals by the pebbly strand,
And cottages for maiden aunts inland,
That go with tea and strawberries and cream
Sweet sheltered gardens by the twisting stream,
Cobb, thatch and fuschia bells, a Devon dream.

Recently the town received an extraordinary gift. An investment banker, Keith Owen – a frequent visitor to Sidmouth despite being based in Canada – contacted the Sid Vale Association to tell them that he had been diagnosed with terminal cancer and that he was leaving his £2 million estate to Sidmouth 'to sustain its ambience and way of life'. 'He was a nice chap, a very unassuming fellow and he really did love Sidmouth,' the chairman of the town council said of Mr Owen in highly Sidmouthian terms. The first spending project was also highly characteristic: the planting at strategic points of 150,000 snowdrop, daffodil and crocus bulbs.

An early connoisseur of Sidmouth's charms – he called it 'a little marine paradise' – was the Reverend Sydney Smith, who brought his family down from his parish in Somerset most summers between 1830 and his death in 1845. Smith was an oddity, a man celebrated not for his work – he was a dutiful clergyman, no more, and wrote nothing of lasting value – but for his jokes. Just about everyone who knew him considered him the funniest man alive; his friends were often reduced to tears of laughter by his jests, and their servants to unseemly displays of hilarity. Of Macaulay, Sydney observed that 'he has occasional flashes of silence which make his conversation perfectly delightful', and of someone else that 'he deserves to be preached to death by wild curates', which I think is still funny.

His most notable intervention in public life followed the infamous rejection by the House of Lords in 1831 of the Reform Bill proposing a modest extension of the franchise. In a speech in Taunton, Smith drew an extended parallel between the behaviour of the Lords and that of a resident of Sidmouth, 'the excellent Mrs Partington', when confronted by the epic flood of 1824. Dame Partington, Sydney related, was to be seen at the door of her house 'trundling her mop, squeezing out the water and vigorously punching away the Atlantic Ocean.' His comic climax achieved immortality: 'The Atlantic was roused. Mrs Partington's spirit was up. But I need not tell you that the contest was unequal. The Atlantic Ocean beat Mrs Partington. She was excellent with a mop or a puddle, but she should not have meddled with a tempest.'

The tempest in question was no joke for Sidmouth or any of the other ports and settlements battered by one of the most violent Channel storms ever recorded. The harbour at Lyme Regis was wrecked, Christchurch was flooded, Weymouth lost its esplanade and most of its pier, scores of houses on Portland were destroyed and the village of Fleet, well behind the Chesil Beach, was completely inundated. Hundreds of seamen were drowned as their ships were wrecked, and scores of people on land were drowned or killed by flying slates, or falling chimney stacks and trees.

In Sidmouth the sea invaded the town in the early hours of 23 November. Mrs Mogridge in York Terrace was awoken by the noise of boats banging against her front door. Mr Hall the draper reported sailors rowing across the market place to rescue distressed ladies. In the library the billiard table was smashed against the fireplace and the piano was washed into the sitting room. The landlord of the London Hotel watched a giant wave sweep into the chemist's and retreat bearing bottles and pill boxes. At dawn Mr Yeates struggled to the beach and saw that the great local landmark, a forty-foot-high stack at the mouth of the harbour known as the Chet Rock, was no more.

The details were recorded by the town's resident antiquarian, Peter Orlando Hutchinson, a magnificently quirky example of the species. Hutchinson came to Sidmouth with his family at the age of fifteen and remained there for the rest of his eighty-seven years. Unmarried (he lived with a cat and a pet raven), he habitually wore a kind of uniform of his own design and went around in a cart pulled by a donkey. He devoted himself to exhaustive investigation of every aspect of Sidmouth's history, legends, geology, flora and fauna, recording his findings in thousands of pages of diaries, and in the five volumes of his *History of Sidmouth*, which was never published.

Hutchinson's friend, the Reverend H. G. J. Clements,

remembered him as 'somewhat original and eccentric in all his proceedings ... a typical antiquary in face and figure ... his very handwriting was a copy from the antique, slowly and deliberately executed, his utterance and diction equally elaborate.' Mr Clements speculated that Hutchinson might have derived his manner from Sidmouth itself 'which has been (and I hope may continue to be) a very deliberate sort of a place'.

It certainly remains a very handsome and well-kempt resort, with fine terraces and crescents of elegant town houses, and a glorious cricket ground (though the secondhand bookshop I remembered from twenty-five years ago has gone). What passes for controversy in Sidmouth rages over such issues as the management of the beach huts, whether or not the Mayor should get a new mayoral chain and the discovery of a used condom outside the new Jurassic Coast Interpretation Centre. A council comment on this last scandal – 'this is nothing new ... we've had reports of people getting completely naked and using the open-fronted showers next door' – hinted at a degree of depravity that would have set Betjeman's admirals and maiden aunts all of a-quiver.

Sidmouth is at one end of the holiday spectrum. Ladram Bay Holiday Park, a few miles along the red cliffs, is at the other. Ladram Bay unspoiled must have been extraordinary. A geological quirk has thrown up stacks of sandstone just yards from the beach, which have been gnawed into horizontal corrugations by the wind and the sea over their 240 million years of existence. The blue of the water and the sky, the blood red of the flanking cliffs and the pillars of stone, the green of the fields made for a dramatic and beautiful visual composition – until the great host of caravans spilled down towards the sea and across the flanking slopes. It is irredeemably blighted, yet it gives great pleasure to countless holidaymakers who would never have a place at one of Sidmouth's plush hotels.

* * *

Otter estuary, Budleigh Salterton

I approached Budleigh Salterton by means of a footpath along the river Otter from Otterton. The Otter was another Devon stream I had not encountered before. Alternating between gravelly riffles and slow, contemplative pools, it looked full of trouty potential. It flowed clear but dark, on account of the dark streambed. The far bank sloped steeply up, the red earth nourishing a thick band of alder, oak and the odd willow.

As it nears the sea, the river dissipates its energy in a marsh of lagoons and mudflats before gathering itself to end its journey at the eastern extremity of Budleigh Salterton's shingle beach, beside a knob of rusty sandstone. The path swings away before the end, and curves along the edge of the saltmarsh and around Budleigh Salterton's charming cricket ground. Practice was in progress: boys were being drilled in their forward defensives and slip catching. It was clear evidence of something that I otherwise might have doubted – namely that there were children in Budleigh Salterton, and people of child-bearing age.

What a curious place it is, starting with the abnormal size, smoothness and roundness of the quartzite stones that make up its beach. It is a seaside town, very appealingly situated, but in no sense a seaside resort, because there is almost nowhere to stay. As recently as the 1960s there were as many as thirteen hotels on or near the seafront. Now there is not a single one. Following the closure of the railway in 1967 they were all either demolished to make way for flats, or themselves were converted into flats, nursing homes or residential homes.

I became anxious about my bed. The one B & B was full, and I became more anxious. Eventually I did locate a hotel, a considerable distance inland; and very welcoming they were, Brian and Lorraine, and the breakfast the next morning was everything I had hoped. But before breakfast came dinner, and they had no restaurant. Where to eat? My question had the edge of desperation.

They suggested the Salterton Arms and gave me directions. I found the place, which seemed extraordinarily busy for a

Tuesday evening, drained a much-needed pint and asked for the menu. No food on ukelele night, the barmaid said. I looked around more attentively. They all had ukeleles. Some were strumming them purposefully and a collective outburst of ukelele was clearly imminent.

The barmaid sent me across the road to the chippie. It was ten minutes past eight. A schedule of opening hours on the door revealed that it closed at eight. I went back to the Salterton, had another pint and sought more advice. The only hope was the other pub, the Feathers. I arrived panting. The barman looked at his watch in answer to my question. Seven minutes till last orders, he said. Home-made faggots with onion gravy and mash, plus more beer, repaired my morale. I felt as if I had been plucked to safety from dangerous seas.

When I came out of the Feathers the light was fading and the town had pretty much shut down. I was startled to find someone having a barbecue on the beach, infringing heaven knows how many Budleigh Salterton bylaws. On the wall nearby was a plaque recording that Millais painted his *Boyhood of Raleigh* there; across the road was the octagonal house where he stayed. That largely exhausts the town's cultural heritage, unless you count various mocking barbs at its expense – as in Coward's *Blithe Spirit*: 'No one but a monumental bore would have thought of having a honeymoon in Budleigh Salterton. I wanted glamour and music and romance. What I got was potted plants, three hours every day on a damp golf course and a three piece orchestra playing *Merrie England*.'

Budleigh Salterton is a place to live long and die respectably. The town is slightingly referred to (as are Eastbourne and

Bournemouth and Florida and doubtless other locations too) as God's Waiting Room, and these days God is waiting longer and longer. My landlord Brian told me that if anyone was recorded by the local paper as having died under the age of eighty-five, it was assumed to be a misprint.

It is not easy to conceive of strong passions being aroused in Budleigh Salterton, but if they are, the likeliest setting is surely the clubhouse of the Budleigh Salterton Croquet Club, or somewhere on the ten velvet-smooth croquet lawns outside. Croquet may be a joke elsewhere, but in Budleigh Salterton it is a serious business. The club is celebrated across the croquet-playing world for the splendour of its facilities and the richness of its history, and they come from all over the world to play there.

It is not a gentle game. A notice beside the lawns hints at the hazards: *Danger. Beware. Injuries Can Be Caused By Fast Moving Croquet Balls.* As for passions, the club's history – available for inspection on its website – is understandably reticent. There is a good deal about the comings and goings of various grounds-men, some of it suggestive of dramatic possibilities: 'Creasey went and Hutchins replaced him. Hutchins was not satisfactory and Till came ... Till was discharged for unsatisfactory service, to be replaced by Lawrence.' This sentence, I think, defies analysis: 'Dolfuss was murdered by the Nazis in 1934 and Hitler came to power in Germany but there was no foreboding in Budleigh Salterton.'

In 1953, Coronation year, Miss Sutton was appointed canasta hostess and the club acquired a new flagpole, but the committee decided against taking part in the town procession. Three years later there were tributes to Lord Clinton, who had died after forty-six years as President; and 'Mrs Lanning resigned after many disagreements with Mrs French.'

Who knows what dramatic scenes informed these simple sentences, what furies took wing, what feuds boiled and festered, what injuries and slights were suffered, what pride came before what fall, what revenge was taken?

16

GULLS AND GROCKLES

Exmouth and the Exe estuary

Exmouth has a slightly forlorn air about it, as if it had come off second-best in a fight or an argument and still felt aggrieved about it. The town centre is well away from the waterfront and is distinctly shabby. The docks were once the heart of the town, handling biggish ships on behalf of Exeter and supporting a fishing fleet to harvest the herring and mackerel. Now it just has a marina hemmed in by brightly coloured, gormlessly derivative boxes of 'luxury apartments'.

The seafront has a long beach of reddish sand, a sea wall, a road, a line of serviceable nineteenth-century houses and a standard range of visitor attractions. I'm afraid that as a resort Exmouth lacks class, and always has. Our old friend Charles Harper – now onto *The South Devon Coast* – found it overrun on Sundays with excursionists from Exeter – 'tradesmen's assistants, clad in the impossible clothes pictured on provincial advertisement hoardings, laughing horse laughs, singing London's last season's comic songs, wearing flashy jewellery, smoking bad cigars . . .'

But Exmouth's consolation is the glory of its situation on the estuary of the Exe. An estuary is a mysterious and subtle place, belonging neither to sea nor river but taking from both to create its own shifting, dynamic water world. At full water the six miles or so of the Exe estuary from Exmouth to Topsham is a great, brimming lake held between slopes to the east and west. Then, as if a stopper had been eased out, the water rushes out through the gap between Exmouth and Dawlish Warren, straining buoys against chains and boats against ropes, setting ridges of wavelets dancing and dashing across the sandbanks.

The colour and texture of the whole sheet of water changes as the mudflats and sandbanks loom beneath then break the surface. The navigation channel follows the western shore, twisting like a dark snake around quaintly named hazards: Great and Little Bull Hill, Shaggles Sand, Cockle Sand, Greenland, West Mud. With the paling of the water's face come the changes in light. A gust of a breeze roughens the surface, the sun goes behind a cloud, a bank of fog rolls up from somewhere and clears. The wind quickens and the cloud gathers, the whole scene becomes grey. Come evening, the sky clears in the west as the sun goes down and everything is burnished in gold. Then the moon rises and brightens, spreading silver.

And so on: a thousand modulations a day, like a book of Bach's 48 Preludes and Fugues transposed for light and water.

There is a fine chronicler of Exmouth and its estuary who calls himself Wayland Wordsmith. I have no idea who he is – except that he is a poet, a historian, an antiquary of the old kind, a sailor, a fisherman, an explorer, a lingerer over sunsets and dawns, a fierce enemy of the enemies of his town, a philosopher and a gifted writer of a terrific blog. From it I gather that he is around my age, early sixties; that he used to do some netting for salmon when there were still enough salmon seeking the Exe to make it worthwhile; that he has a boat and a family; that he spends a good deal of his time hunting out arcane stories and nuggets of information from piles of old newspapers and books.

I confess that I have borrowed freely from him, and without shame, because I am pretty confident he won't mind. I'd like to meet him and tell him what a debt I owe him.

Exmouth has no Grand Hotel but it does have the Imperial, which looks across its own lawns and the esplanade to the sea. One of Wayland Wordsmith's titbits concerns an interview conducted in February 1918 by a correspondent from the local paper with 'the wealthy and somewhat eccentric Australian inventor Thomas Mills', who was then occupying a suite at the hotel.

Thomas Mills was in Exmouth to do his bit for the war effort. Like many other patriots, he had been appalled by the dreadful toll of merchant shipping taken by the German U-boats. It occurred to him that if the German subs could be detected at sea before they attacked, they could be neutralised. His brainwave was to train seagulls to find them. To that end he had constructed a dummy submarine with an imitation periscope from which food congenial to seagulls was expelled at intervals. His plan was to get the association between periscope and nourishment lodged in their avian brains, rather in the way that their descendants have become accustomed to feeding on municipal rubbish dumps, and then to send them to locate the real things.

The Admiralty gave Mr Mills some encouragement, but not much. One senior officer asked him – quite reasonably – how the seagulls would be able to tell the difference between German subs and British subs. Mills replied that if our subs were confined to port, it would follow that any still at sea must be hostile.

The trials he organised in Exmouth were, in the view of Mr Mills, successful enough for the seagulls to be deployed for real. But his view was not widely shared. By then the adoption of the convoy system, in which merchant ships sailed together guarded by warships, had significantly reduced the depredations of the U-boats; and in any event the signing of the Armistice in November 1918 rendered the whole exercise somewhat redundant. Mr Mills was and remained extremely bitter about the way he was treated by the Admiralty and vented his spleen in a book to which he gave the arresting title *The Fateful Seagull*, which I'm afraid I have not read.

*

According to Wayland Wordsmith, the most famous son of the estuary (born in Starcross) was Captain George Peacock, not exactly a household name. He does, however, warrant an entry in the *Dictionary of National Biography* detailing his extensive surveying work in the 1830s and 1840s in South and Central America. The *DNB* is a little snooty about this, recording that 'he seems to have persuaded himself' that he was the first to survey the route of the Panama Canal, even though 'the routes he recommended were known to the Spaniards from the earliest times.'

In time the Captain retired to Starcross and had built for his amusement an unusual pleasure boat called the *Swan of the Exe* that became a familiar sight on the estuary. Described by the *Illustrated London News* as 'the very similitude of a gigantic white swan' she was only 17-and-a-half feet long but so broad in the beam that the saloon could fit a table for ten. Her sails were folded to look like the bird's wings, and additional power came from the two webbed feet operated by lever. The saloon was originally fitted with a hatch for bathing, but Captain Peacock scrapped it after one of his guests got stuck in it and nearly drowned.

The *Swan of the Exe* was launched from Exmouth in 1860 in front of a large and excited crowd, while the town's brass band played 'Rule Britannia'. She proved to be surprisingly durable and was still being sailed by Captain Peacock's grandson in the 1920s. By then she was accompanied by a tender, the *Cygnet*, which may still be admired in the museum at Topsham, her parent having finally perished in a fire.

*

In the interwar years Dawlish Warren, the thumb of sand squeezing the southern side of the estuary opposite Exmouth, played host at its sea end to an impromptu community of shacks and chalets brought by boat and installed wherever a reasonably firm foundation could be found in the dunes. One belonged to the family of Raymond Cattell, who became an extremely distinguished psychologist in post-war America. Before leaving England for good in 1937, Cattell wrote an intermittently diverting book called *Under Sail Through Red Devon* recounting his adventures with various boats and companions along the south Devon coast. He recalled carefree times at Dawlish Warren where 'peculiar people have built themselves habitations in which they live in precious freedom and isolation.' They were, he said, philosophers rather than artists – 'they live in strange, parti-coloured wooden bungalows which hide themselves between high banks of sand . . . others ride like ships on the rolling dunes . . . two, raised on stilts, permit the waters of the estuary to flow beneath . . . at night they send their twinkling lights over the water like small Venetian castles.'

Some of the chalets, Cattell recorded, were strong and protected enough to survive several winters. Others were blasted to smithereens by the storms and scattered on the waters. After the war the originals were joined by cheerfully painted beach huts, which were generally taken away by boat at the end of the season and reappeared like migrating birds the following spring.

Such free-and-easy behaviour was, needless to say, anathema to officialdom. In the 1980s the council decreed that henceforth only huts of an approved uniform design would be permitted. The old ones that were not claimed and removed by their owners were burned on the beach. At around the same time the old custom of pootling over from Exmouth in fine weather to camp on the dunes was outlawed.

In the spirit of modern times, part of the Warren was declared a nature reserve, these days policed by wardens on quad bikes. The rest is shared by a golf course and a large amusement park. Meanwhile the hinterland beside the coast road has been annexed by a cluster of campsites, caravan parks and chalet settlements, which during the season release a flood of humanity across the Warren and neighbouring attractions. 'Balancing visitor use with the needs of rare and important wildlife' is part of the nature reserve's mission statement; which means, in effect, the wildlife keeping out of the way.

I headed for Dawlish along the sea wall by the Red Rock Café. It was almost high tide and the sea was licking at the fringe of terracotta sand at the base of the wall. Further on it struck against the wall itself, a heavy hollow thump like distant artillery fire.

Dawlish

With its black swans and neat gardens and fudge shops and polite cafés Dawlish is pleasant enough on a sunny day. It's a place for an outing rather than an extended stay; to wander around The Lawn and listen to the tinkling of the stream, paddle along the dark-pink beach when the tide is out, have an ice cream and a clotted-cream tea.

It once had hotels and pretensions to be a resort of special elegance. Some bright spark coined the slogan 'Dawlish is Dawlicious', but the coming of Brunel's famous railway put a stop to that. It cheated the town of its seafront and became a kind of psychic prison fence between it and its sea. The building of it displayed the contempt of those Victorian entrepreneurs and their engineers for the interests of local people and the preservation of landscape at its most gross. The railway company simply bought up the land it wanted, booted the locals out, flattened what it needed to lay track and kept the rest.

Brunel's belief in his own vision and disdain for those who refused to share it was boundless. He was repeatedly urged to build the line inland; he told the shareholders that running it along the shore between Dawlish Warren and Teignmouth would be cheaper and more efficient, and he dismissed any suggestion that the storm-driven seas beating at his embankment would cause trouble. Brunel created an undeniably wondrous rail experience. But the price to be paid for the little man's hubris was brought home in spectacular style by the complete collapse of the track under the impact of the storms in early 2014, which closed the line for weeks, inflicting untold damage on the economy of the whole south-west and landing Network Rail with a bill for many millions.

West from Dawlish the railway line takes to a series of tunnels to penetrate the cliffs, and there is no sea wall or path of any kind until it emerges beyond the pair of red stone stacks known as the Clerk and the Parson. I had a sweaty climb out of Dawlish on the A379 then a steep descent of Smugglers' Lane (what other name could there be?) to rejoin the wall.

I had cycled along it improperly but quite safely between Dawlish Warren and Dawlish and intended to do the same to Teignmouth. But I was intimidated by Network Rail crews in electric-orange jackets so I got off. I asked one of the Network Rail men why they were so down on cycling. 'It's a bylaw,' he replied. I refrained from pointing out that this was not a reason. 'Well, it would be down to us if you went over,' he said. 'Think of the bloody paperwork.'

It was good luck for Teignmouth that it escaped the Brunel blight. The line cuts away from the sea at the eastern edge of town and proceeds discreetly via a deep cutting through the railway station and up the side of the Teign estuary towards Newton Abbot. Its bad luck was, and is, the main road. As a result of a particularly brutal 1970s 'improvement scheme', this cleaves its way around the back of the old town to get to the Shaldon Bridge over the estuary. Scores of houses and shops and pubs were swept away to make room for this monstrosity, which has done nothing to relieve traffic congestion and acts as a car-clogged barrier between the residential district to the north and the docks, harbour and retail heart of Teignmouth, not to mention its seafront.

Nevertheless the town has managed to hang on to a good deal of the charm and vivacity that have beguiled visitors for

200 years and more. I wanted to share this with my family, so at the end of August 2013 we came down for a night and the best part of two days. The blissful weather that had spread a smile around our seaside resorts for much of that summer was holding on. We stayed in an astonishingly inexpensive hotel off the Dawlish Road, in a spacious suite looking out over the blue sea. There was a gate at the bottom of the hotel's grounds which took us out near the sparkling Lido, whose reprieve from closure a few years back displayed a grasp of priorities rarely encountered among local authorities.

We swam in the Lido and we swam in the sea. The girls splashed around in a cheap inflatable boat until it burst. I hired a deckchair and read and daydreamed and watched other families helping themselves to the sweet and innocent fun that the seaside, at its best, dispenses so liberally. We wasted a heap of coins in the arcade on the pier – which they call the Grand Pier but is anything but – and joined everyone else wandering around The Den, the big grass oblong that separates the seafront from Teignmouth's most gracious residences.

For lunch we ate prawn and crab sandwiches, sitting on a wall at the quayside looking up the estuary. The view was framed by Shaldon Bridge ahead, and by the town and Shaldon village either side, with rising ground beyond. A multitude of sailing boats bobbed at their moorings or lay slumped on their sides on the mud, stranded by the retreating tide. Two girls were diving and swimming between their boat and a pontoon. A boy threw a stick for the family dog until his dad said he was wearing the poor creature out. In the port proper, a freighter was unloading, a reminder that Teignmouth's long history as a minor but significant port was not yet over.

Later we wandered through the narrow streets behind the quayside, bought buttered Brazils and sherbet lemons and cola cubes at the sweet shop, peered through windows at knick-knacks and tattooists at work. We went across to Shaldon on the ferry in the evening. Anglers were lined up along the spit at the mouth of the estuary casting into the running tide in the hope of a bass.

We left the next afternoon after scones and strawberry jam and clotted cream in the café near the Lido, scoffed amid a cloud of wasps. I thought again – not an original thought by any means – that when the breeze is in the south and the skies are clear enough for the sun to show, there are few things in life better than a day at the seaside in Teignmouth or a place with the same spirit about it.

Fanny Burney liked Teignmouth too. In 1791 she spent three months there with her sister, Maria Rishton. Maria was distinctly free and easy in her ways, wearing nothing fancier than 'a common linen gown' and swimming in the sea every day. Fanny thought Teignmouth 'situated the most beautifully of any town I ever saw'. She took up bathing herself, attended an ass race on The Den featuring sixteen 'of the long-eared tribe' and watched a rowing race between two teams of females, one from the town and one from Shaldon, which was distinguished by 'the barbarous dress' of the Shaldonians, who wore no shoes or stockings and were 'naked to the knee'.

The Devon heritage people are not that interested in Fanny, who is not sufficiently A-list, but they are obsessed by Keats, who spent several months in Teignmouth over the extremely wet spring of 1818. There are Keats plaques, a Keats trail and even some indifferent lines of his about local beauty spots on an outside wall of the New Quay Inn. Much is made of the fact that he finished off his one epic poem, *Endymion*, while he was there; rather less of his opinion of Devon, 'a splashy, rainy, misty, snowy, foggy, haily, floody, muddy slipshod county.' I'm with Wayland Wordsmith, who complained vigorously about the 'unreasonable monopoly' exercised by Keats on Teignmouth in particular, and by dead poets generally.

There are at least two genuine local notabilities deserving attention as well. One is that most dashing frigate captain of Nelson's day, Sir Edward Pellew, whose fine mansion, Bitton House, is now the headquarters of the local council. Admittedly Pellew was – for obvious reasons – very rarely there, but the heritage squad might consider replacing the endless photographs of departed aldermanic worthies on the walls of the house with some decent naval memorabilia to complement the pair of cannon on the terrace outside.

Teignmouth's most distinguished native son was known in England as the King of Harpists and in Vienna – where they adored him – as *Der Paganini der Harfe*, because the brilliance of his playing reminded them of the diabolically virtuosic Italian violinist. I freely admit that I had never heard of Elias Parish-Alvars until I picked up a monograph about him from the Teignmouth Museum (he was born plain Parish, and added the Alvars to make himself more exotic). But for a while he was a celebrity – Mendelssohn was his friend, Liszt admired him and Berlioz was quite bowled over:

'I met the prodigious English harpist Parish-Alvars . . . the man is a Liszt of the harp. You cannot conceive all the delicate and powerful effects that he manages to produce from an instrument in many respects so limited. His fantasy on *Moses*, his Variations on the Naiads' Chorus from *Oberon* and a score of similar pieces delighted me more than I can say.'

Parish-Alvars wore himself out playing and touring, and died in Vienna in 1849, the same year as Mendelssohn. As a boy he had been much encouraged by a prominent Teignmouth figure, Sir Warwick Tonkin, who – when he heard of his death – wrote some memorial verses for the *Exeter and Plymouth Gazette*:

> *O'er Mendelssohn the cypress tree*
> *Was scarcely planted near,*
> *Ere weeping willows bend, we see,*
> *To shadow Alvars' bier . . .*

* * *

The ride from Shaldon to Torquay is not one I would care to repeat. Not only is it atrociously steep, but there is no realistic alternative to following the main and extremely busy A379. Cyclists moving at less than 3 m.p.h. are not popular with motorists. Impatience is palpable, hostility often open.

The road passes through a succession of places with names ending in 'combe' – all once separate villages but now forming together the northern limb or tentacle of the Torbay urban spread. The last is Babbacombe, below which the land drops down to the sea at a beach called, not Babbacombe, but Oddicombe. Early in 2013 a large section of the cliff slid into the sea, staining it blood red for weeks and bringing down with it part of a large house which – perhaps imprudently – had been bought at an auction by a retired London police officer without looking at it.

The unstable rock at Oddicombe is not the mudstone of Sidmouth but Permian breccia – interestingly different for geologists, but for the rest of us very similar in its redness and its habit of falling on incautious heads. At Oddicombe it is flanked to north and south by outcrops of grey Devonian limestone, foretastes of major changes to come.

It was here that a remarkable, self-taught Victorian naturalist, Philip Henry Gosse, and his young son poked and pried and delved into the rock pools exposed at low tide. Their relationship, which must have seemed then so natural and instinctive, would much later provide the material for a haunting and unforgettable exercise in rearranging the past, Edmund Gosse's *Father and Son*.

The son's version of the story tells how Henry Gosse, a rigid and fervent member of the fundamentalist Christian sect, the Plymouth Brethren, tried to shape his only child into another warrior for Christ; of the rupture between them, and of the agony of mind caused by the conflict between the father's creationist beliefs and the evidence of the world's great age he found staring him in the face from the pools.

The most extraordinary thing about *Father and Son* – demonstrated by Ann Thwaite in her biographies of the Gosses – is the way in which the son so carefully distorted the portrait of the father and the nature of the bond between them. Edmund Gosse called it 'a genuine slice of life' and insisted that it was scrupulously true. Henry James was nearer the mark when he said of Gosse that he had a 'genius for inaccuracy'. The mystery is whether or not he was aware in his heart that he had manipulated a whole series of incidents and encounters to support a version of his father that those who knew him found unrecognisable; and if he was aware, why did he do it?

Curiously, Henry Gosse had a much greater influence on his age than Edmund on his. The son was an industrious professional writer, his many volumes of poetry, literary criticism and biography mildly admired in his time and subsequently wholly forgotten – apart from *Father and Son*. The father wrote a series of bestsellers about the wonders to be found where the land meets the sea – most notably *A Year at the Shore* – which set off a Victorian craze for rock-pooling. Gosse came bitterly to regret his part in the invasion of the shore by 'crinoline and collecting jar'. 'You may search all the likely and promising rocks within reach of Torquay,' he wrote, 'which a few years ago were like gardens ... and come home with an empty jar and an aching heart, all now being swept as clean as the palm of your hand.'

This excessively sensitive and remarkable man died in August 1888, not long after a final drive along the Torbay coast with his son. He had always prayed fervently that his destiny would be to witness the Second Coming and be chosen as one of the 'favoured saints who shall never taste of death'. Edmund Gosse claimed much later that in his final hours his father had turned on his God, rebuking him bitterly for the deception. Is he to be believed?

Torquay is the most westerly of the major Channel resorts and historically the one with the highest opinion of itself. Its growth in the nineteenth century owed much to the natural advantages of its position and the allegedly exceptional balminess of its climate. Its promoters invoked a parallel with the South of France and suggested that Torquay had somehow managed to import its unique microclimate from the Mediterranean and reposition it on a bay along the rugged, storm-tossed coast of Devon.

Investors fell for the lure of the English Riviera. Military men, retired naval commanders, doctors and solicitors, respectable merchants and provincial bankers all scurried west to snap up sites on one or other of Torquay's five or six or seven hills (opinion is divided on the exact number). They built spaciously and elegantly, chose their neighbours with care, brought with them the values and standards of moneyed, middle-class Victorian England.

An early expression of Torquay's idea of itself is Hesketh Crescent, a bow-shaped row of exuberant early Victorian town houses looking out to sea from the north side of Tor Bay. Charles Harper claimed that early on summer mornings the retired generals and colonels of Hesketh Crescent set forth for their morning dip 'clad in gorgeous dressing-gowns, shuffling in bath slippers to the sea, the bright sun making heliographs of their bald and shining pates.' But even Hesketh Crescent, Harper bemoaned, was subject to changing tastes. 'To Let' boards had appeared; the generals and colonels were too close together for comfort. Detachment was the rage – 'a multitude of discreet villas, each enclosed in its grounds behind inclosing walls and shrubberies.'

Torquay's retirees continued to maintain a tight control over its development. To be 'select' was the guiding principle. Exmouth, Paignton, Ilfracombe on the north coast, were all welcome to pull in the hordes of eager trippers. Torquay, like Sidmouth and Budleigh Salterton, did its best to keep them out. In the years between the two world wars, Torquay Council invested consistently in appropriate amenities. It built a pier, a magnificent Pavilion and a bandstand, installed pleasure gardens and shaded walks fitted with many benches, provided a boating lake and bowling greens and tennis courts as well as anchorages for yachts and pontoons for cruises by motor boat.

The 1932 official guide stated Torquay's philosophy plainly: 'Those whose idea of a holiday is compounded of big wheels, paper caps, donkeys, tin whistles and generally a remorseless harliquinade turn their backs on the town ... the residue, the thoroughly normal, healthily educated people who are the backbone of the nation, love Torquay.' Sunday trippers were banned, but seductive posters illustrating Torquay's sun-drenched charms shone down from the portals of Paddington Station. The *Times* approved: 'Torquay is certainly the English equivalent of Cannes ... there is no other resort which, apart from a certain prim austerity in the administration of the licensing laws, comes nearer in character and amenities to the most progressive of Mediterranean towns.'

The 1939–45 war changed everything. But it took Torquay some time to wake up to new realities. In 1949 Alderman Edward Ely addressed the council thus: 'We have to make up our minds if we are to continue as a snobbish seaside resort, which I and many other people prefer. If Blackpool sells tripe, that is no reason why we should.' The council voted for business as usual and reaffirmed its ban on Sunday games. But this was post-war England, a very different place, and business could not be as usual.

The fate of the wonderful Pavilion illustrates the point. When it opened in 1912 this stately pleasure house embodied and symbolised Torquay's pride in itself. Faced in gleaming enamelled tiles, its central dome supported a full-sized figure of Britannia, with statues of Mercury above the two smaller domes. Outside, it had a promenade deck, octagonal bandstands, floral swags, urns topped with pineapples, carved scrolls, ferns and cherubs, an amazing wealth of decorative ironwork. Inside, there were sumptuous lounges, a café, an auditorium panelled in oak and embellished with mouldings. The Torquay Municipal Orchestra played mornings and afternoons, the concerts often broadcast by the BBC.

The Pavilion was always a heavy drain on the council's budget, but one it was prepared to carry to maintain the dignity and prestige of a premier seaside resort. But after 1945 costs rose as income fell, and the tone was inexorably lowered. The orchestra was disbanded, a body blow to civic pride. They tried variety, bingo, roller-skating, ice-skating. The final live entertainment, in 1976, was the *Eric Sykes Show* with Hattie Jacques and Deryck Guyler – a far cry from the opening night of the 1926 season, *The Farmer's Wife*, starring the young Laurence Olivier.

Two schemes for demolishing the Pavilion and developing the site were proposed in the 1960s, but campaigners shamed the council into rejecting them. It reopened after a refit in 1987 as a complex of small shops and survived in this form until 2012, when the traders were evicted in preparation for another grand hotel/shopping/car park redevelopment vision. The Pavilion, by now looking very sad and shabby, was shut. And that is how it remains, sadder and shabbier still, now dwarfed by yet another Big Wheel.

In the 1980s the council was persuaded that the town's flagging economy could be revived by the provision of a venue for conferences and year-round events on the lines of the one in Bournemouth. The demolition of the elegant old Rosetor Hotel on Chestnut Avenue provided a prime location for what was to become the English Riviera Centre. The firm responsible for Bournemouth's BIC, Module 2, was hired; the predictable result was a hideous grey slab with six stunted turrets topped in green. Now renamed the Riviera International Centre, it welcomes visitors in eleven languages. It remains a dispiriting sight in all of them, its ugliness the more striking because of its close proximity to the glorious medieval Torre Abbey, while continuing to cost the council an arm and a leg to keep it from falling down altogether.

By then the responsible local authority was Torbay Council, which had swallowed up the old Torquay Council as well as those of Paignton and Brixham. The change reflected the dilution of Torquay's once impregnable exclusivity. In the 1960s it became for a time a favoured destination for disaffected youth seeking sunshine, loud music and freedom from the stifling confines of home. Their clothes, hair, unwashed feet and apparently casual morals were repugnant to Torquay, and the town's Trades Council passed a motion imploring the police to get rid of 'these so-called Beatniks'.

According to Torquay's inquisitive historian, Kevin Dixon (see www.peoplesrepublicofsouthdevon.co.uk for a full selection of his work) this invasion was blamed on a 1964 film set in Torquay, *The System*, in which a group of hormonally vibrant young men, led by a startlingly youthful Oliver Reed, hunt for complaisant girls among the summer influx. Incidentally, the film is also credited with popularising 'grockle' as a derogatory term for tourists. Kevin Dixon records that a swimming-pool attendant in Torquay referred to an elderly female swimmer as The Grockle because she reminded him of a dragon so named in a cartoon in the *Dandy* comic. It caught on among locals as a label for all visitors, and was picked up by the film's script-writer.

Whatever the Trades Council and the residue of the retired generals and colonels might think, Torquay had to go down-market. The question was – and remains – how to manage that descent. Tourism is the town's lifeblood. Keeping it flowing is a struggle, with casualties on the way. One has been the resi-dential hotel of the type immortalised in John Cleese's *Fawlty Towers*. A more recent example was the Grosvenor, whose progress onto the rocks under the hand of its bouffant-haired owner, Mark Jenkins, was charted in squirmingly embarrassing detail by a Channel 4 series, *The Hotel*. Plenty of Torquay's hotels have sunk; others remain just afloat in a condition that challenges belief. But some cruise along because they success-fully manage the balance between quality and quantity – between the discriminating visitor and the necessary coach party – to the satisfaction of both.

Torquay is blessed by natural advantages: its hills, the sweep of its bays, its sand, its blue sea, the way it is cradled between its headlands and the rising land behind. Speculators and develop-ers, aided by successive generations of councillors and officials, have committed many crimes against the town, but not enough of them to despoil it.

One of the particular pleasures of Torquay is to arrive at its elegant railway station and walk across the road to the wedge of green that is the home of its rugby, cricket and bowls clubs. How delightful it is to have these sports at the heart of the place instead of banished to some faraway windswept tract of reclaimed wasteland. I walked from the bowls club's cheerful black-and-white clubhouse through the gardens in front of Torre Abbey, registering the presence of the Riviera Centre with a shudder, and onto the beach. It was a soft, mild day in late February, balmy enough to sustain Torquay's climatic pretensions. I met a chap doing early maintenance on the wooden platform on which the family beach hut would sit for the summer. Torquay born and bred, he told me the town was on the slide; and to illustrate his argument pointed out to me the roof of the Grosvenor Hotel where Mr Jenkins had just finished making a considerable ass of himself for the TV cameras.

The tide was almost in and I strolled along the sea wall, admiring the recently repaired Royal Terrace Gardens soaring above the pier and the Princess Theatre and the marina. Beyond the harbour the road climbed past the Imperial Hotel, which was in need of a lick of paint and struck me as rather less imperial than the Grand was grand. I picked up the coastal path which twists and turns up a steepening slope among choice villas glimpsed behind hedges and walls – some banal in design, some outlandish, some rather sweet. Eventually I came out at Babbacombe, stopped in my tracks by the appearance of the Palace Hotel, itself appropriately characterised by Pevsner as 'an unprepossessing monster' but redeemed somewhat by its very splendid grounds.

It was a good long walk, but the best of it was the promenade along the seafront between the pier and the Grand. It is a curious word, promenade, meaning both the activity and where it takes place. The pleasure of it is at the heart of the pleasure of the seaside town: the stroll from nowhere in particular to nowhere in particular and back again, in no kind of hurry, with no particular purpose in mind except to pull the sea air deep into the lungs, feel the rhythm of the sea and match it to the rhythm of your heartbeat and the tread of your feet, and to notice and delight in the incidentals.

17

MINE GOOT PEOPLE

I was looking for Oldway Mansion, which is the marvel of Paignton, when I bumped into an elderly woman and her daughter walking companionably along a leafy avenue away from the seafront. She gave me directions, and I asked her how she liked Paignton. She said she had been evacuated to Torquay from London in 1939, and had come back thirty years later with her husband to live there. 'Then we moved to Paignton. Torquay used to look down on Paignton, now it's the other way round.' She said she walked down to the seafront most days, had a cup of tea, watched the world go by. 'I really like Paignton,' she said. 'I always have.'

Paignton's holiday trade is of the cheap-as-chips variety and that is the flavour of its seafront: cheerful, noisy, dare one say it, a touch tacky. Under the June sunshine the red beach shone with oiled flesh. The smell of batter spread from the several chippies. The pier reverberated to the clash of dodgems and the clang of slot machines. The multiple attractions of the Green – the broad open space between the sea and the handsome white-and-cream villas along Esplanade Road – seethed with families unashamedly drawn to Paignton by the cheapness of the abundant self-catering accommodation. It declared itself consciously to be the polar opposite of Torquay, and proud of it.

Yet away from the seafront they have a good deal in common. Paignton's town centre was laid out in the 1870s and 1880s in expansive style by George Bridgman, a local architect of taste and vision. Many of the handsome terraces of town houses and the villas and public buildings from that era survive and convey an atmosphere of genteel and comfortable living far removed from the raucous fun required by the holidaymakers.

In 1870 George Bridgman was introduced to a large American with a luxuriant white beard and wealth to match. Isaac Merritt Singer, the sewing-machine magnate, had arrived in south Devon by a circuitous route. He had left America for Paris a few years before to escape from a remarkably complicated and scandalous domestic situation involving the fathering of at least a dozen children through various marriages, bigamous and otherwise, and amorous entanglements. In Paris he lived contentedly enough with Isabelle Boyer, the last of his wives, who provided him with six more children, until the outbreak of the Franco–Prussian war in 1872 persuaded them that England would be safer. He visited Torbay and liked what he saw. Land was available in Paignton and he set about buying up as much of it as he could lay hands on.

Singer took a shine to young George Bridgman, and commissioned him to design a residence on a rather grander scale than Paignton was used to. It was to be a mansion in French Renaissance style, which Singer insisted should be called The Wigwam to remind him of home. In addition he needed somewhere to exercise his horses by day and entertain by night, so Bridgman supervised the construction of a round red-brick pavilion with a low conical roof, called the Rotunda.

The horses were exercised and the invitations were issued. But the snobs of Torbay were not impressed by Singer's Rotunda or his horses or his money or – least of all – by his reputation, and turned their backs on him. The traders and merchant classes were less choosy; on New Year's Day 1874 all the children of Paignton were invited to inspect Singer's 26-foot Christmas tree and receive presents from the man himself. Meanwhile work on The Wigwam proceeded, but before it was finished, Isaac Singer dropped dead from heart failure. The funeral was the kind of spectacle he relished. Eighty carriages formed the procession to the white marble Singer mausoleum in Torquay's cemetery, stretching back three–quarters of a mile through the streets and watched by tens of thousands. His body was dressed in black coat, trousers and slippers, white shirt, waistcoat and gloves. It was placed in a cedarwood coffin inside a lead coffin inside an oak coffin.

The Wigwam was finished in 1878 but by then Singer's widow had moved back to France. Eventually it came into the hands of her son Paris, the third in the last batch of Isaac Singer's offspring. Paris had studied architecture and felt he could do better than a mere château with a comical name. He shared Louis XIV's taste and commissioned a French father-and-son team of architects and garden designers, Henri and Achille Duchêne, to transform The Wigwam and its grounds into a Devonian version of Versailles, to be renamed Oldway Mansion.

As a result three of the four walls of the original house disappeared behind façades of stone slabs bristling with pillars, porticoes, loggias, niches, statues, marble embellishments and other pseudo-classical clutter. The interior was remodelled to contain a hall of mirrors, a ballroom, a study lined with Corinthian oak columns and figures from classical allegory, and a gigantic double staircase of white marble with bronze balustrades leading to Jacques-Louis David's absurdly over-the-top depiction of Napoleon placing the imperial crown on Josephine's head with Pope Pius VII looking impotently on. Outside, the Duchênes laid out an epic composition of parterres, lawns, gravel walks, formal beds, terraces, an orangery, grotto, hippodrome, rock garden, bowling green, tennis courts – all thickly populated with statues of Pan, Bacchus and a supporting mythological cast.

Needless to say, this display of boundless wealth and ambition brought its owner no happiness. Separated from his wife (and the mother of his four children), Paris Singer embarked upon a troubled affair with the dancer Isadora Duncan. After the birth of their first child she came to his palace in Paignton for the summer. He mostly stayed on his own in his room, tormented by digestive difficulties, while she watched the rain. 'I had not reckoned with the rain,' she wrote to a friend. 'In an English summer it rains all day long. The English people do not seem to mind at all. They rise and have an early breakfast of eggs and bacon and ham and kidneys and porridge. Then they don mackintoshes and go forth into the humid country until lunchtime when they eat many courses ending with Devonshire cream.'

No family ever lived in this most unfamilial place. It was used as a hospital during the 1914–18 war, and later became a country club. In 1946 it was bought by the local authority from the Singer family and was converted into council offices. The council finally moved out in 2013, leaving the place looking sadly neglected: the roof lead hanging in sheets, the plasterwork stained, the parapets cracked, weeds bursting through the paving on the terraces. It is now awaiting conversion into a 'luxury spa hotel' with indoor bowling and apartments – its only possible salvation, although some might think demolition a kindlier fate.

* * *

There were plenty of fishing boats in Brixham Harbour: big beam trawlers, smaller inshore trawlers, day boats, stubby little crabbers. The smell of fish was insistent, mixed with fumes of diesel, tar, anti-fouling paint. Heaps of netting and stacks of crab and lobster pots shared the quayside with coils of rope, rusted chains and winches, bits of old engines, fuel cans, paint cans, cans that had once held putty.

The port and the fishing constitute the beating heart of Brixham, but there have been plenty of times when the pulse beat very faint and the town wondered about its survival. It was Brixham men who showed the other British ports how to use the beam trawl – a big bag of netting attached to a rigid beam which was dragged along the seabed. In the 1830s a Brixham skipper, James Stubbs, who was fishing out of Hull, dropped his gear into the Silver Pit, a deep hole near the Dogger Bank, and took four thousand sole in a single trawl. In a classic illustration of the destructive potential of new technology, the Silver Pit was soon being fished night and day; the price of sole fell to five shillings a truckload and within three years the location was fished out.

Brixham boats and skippers led the expansion into the fabulous cod grounds off Iceland. By 1850 more than 200 boats were registered there and the extension of the railway across south-west England opened up yet more outlets. But the outbreak of war in 1914 was a catastrophe for the port in more ways than one. Its finest and fittest fishermen were called up for naval duties, and many of the boats which were able to find a crew were sunk by German U-boats. By 1918 the number of vessels had halved, and many of the fishermen who did come back were forced to seek work in new ports such as Milford and Fleetwood.

By 1939 only six boats were still registered in Brixham. The 1939–45 war gave a boost to fish stocks, and afterwards the combination of new diesel-engine technology and bigger trawlers brought Brixham's fishing industry back to life. The fleet swelled and in 1971 a new quay was opened to deal with the catches. By 1991 more than a thousand people worked in fishing; ten years later Brixham had established itself as the premier fishing port in England and Wales.

On the harbour wall – streaked in gull shit and, more often than not, with a gull perched on its head – is a statue of the man responsible for Brixham's one moment of real historical importance. He was a Dutchman, small, thin, severe-looking, with a hawk's nose and piercing eyes; reserved in manner to the point of moroseness, with no inclination for social life or amusement apart from hunting, driven by a powerful sense of duty and equally powerful Calvinist convictions. Just the man, in fact, to drag England out of the mess in which James II was doing his utmost to land it.

The story of the arrival in Brixham in 1688 of the invasion force led by William of Orange became embellished with exaggeration and invention so rapidly that later historians were hard-pressed to disentangle what happened from what the locals had made up. It was said that William's boat was greeted by a local fisherman called Youldon and that the Duke was actually carried ashore by 'a little man' called Peter Varwell, and that on putting his foot upon the first step of the pier William asked 'Welcome or not?' Whereupon the people huzzahed and cried 'Welcome!' Thereafter – the story went – the Duke was addressed by Youldon thus: 'As it please your Majesty King William / You're welcome to Brixham Quay / To eat buckthorn and drink bohea / Along wi' we.'

Alas, 'tis all nonsense – apart from all the other improbabilities, bohea, a species of strong dark China tea, was a rare luxury even in London and could not possibly have been the brew of choice for common Devonians. Nor, as was also related, did local orchard keepers have apples rolled down the narrow streets to cheer up William's weary men, nor did Peter Varwell ever travel to London to claim a reward of £100 from the new King and use the money to build a fine mansion (another version has him being cozened by sharpers in London, repulsed from court as an impostor and returning home 'never to hold up his head again').

However, it is possible – just possible – that the man who would be William III did say as he stood on English soil: 'Mine goot people be not alarmed, I am only here for your goot, for all your goots.' His English was not fluent and the sentiment was in character, so I like to think he did.

*

264

A little way up the hill from the harbour is the fishermen's church, All Saints, where they were paying respects to Brixham's scaly heritage at the annual Festival of the Sea. The interior was hung with nets and ropes, buoys and anchors, pennants and chains. There were models of fish, paintings of fish, fish made of sugar, photographs of old boats and old salts and harbour scenes. There were also fish, real fish fresh that morning: whiting, sole, cod, gurnard and several heads of monkfish split wide in cavernous grins.

The display was being orchestrated by John Lovell, a longtime Brixham trawler skipper. He sees it as his mission to show something of the town's history and the part of fishing in it to Brixham's incomers. 'When I was a lad,' Lovell says, 'the port and the boats, that was Brixham. After school every lad and lass came to the quay to watch the boats come in and unload the catch. Some of the kids these days never eat fish, except fish fingers.' So they have fish in church and Lovell coaxes them up to touch the skin and feel the teeth. 'It's important they understand what fish means to this place,' he says.

It was just my good luck he happened to be there. I had come to All Saints to hear the carillon, which at noon each day plays one of the great English hymns, 'Praise My Soul The King of Heaven' – the one that goes on, 'To his feet thy tribute bring / Ransomed, healed, restored, forgiven / Who like me His praise should sing? / Alleluia! Alleluia! / Praise the everlasting King'. Noon struck and lo and behold, what a disappointment! Instead of the familiar march tune 'Lauda Anima' that has lifted the roof off a thousand churches (composed in 1869 by the long-serving organist of St Paul's London, John Gross), I was treated to an insipid and inferior substitute. It was a sad anticlimax.

Those stirring words were written by Henry Francis Lyte, minister at All Saints for twenty-three years until his death in 1847. By all accounts Lyte was an exceptionally high-minded minister, a gentleman, a poet, a man of science, a fierce enemy of slavery, passionate in his religion and in his devotion to his rough parishioners who came to church in thick jerseys, red woollen caps, blue trousers and white braces. But he was also a poignant figure, progressively undone by the ravages of TB and by the religious currents of his time which flowed as strongly as the currents off Berry Head.

In the course of his ministry his once large and loyal congregation thinned to a mere handful. Some were offended by his introduction of High Church ritual, others were seduced by the fiery evangelism of emerging non-conformist groups, particularly the Plymouth Brethren. Many of the deserters were young men from respectable local families whom Lyte had picked and then trained to go out into the countryside to spread the word among rural labourers and their families. The final disaster was the defection of the choir, whose members also taught in the once-thriving Sunday school. None ever set foot in All Saints again, and according to his family and friends, their desertion caused Lyte immense grief.

In September 1847, after preaching a last sermon at All Saints, Henry Lyte left Brixham for Italy, where his doctors had advised him to spend the winter. He got as far as Nice where he died in November. It is often stated confidently by those who do not know what they are talking about that Lyte wrote his immortal hymn 'Abide With Me' in a fever of inspiration on the afternoon of that Sunday when he preached his last sermon. The story goes that he was sitting in the study of his house at

Berry Head looking out across the waters of Tor Bay when the words came to him. In fact Lyte's biographer, B. G. Skinner – himself a vicar of All Saints – presents convincing evidence that the hymn had reached its final form earlier that summer, although elements may well date from much earlier.

What is sure is that it speaks with the voice of a man who knows death is near and is not ashamed to address his God in the most intimate terms, almost as a friend who will not and cannot let him down as others have. It is a hymn of ending, of passing, suffused with the sadness of looking at things for the last time, suffused also with the confidence of redemption.

Lyte himself wrote a tune to accompany it, but it was not until it was joined – long after his death – with William Monk's great and ineffably sad tune 'Eventide' that it acquired its classic status. It remains one of very few hymns – 'Jerusalem' is another – to have escaped far beyond the confines of the church. It is sung at the FA Cup final and the Rugby League Challenge Cup final and is played on India's Republic Day by the combined bands of the Indian armed forces.

Henry Lyte's house at Berry Head is now a handsome and smart hotel, where there is a plaque recording the spurious version of the hymn's composition. Berry Head itself is composed largely of Devonian limestone, hard, grey, rich in fossils. It marks the end of Red Devon whose last appearance is a low outcrop of Permian breccia between Paignton and Brixham known as Roundham Head. It also concludes the adventure recorded in Dr Ian West's great geological website. I wish he and his helpers had gone further, but all good things must come to an end, and this is a very good thing indeed.

18

Coots and Crabs

It is a very different coastline that reveals itself south-west of Berry Head. Even on a fairly benign summer's day there seemed to my landsman's eye a suggestion of a threat about Start Bay, the great crescent of sea stretching away to the dark finger of Start Point. The blue water was roughened by the breeze into white crests. There were no boats out and the empty sea looked wide and unfriendly.

It calls itself a bay but it offers precious little in the way of protection in stormy weather. When the wind is from the east or south-east it is horribly exposed, and its bed is littered with the wrecks of vessels driven in and either smashed on rocks or battered to pieces on the shore.

There is one gentle refuge at the north end of the bay, where the high ground steps back to make room for a quarter moon of smooth shingle beach. It is known as Blackpool Sands, just as the shingle at Slapton is known as Slapton Sands. I'm sure there's a perfectly sound reason why Devon chooses to refer to pebbly beaches as sands but I don't know what it is, and I would like them to know that it is rather confusing.

A beast of a hill leads up from Blackpool Sands to Strete, a village perched on top of a cliff with a handsome pub, the King's Arms, distinguished by some very pretty decorative ironwork along its first-floor balcony. A plaque across the road records the sad fate of three little thatched buildings – one of them a reading room run by the Women's Institute – which were destroyed by a stray shell during artillery practice in 1944.

It is a reminder that this whole area between Blackpool Sands and Torcross and extending several miles inland played a vital role in the great turning point of the 1939–45 war – vital, painful and largely unsung. In November 1943 Devon County Council was informed that thirty thousand acres of land and foreshore were being requisitioned for military use. The three thousand inhabitants of eight villages and the surrounding farms were given five weeks to leave their homes. A few months later the peace of the countryside was shattered by the thunder of gunfire, and the waters of Start Bay and the shingly shore at Slapton seethed with boats and men and weaponry preparing for the invasion of Europe.

Slapton Sands was the nearest equivalent we had to Utah Beach in Normandy, where the right flank of the Allied invasion force would make landing. Eisenhower, concerned about the lack of battle experience of many of his men, ordered a series of training exercises that would simulate real conflict as closely as possible – including the use of live shells and ammunition. Inevitably there were accidents, such as the unintended bombardment of Strete, and incidents of American soldiers killed by friendly fire. On the whole, though, the rehearsals for D-Day proceeded smoothly enough, until the night of 28 April 1944.

Exercise Tiger had been organised to mimic a full-scale beach landing. The combat assault by the US 4th Infantry Division took place in daylight and passed off without problems. Several hours later, in darkness, a follow-up force of engineers and back-up personnel was to be put ashore with trucks, amphibious vehicles, jeeps and the like, all transported in the flat-bottomed tank-landing ships knows as LSTs under the protection of Royal Navy gunboats. Eight of the LSTs were in Lyme Bay, well to the north of Slapton, when they were attacked by German torpedo boats. Three were hit – one sank almost at once, one burst into flames and the other was crippled. Hundreds of American soldiers and sailors were trapped below deck. A total of 749 of them were killed in the explosions, burned to death or were drowned.

Among those on board were ten officers of particular concern to the command. They all had what was known as BIGOT security clearance, which meant they had detailed knowledge of the invasion plans, including target locations. Had any of them been taken alive and interrogated, the entire Overlord operation could have been compromised. An information blackout was imposed on everyone involved, including the doctors and nurses who treated the injured. In the event the bodies of all ten BIGOT officers were recovered. The secrecy order was not formally rescinded, although an announcement of the deaths and brief details of the disaster were published in an American military newspaper.

Ten years later US General Alfred Guenther unveiled a monument on Slapton Sands to acknowledge the sacrifice of local people in evacuating the district so that the exercises could take place. Although he referred briefly to what had happened during Exercise Tiger, the whiff of mystery and cover-up still hung around the incident, and in time inquisitive nostrils began to twitch. A retired policeman, Ken Small, publicly wondered why there was no comparable memorial to the Americans who had died, and he arranged for a Sherman tank sunk offshore to be salvaged and placed on a plinth at Torcross.

Newspapers in America and Britain picked up rumours that had been circulating for some time: that many of the supposed victims of German torpedoes had in fact been killed by American friendly fire; that a mass grave had been dug on someone's farm to take bodies, and that other bodies had been walled up in tunnels in the Castletown dockyard near Portland; that Eisenhower himself had witnessed the disaster and ordered a cover-up to conceal his own responsibility. It's worth recording that no convincing evidence to support any of these claims has ever been produced. In all probability Exercise Tiger was just a bloody mess, as happens in war.

The straight and blessedly level coast road runs between Slapton Sands and a beautiful and mysterious lake. This is Slapton Ley, the largest natural freshwater lake in south-west England. The upper section, east of the bridge that takes the lane inland to the village of Slapton, is not really lake at all, being choked by reeds and banks of mud with narrow channels of water twisting between. The lower ley, extending to Torcross, is open water fringed all around by reeds, very clear and mostly shallow, with one or two deeper holes. On the far side, away from the road, the reed beds are backed by trees with fields rising steeply behind.

The Ley has long been a haven for waterfowl. Our way is to

nurture and cosset them and peer at them through powerful binoculars, but the inclination of the Victorians was to shoot them. For a long time the Royal Sands, a fine example of that now extinct institution, the sporting hotel, stood at the top of the lower ley near to what is now a car park. Built in sturdy stone, its walls thickly clad in creeper, it catered to the requirements of a steady flow of whiskered sporting gentlemen.

They were catholic in their tastes, those nineteenth-century shooters. Pretty much anything that flew or swam past their gunboats was considered fair game. Bitterns, bean geese, great-eared owls, ospreys, great northern divers and other scarce birds were shot without a second thought. In 1863 a pair of Pallas's sandgrouse exhausted by their flight from Central Asia were incautious enough to seek refuge at the side of the ley, and were promptly slaughtered – 'it seems sad to reflect that these distinguished visitors should have met with so inhospitable a reception,' a local historian commented.

But the chief quarry at Slapton Ley was the humble coot, which thrived there in great abundance; and the great event of the year was the Ley Day in January. A line of boats was stretched across the water near the hotel, each with a boatman and two sportsmen in it, each sportsman equipped with two guns. At a signal the line advanced, driving the coots towards the Torcross end of the lake, where more guns awaited them on the shore. Gradually the birds became more and more tightly packed until panic took hold. In the words of William D'Urban and the Reverend Murray Mathew, authors of *The Birds of Devon*: 'The unfortunate coots ... rose in one dense mass, churning the water with their wings, affording a spectacle long to be remembered by all those who have been fortunate enough to witness it . . . after rising, the birds swept back over the boats, being saluted with volleys from the gunmen . . . the execution was very great and the water was soon covered in the dead and the dying.'

As many as 1700 coots were killed in the course of the Ley Day. But the effect, in the opinion of the authors of *The Birds of Devon*, was largely beneficial: 'We learn that notwithstanding the slaughter, the coots are almost as numerous as ever and the thinning out of the old stock has improved the health of the survivors.'

The angling was as highly prized as the coot shooting. There are records of ninety-one pike being caught in a day by one rod, and 800 perch to two rods. A delightful old-fashioned book called *The Pike-Fisher* by Edward F. Spence looks back over many thrilling days on the Ley. It was nothing unusual to catch twenty in a day averaging six pounds each, and there were plenty of bigger fish. His biggest took a wobbled rudd deadbait: 'The rod was almost torn from my unexpecting hands and when the catch was on the reel it screamed like a heretic being cross-examined on the rack.' Twenty-two pounds she weighed, 'with a face on her as wicked as an Army mule'.

Alas there are no boats on the Ley any more, no fishermen, no fishing. The bird lobby, in the ascendant as usual, has decreed that the mating of great-crested grebes and other sensitive species would be disturbed by the company of anglers. The fact that grebes and fishermen coexist perfectly happily elsewhere, and that anglers have been denied a wonderful setting for their entirely peaceful and spiritually nourishing pastime, counts for nothing. The birders with their 'scopes and glasses and impregnable righteousness run the show. One consequence, inevitably, is that there is now no useful information about how the pike, perch, rudd, roach and eels are doing.

On the beach at Torcross I watched a lone fisherman sort his net close to the sea's edge. He had already been out and had come back with a box of plaice, a sack of good Dover sole and a large ray, which these days is sold as skate. He was a one-man operation, generally fishing a mile or so out most days when the weather was not too fierce, selling his catch directly to the pubs and restaurants and doing all right. While he methodically untangled and straightened and folded his net, a sizeable boat was working very close to the beach not far away. He said it came from Brixham and was dredging mussels. The regulations were that they could only take mussels on the drift, with the engine cut, and not under power. There are a lot of regulations, he said. The bane of the poor fisherman's life.

He was the last regular left, last in a long line. A hundred years ago the shore in front of the three villages of Torcross, Beesands and Hallsands was thick with boats and nets and fishing paraphernalia. Fishing the seine net was a co-operative venture. Acting on the signal of a lookout above the beach, the boats – four men to each one, three rowing, one to pay out the net – swept the water on the ebb tide. When the flood was running, the two ends of the two thousand yards of rope were rowed into the beach for the retrieve to begin. In rough weather trained Newfoundland dogs would be sent out through the waves to bring the rope ends in.

The catch – mainly of mullet, and of sole and other flat fish – was auctioned on the beach. The custom was for the oldest fisherman to take a handful of fine shingle and let it slip through his fingers. Whoever was bidding when the last grain fell took the catch.

Seining alternated with setting pots for crab and lobster along the crustacea-rich ledges west of the Skerries and between Start Point and Prawle Point. The pots were woven from lengths of pliant willow cut from age-old communally owned withy beds maintained in damp groves inland. As recently as the 1960s the willow saplings were still being cut in late winter and stacked to dry out before being woven into pots. But the old ways were on their way out; synthetic materials made for more durable pots, and mechanical winches made it possible to set and retrieve much longer strings than could be managed by hand.

Hallsands was the southernmost of the Start Bay villages. Charles Harper described it as being 'built into the tall, dark cliffs just as house martins plaster their nests against the eaves'. It was precariously placed, but the village lived and breathed and fished (there was no other livelihood). There was a pub, the London Inn, and a shop, and thirty-seven houses with a population of around 120.

It is a grim tale. In 1896 the government's Board of Trade gave the marine engineer John Jackson – later Sir John Jackson – permission to take sand and gravel from the seabed off Hallsands for use in enlarging the Royal Dockyard at Devonport. Dredging began the following year, after Jackson's agents had given assurances that the excavations would soon be filled by shingle naturally shifted from elsewhere on the seabed. Over the next five years 650,000 tons of aggregate were removed, and the Hallsands beach began to sink. By 1903 the fishermen's slipway was three-and-a-half feet above the beach; a year later the drop was six feet. By then the sea wall in front of the London Inn had slipped forward, the road had collapsed and the cottages nearest the sea were disintegrating. Thereafter each winter's storms saw more and more of the village devoured, and in 1917 the decision was taken to abandon it altogether.

Even a hundred years later, the callousness and deceit of the authorities retain the power to shock. Even as Hallsands was literally sliding over the edge into oblivion, the Board of Trade officials were still insisting that it was all due to 'natural causes'. A memorandum from the Treasury warned the inquiry into the tragedy that 'if we offer a grant at once we shall only be pressed for more – the Hallsands fishermen are masters in squeezing.' The masters in squeezing had been offered £1000 compensation between them, later increased to £3250 – less than £30 per person for the loss of everything they had ever known. 'What are we going to do?' asked one of the dispossessed. 'We have spent the whole of our lives here fishing. We know no other trade and we are useless.'

Although most of the village was lost, a few of the houses highest up survived. The last resident of Hallsands, Elizabeth Prettejohn, clung on until her death in 1964; there is an extraordinarily poignant British Pathé News film of 1960 showing her at the age of nearly eighty in headscarf and long skirt, feeding her chickens, while the sea that destroyed her community crashes away below the ruins of the other empty houses.

The Prettejohns were one of the long-standing Hallsands clans. Another were the Trouts, three of whom – all sisters –

later ran a hotel on the clifftop. The last of them, Edith, lived on there as a recluse long after the deaths of the other two and the hotel's closure. She died in 1975, by which time it was semi-derelict. The site is now occupied by a gleaming block of anywhere architecture called Prospect House and divided into 'New England style' luxury apartments.

Below the balconies and tennis courts and swimming pool and electronic security gates, the shattered vestiges of Hallsands still cling to the rock face. At the bottom the sea sucks and swirls over what was once the beach where the fishing boats were pulled up. Looking at the scene from the viewing platform — even the footpath has now been closed — it seems incredible that anyone could ever have lived here, and their way of life seems as remote as that of our Stone Age forebears.

19

POINTS, HEADS AND TAILS

2003 was the summer of superlatives: the hottest for a generation, the driest, the sunniest. The heatwave did not last as long
as the one in 1976 but over the month of August the temperatures were higher. Across continental Europe it was the
most intense for five hundred years. Forest fires raged, crops
withered and perished, thousands of elderly people died of
dehydration.

The Forts were short of cash that year so we decided to holiday cheaply. We bought a big tent on eBay and booked a pitch
for a fortnight at a campsite a mile or so inland from
Lannacombe Bay, which is roughly halfway between Start Point
and Prawle Point. I had never camped before. I had no idea
how to put up a tent, how to organise camp life, how to live
cheek by jowl with strangers, how to cope with shared showers and fridges and the like.

In many ways it was like being back at boarding school, in
the lack of privacy and quiet and in the consuming nature of
the institution. We made friends with the family next door, the
kind of friendship that of geographical necessity is suspended
when the fortnight is up. I found, to my surprise, that I loved

the simplicity of the life, the demands of the routine, the physical closeness of the grass and the earth. I also found the study of my fellow campers infinitely absorbing.

Each morning the sun rose somewhere over Start Point into a pale, flawless sky, irradiating the dew and the night's cobwebs. Each night it sank beneath a band of crimson somewhere beyond Prawle Point, leaving the stars to prick the deep-purple sky. Each day we went down to Lannacombe Beach, a small wedge of pale sand caught between rocky outcrops at the end of a narrow, wooded combe between humps of grazing land.

The sea temperatures that summer were the highest yet recorded (the record was beaten in the summer of 2014), and the swimming in that clear blue sea was pure bliss. The oyster sand, the waving kelp, the rolling shoals of sand eels flashing like coins at your feet, the water easing around legs and shoulders, the sun warm on your head, shouts and splashes, children poking in rock pools, toddlers shaping castles in the sand, grandfathers bowling tennis balls at grandsons, grandmothers in chairs under umbrellas knitting or studying horoscopes, the lap of gentle waves on dark rocks, the feel of salt drying on your skin and of sand between your toes, the lengthening shadows and inescapable weariness of the return – these were just some of the elements of another enchanted day at Lannacombe. Fortunately memory combs out the other stuff – rows, tantrums, sunburn, gashed knees, altercations over bad parking and the rest – and leaves only the enchantment.

This stretch of coastline – hard Devonian schists broken and blasted into jagged, misshapen teeth – readily presents other, less kindly faces. The Start itself, with its white lighthouse, thrusts a fissured fist of rock out towards the Skerries, causing a rip of tide across its foam-white knuckles. On the balmy day of our visit to the lighthouse, the guide reeled off a litany of the ships that had come to grief in this treacherous place, and it all seemed rather interesting and slightly far-fetched. But take, for instance, a night in March 1891, the 9th, to be precise.

A collision between a high pressure weather system over the Atlantic and a deep low over northern France drove a succession of blizzards on a furious easterly gale against the coast of south Devon and Cornwall. With the light almost gone, the wife of one of the Start Point lighthouse keepers glimpsed a cargo ship looming out of the snow just beyond the rocks. As she reached another window she saw the SS *Marana* strike and begin to break in two. The crew managed to launch their two lifeboats into tumultuous seas. One foundered and all on board were lost. The other was forced east towards Prawle Point and was smashed against a ledge. Five men managed to reach the shore, of whom one died of his injuries, one froze to death and three survived to tell their appalling tale.

But the horrors of that night were not finished. A few hours later a Liverpool sail ship, the *Dryad*, with twenty-two men on board, was also driven onto the rocks below the Start Point lighthouse. Only one man succeeded in struggling ashore, but when the rescuers threw him a rope he had not the strength to grasp it and was swept away.

Prawle Point is faced across the mouth of the Kingsbridge estuary by the equally stern and rugged heights of Bolt Head. Sitting in a self-satisfied way at the narrowing of the estuary is Salcombe. I have been to Salcombe many times and have usually enjoyed myself there: netting prawns in the creek at the back of town near the slipway, watching lines of boys and girls crabbing off the walls, slurping at ice creams, walking out on the cliff road to the lovely gardens at Overbecks. But I have never been there without thinking that if there were to be a revolution, Salcombe would be as good a place as any to start it.

I am sure there are genuine Salcombites born and bred and resident year-round but in the season they are hardly to be seen. The town is occupied by *Genus salcombii*, blonde women in skinny jeans and £200 haircuts engaged in deep conversations about school fees, A-level choices and au pair problems; blokes in pastel polo shirts, shorts and canvas shoes nodding over their smartphones or discussing the preposterous cost of property in a purposeful way, as if they were actually thinking of buying. To encounter them swanning along the narrow streets with their intensely tutored offspring filling the air with their Sloanese drawling is to feel again for a moment the keen longing of forty years ago to change the world.

The climb from Overbecks to Bolt Head is a strenuous one, very strenuous if you are encumbered with a bike. The problem I was encountering as I went further south-west was the absence of suitable lanes or bridle paths to get me to where I wanted to be. This left the coastal path, which you are not supposed to cycle. I admit that I did cycle some stretches when I felt I had to. I always felt slightly uneasy doing so, as I am by nature law-abiding, but not that uneasy. When walkers objected, as happened once or twice, I always dismounted out of respect for their injured feelings and did not get on again until they were out of sight.

On a day in high summer 1588 thousands gathered on Bolt Head, eyes trained on the terrifying spectacle at sea. They had heard that the King of Spain, wherever that was, had sent a fleet, an Armada he called it, to conquer England because he was a Catholic and considered it his divinely appointed duty to overthrow our religion and replace it with obedience to Rome. It was a sight to inspire terror and awe: a crescent of great galleons, galleys, galleasses, hulks and support ships, 150 vessels in all; seven thousand sailors, 19,000 troops, enough firepower to sink the very much smaller English navy several times over. The spectators must have thought they were witnessing the prelude to catastrophe, and how nearly right they were.

The Armada had first been sighted off the Lizard on 19 July. The English fleet under Lord Howard and Francis Drake put out from Plymouth but did not engage, keeping their distance as the Spaniards laboured up the Channel. It must have been during that manoeuvre that the Armada passed Bolt Head. On 23 July there was an indecisive engagement off Portland Bill, and four days later the Spanish fleet anchored off Calais. It was supposed to escort the Duke of Parma's invasion force across the Channel to England, but neither the Duke nor his army were ready. Ten days later the Armada was decisively defeated off the port of Gravelines, and England and its Protestant Queen could breathe again.

It is small wonder that the Spanish became convinced that God had turned against their crusade. Poor preparation and leadership on their side, and superior English seamanship on the other, were certainly factors in the disaster. But they also suffered an ill-fortune with the weather so consistent and extended that divine displeasure seemed the only possible explanation. As it was, the wind that gave Lord Howard's ships the weather gauge at Gravelines then turned into a full-blown westerly storm. The Channel blocked, the Armada sailed north, for home as they prayed; and the storm turned into a near hurricane, and half the ships were lost on the coasts of Scotland and western Ireland.

A footnote to the calamity was the fate of one of the Armada's two hospital ships, the *Saint Peter the Great*, which somehow or other managed to find herself back in the Channel in November and was wrecked at the entrance to Hope Cove, a few miles west of Bolt Head. Her medical supplies and valuables were thoroughly plundered by the locals, but her starving and demoralised crew and officers were looked after kindly and eventually sent back to Spain. It is said that the timbers from the wreck were incorporated into a number of houses at Hope as well as the roof of the school in Tiverton and the pulpit of Exeter Cathedral.

Below Bolt Head to the west is Soar Mill Cove, a little bowl of sand in the cliffs which at low tide in fine weather is the most delightful place to lounge and swim. There is a rather swish hotel up the path, discreetly built into the hillside. The tract of countryside behind the hotel, between Salcombe and Hope, is remarkably deserted except for a few cottages and farms. The western portion, towards the sea, is known as Bolberry Down, and somewhere there is, or was – I never found it – a chalybeate spring.

Chalybeate springs were once centres of healing. The waters contained a cocktail of minerals recommended to treat colic, melancholy and the vapours, to kill worms and dry the over-moist brain, to combat hysteria, to make the fat lean and the lean a bit fatter. Some of the springs, such as those at Tunbridge Wells in Kent, became medical centres of considerable economic importance for their localities – which is what John Cranch of Kingsbridge hoped for the chalybeate spring on Bolberry Down.

'In combination with the advantage of marine air and water, sea bathing, the fisheries etc.,' Cranch wrote, 'I consider this spring as inestimable and that it will one day be the means of drawing to the vicinity a great resort of wealthy invalids and others and make the neighbourhood rich and prosperous.' These words were quoted in a sweet little volume, *Kingsbridge and its Surroundings*, by Sarah Prideaux Fox, who added: 'This expectation, however, has not yet been realised.' Not by 1874, when her book appeared, nor by 2013. The unfortunate John Cranch volunteered in his early thirties to serve as the zoologist on Captain James Tuckey's 1816 voyage up the Congo River in Africa, on which he and all the other members of the expedition died of fever.

The dark schist cliffs between Bolt Head and Bolt Tail are menacing enough on a decent summer's day, and must present a terrifying sight from the sea in a storm. The *Ramillies* was the oldest ship in the King's navy when, in February 1760, she was sent from Plymouth to join the blockade of French ports organised to stop yet another projected invasion. She wallowed down the Channel and ran into a south-westerly storm which drove her back to the north-east. Her master, deceived into believing that Bolt Tail was Rame Head and that he was back off Plymouth Sound, steered towards the cliffs. Realising his blunder he tried to turn her. The main mast and the mizzen crashed down, and when they tried to hold her with anchors, the anchors pulled and the *Ramillies* struck stern first against a cave at the foot of the sheer cliffs of Bolt Tail.

In terms of loss of life, this was the worst disaster in the history of Channel seafaring. Of the 734 men on board, just twenty-six survived. Part of the hull of the ship still lies just off the mouth of the cave, while three of her cannon and her rudder are said to be lodged in the sand inside. I did not feel inclined to descend the cliff to check the accuracy of these reports.

I did, however, drop in at the Cottage Hotel in Hope and took liquid refreshment in a little cabin next to the bar which is lined in timbers from another victim of this ship-hungry shore. She was the *Herzogin Cecilie*, one of the last of that most romantic breed of trading vessel, the grain ships. With her steel hull and four masts, she carried thirty-five sails under full sail and averaged under 100 days on the run from Australia.

On her final voyage, in 1936, she reached Falmouth from Port Lancaster in South Australia in eighty-six days. From Falmouth she set sail for Ipswich, but in dense mist she ran onto Ham Stone, just off Soar Mill Cove. Without auxiliary engines she was helpless, and eventually drifted onto the rocks below Bolt Head. She was stuck there for seven weeks while her cargo swelled and fermented, straining and finally bursting the timber deck and releasing an atrocious stench for the benefit of the crowds of visitors who turned out to gawp at her.

Eventually enough of her evil-smelling cargo was taken off for her to be refloated. Her skipper asked Salcombe for a safe berth but the harbour authorities there refused on the grounds that she might threaten public health, so she was beached at

Stair Hole Bay. A month later a gale blew up and pounded her until her back broke and she sank.

The story of the dashing life and lingering death of the *Herzogin Cecilie* is enough to stir even a convinced landsman like me. The many photographs of her under sail reveal a thoroughbred of surpassing beauty: a slender blade of a ship slicing through the seas under a soaring cloud of canvas. Her remains – some decking, iron plates, part of the bow, pulleys – are still scattered about the seabed, melancholy reminders of the startlingly recent passing of the age of sail.

The Cottage Hotel at Hope Cove is a most respectable establishment. It is difficult to imagine anything untoward happening there, except possibly a highly discreet exercise in adultery. The restaurant, the lounges, the oak-panelled corridor, the carpets and curtains are suffused with genteel good taste. The bedrooms murmur pastel pedigree, the puddings come on a trolley, the scampi in breadcrumbs, the cream-cheese sandwiches with slivers of cucumber.

'Our regulars do not like change,' one of the owners said to me. 'The biggest revolution we've had was changing from willow-pattern china to modern white.' She laughed. 'People come here for a certain thing, made up of the sea, the air, the view, the quiet and the hotel. We are old-fashioned and proud of it.'

Hope is a pretty place and the hotel has a lovely position, and speaking for myself, I would be very happy to spend a few days and nights there wandering the cliffs, stuffing myself with cream teas and slumbering in a bed made up by someone else. Like all these coastal villages, it once depended on fishing and now depends on tourism. A century ago it supplied crabs and lobsters all around, and the smell of the pots stacked to dry along the sea wall was the cause of adverse comment among visitors. But even then Charles Harper noted that 'villas and bungalows are putting the old cottages of cob and rock to shame.'

The path west from the cove threads its way along the top of the cliffs. Thurlestone shows itself ahead, a bigger settlement but similarly composed of an old village swamped by later accretions of housing (though it is the opinion in Hope that Thurlestone considers itself a distinct cut above its neighbour). The most select properties in Thurlestone border the eastern arm of the golf course, which separates the village from the sea.

I stopped for a while to chat to a fit, white-haired chap walking with his dog. He was on holiday with his wife and friends as he had been every summer for forty years. They had been to Thurlestone before children, with children, after children and now in retirement, and his affection for it was undimmed. What was it? I asked. The air, walking, swimming in the sea, tennis, golf, nothing changing much, the comfort of the familiar – those were the elements of his answer.

Thurlestone's severe grey stone church stands on the northern edge of the village, the top of its lofty tower looking across to the arched rock – or 'thirled stone' – on the shore. One of its stained-glass windows honours the memory of the Reverend Peregrine Ilbert 'who for fifty-five years lived among and for his parishioners'. Miss Sarah Prideaux Fox commended him warmly for his 'determination to prevent the opening of any place for the sale of strong drink, knowing full well its demoralizing effect on the rural population'; although whether the rural population – without a pub for miles around – shared her admiration may be open to question.

It would not be surprising if strong drink played a part in the most shameful episode in Thurlestone's history, which followed the wrecking of the brig *Chanteloupe* in September 1772. She was bound for London from the West Indies with a cargo of coffee, sugar, rum and Madeira wine when she was driven onto the rocks. Among the passengers were a John Burke and his wife, on their way home after selling their plantation in Jamaica for a handsome sum, and the rumour soon spread that there had been gold and booty aboard.

A great crowd gathered on the beach and went to work. According to an eyewitness, twelve of the bodies of the drowned were stripped naked and abandoned on the sand. The wretched Mrs Burke was seen alive, clinging to a rock, but no one would go to her aid. She had put on an array of rings and other jewellery in the hope of saving them, and when she was finally washed ashore, still alive, her fingers were cut off and her ears mutilated to get the precious stones off her. She was then finished off and buried in the sand, only to be dug up a few days later by a dog, which at least made it possible for her to have a Christian burial.

20

HUE AND CRY

Thurlestone is separated from Bigbury by the mouth of the Avon. There is a foot ferry across, operated by the master of Bantham Harbour, Bantham being the little village of thatched stone cottages tucked into a steep, protected haven on the south side of the estuary. I asked him what the headaches were for the harbour master in such an idyllic spot. Idiots, he said forcibly, specifically rich idiots with smart boats but no idea what to do with them. And illegal netting for bass. I wanted to know more but the journey took less than five minutes and there were walkers on the far side waiting to be whisked back to Bantham.

This Avon is one of many Avons (it is the Celtic word for 'river') and a fairly insignificant one once the long estuary peters out a few miles inland. But the mouth is still deep enough not to be wadeable even at low tide, which does not stop other idiots trying it. A young female lifeguard at Bigbury said I wouldn't believe how stupid people could be. Try me, I replied. What about trying to push a buggy with an infant across? I believed her.

The life-savers are stationed on the shore at Bigbury, which is another shapeless blotch of bungalows, villas and holiday apartments around a few old cottages. The tide was out but on the turn and the distant breakers were spotted with the black forms of surfers and bodyboarders. Transit vans were lined up in the car park disgorging squads of youngsters clutching their boards and wetsuits.

Under a clearing sky, with waves creaming out of the blue sea against the fringe of a wide expanse of golden sand, Bigbury Bay made a fine sight. In the middle is Burgh Island, with its well-known 1930s art deco hotel. The island is steep and rugged where it faces the sea, but the landward side is a smoothly sloping sward of grass. There was once a monastery roughly where the hotel now stands, with a little chapel on the summit above. The monastery went the way of others under the direction of Thomas Cromwell, and the chapel was put to a more immediately practical use than worship.

Burgh Island

Nowadays pilchards are marketed as Cornish sardines and their soft, oily flesh is prized by chefs and lauded by dieticians. But for centuries they were food for poor people, and the lifeblood and economic mainstay of every fishing village up the Channel from Land's End to Bigbury Bay, as well as along the north Cornish coast to Padstow.

Generally the first great shoals appeared in July, far out beyond the Isles of Scilly, after wintering in the depths of the western Channel. The shoals moved steadily inshore, turning the sea dark and oily. Each village had a lookout perched at a clifftop vantage point; this was the use to which the old chapel on Burgh Island was turned. He was known as the huer, and when he sighted the shoals he would cry out the alert.

At the signal the entire village bar infants and the infirm would converge on the shore. The open boats were launched, two boats to each seine net, seven men or good strong lads to each boat, four rowing, three working the net. There was a master of the fishery, charged with commanding where the nets should be shot. The aim was to circle the shoal with nets from the seaward side and draw it towards the shore, while a smaller boat known as the lurker positioned itself at the opening, dashing its oars at the surface to deter the fish from escaping. Come evening the whole trap was pulled inshore until it was possible to turn out the catch onto the fringe of the beach in stages, to prevent the pilchards being injured and dying prematurely.

At the sea's edge the villagers waited with hand nets and shovels and barrows. Part of the catch was taken away by cart to be sold fresh in the locality. But the main business was conducted in the salting-houses, the stone cellars built into the sea walls of every village. Here the women stacked the fish, layered with salt, until they reached the ceiling and all the space was filled. There were runnels along the floor leading to wells; as the fish dried and shrank in the salt, the oil ran away to be collected and used or sold to light lamps and for cooking.

After thirty days the pilchards were ready. They were thoroughly washed to rid them of the dirty salt and packed into hogsheads and re-salted. The contents of each cask were progressively compressed by boards, and more fish added, until the overall weight reached 476 pounds. The cask was then sealed and marked ready for export. The principal markets were Spain and Italy, where salted pilchards formed a staple of the Lenten diet. The poorest Italian families used them throughout the year, crumbled in small quantities onto the eternal pasta. Thus it was that Cornish and Devonian fishermen, most of them Methodists or Protestant dissenters, supplied the needs of faraway Papists.

In good years the exports from the Cornish fishery alone reached fifty thousand hogsheads. With an average of 2500 to 3000 pilchards per hogshead, the numbers of fish taken were enormous. Sometimes the abundance was such that a proportion of the fish were simply spread on the fields as fertiliser. The irreplaceable value of the pilchard harvest, the almost ritualistic regularity with which the shoals arrived and the communal endeavour required, meant the fishery occupied a uniquely important place in the life of those isolated, self-reliant communities. Wilkie Collins, of *The Moonstone* and *The Woman in White* fame, captured its flavour in an entertaining travelogue called *Rambles Beyond Railways*:

Boys shout, dogs bark madly, every little boat in the place puts off crammed with spectators, old men and women hobble down to the beach. The noise, the bustle, the agitation increase with every moment. Soon the shrill cheering of the boys is joined by the deep voices of the seiners. There they stand, six or eight stalwart sunburned fellows ranged in a row, hauling with all their might and roaring the regular nautical Yo–Heave–Ho in chorus . . . the water boils and eddies, the net rises to the surface and one teeming, convulsed mass of shining, glancing silver scales . . . the noise before was as nothing compared with the noise now . . .

Some observers found an inevitable concomitant of the pilchard fishery difficult to stomach. 'There is but one odour,' one wrote, 'and that is the reeking odour of pilchards. We ordered roast beef but fancied we dined off pilchards. We ordered brandy and water but the pilchards had polluted the brandy. We went to bed at nine to avoid the pilchards but they seemed to be over and under the bed, in the walls and the bed-curtains, in the cupboards and the pillows.'

Inevitably there were poor years as well as years of plenty. Towards the end of the nineteenth century the shoals diminished sharply, almost certainly as a result of overfishing. They no longer came inshore, and bigger boats had to go further out to find them. The fishery survived into the twentieth century in a much reduced form, and after 1945 the demand from southern Europe began to slacken. The last factory still pressing the pilchards in casks – at Newlyn in Cornwall – closed in 2005. By then pilchards were no longer pilchards but Cornish sardines, and in that form – fresh under the grill or on the barbecue – they continue to sustain a small-scale but valuable fishery, which also supplies fish for upmarket canning.

It is a very long time since the huer's cry has been heard, and the shoals of pilchards no longer darken the sea. The stone-built cellars where women sang and gossiped and cursed as they stacked the fish are gone, or have been converted into characterful holiday homes.

* * *

A succession of deep clefts enclosing river estuaries fractures the western part of Devon's Channel shore. The rivers – the Avon, the Erme and the Yealm – are insignificant inland but considerable obstacles to the coastal traveller. There are seasonal ferries across the mouths of the Avon and the Yealm, if you get your timings right and can summon the ferryman. But the Erme is a damn nuisance.

Charles Harper helped himself to someone's boat and rowed himself across, which is something I would not have the balls to do. According to various authorities the estuary is no more than knee deep at low tide, but I did not fancy trying it with my bike held overhead, particularly as a heavy blanket of fine, drenching rain had settled, restricting visibility to about fifty yards even after wiping my specs. So I was forced inland, and eventually found myself in a small town called Modbury, by which time I was as wet as if I had swum the Erme at full flow. I also had a puncture.

The consequence of all this was that I did not get back to the sea until I was beyond Mothecombe, the famously lovely house and estate on the Erme estuary. It was acquired in the 1870s by

Henry Bingham Mildmay, a partner in Barings Bank. Mildmay's wife was Georgiana Bulteel, whose sister Louisa was married to Edward Baring, senior partner in the bank and owner of the neighbouring Revelstoke estate with its great mansion, Membland. It was Baring who was largely responsible for the South American investment strategy that precipitated the collapse of the famous firm in 1890, triggering a global banking crisis.

By then 'Ned' Baring had been raised to the peerage as Lord Revelstoke and had aggrandised his Devon property in a manner correspondent to his position and enormous wealth. Membland Hall was expanded with a new east wing and tower – 'a very prominent example', Charles Harper judged, 'of great cost, much pretension and very little art.' Baring bought the village of Noss Mayo, which looks down on the estuary of the Yealm from the south side, and all the land east to the Mildmay estate. He had a carriageway nine miles long laid along the clifftop for his guests to enjoy views of the Channel and Plymouth Hoe. There was a steam launch, a schooner, a cricket ground and pavilion, and a host of new buildings in the approved William Morris *cottage ornée* style with paintwork in Revelstoke blue.

And all this pride came crashing down. By the time of Baring's death in 1895 his fiefdom by the sea was gone. Although the bank was kept afloat as a result of a Bank of England rescue, the directors were made personally responsible for the debts. The Revelstoke estate was broken up and Membland Hall was sold (it was demolished in 1927). Henry Mildmay, very much less to blame for the crash than Baring, managed to cling on to Mothecombe, which remains in the family today.

*

One of Ned Baring's projects was to build a new church in Noss Mayo. It replaced the previous place of worship, a small and ancient slate and stone building inconveniently but very picturesquely perched above the sea at Stoke Beach. It was known as the Church of St Peter the Poor Fisherman, and what is left of it still stands down a steep track from Lord Revelstoke's carriageway, nestled in a grove of trees, the sea surging around and over the jagged rocks below it.

It remains a highly atmospheric spot, even though its isolation has been mitigated by the proximity of a very discreet caravan park. The rough stone walls are green with moss and darkened by damp. Much of the roof has gone, leaving the stone slabs of the floor spattered with bird droppings. Some of the simple old pews in the south transept have been left for the occasional services that still take place. It is less than whole but much more than a ruin, retaining the feel of sanctity, of a place to seek and find solace.

Outside, leaning at angles in the shade of the trees, are the gravestones. One records the death in infancy of one of Ned Baring's sons, Rupert. Another son, Maurice Baring, became a novelist and poet of some standing, although he is now pretty much forgotten. He described the church in his autobiography: 'by the sea shore right down on the rocks, grey and covered in ivy and surrounded by quartz tombstones that seemed to have been scattered haphazard in the thick grass.' As I left in the rain, the wind pulling at the branches of the oaks, I wondered if all our churches might be like this one day, roofless and abandoned, the cause of questioning as to what they were for.

*

The Yealm estuary has two arms, one leading to the stream itself, the other to a creek which has Noss Mayo on one side and the village of Newton Ferrers on the other. The ferry crosses the narrows where the two arms come together, and is summoned by opening a hinged white disc visible from the ferryman's house. It is a necessarily leisurely business getting across. I was the only passenger and the charge was, I think, £2.50 for me and the bike. The Yealm ferry must be a strong contender for the title of least commercially dynamic transport service in the country.

I was put ashore on the western side and followed a narrow footpath past several gardens which eventually turned into a long and bumpy bridle path, minimally signposted. I kept going and eventually hit the coastal path which took me along the cliffs and down to the Church of Saint Werburgh, standing very bold and defiant on an outcrop over the sea.

Geologists get quite animated about Wembury Bay on account of the great age and interesting formations of the Devonian mudstone and siltstone. Anyone else, however, may find this stretch of coastline somewhat dour. The predominant shade of the rocks and low cliffs is grey, and there are no beaches, only odd patches of gritty shingle. Its appeal is of the rugged and rough kind, as a result of which it is largely undeveloped for holiday use. Curiously enough, though, the ruggedest section – opposite where the Great Mewstone rears its angled crest two hundred feet above the water – was once occupied by the Wembury Holiday Camp, where pleasure-seekers from Plymouth and elsewhere enjoyed seaside fun and games in the 1930s. There is not much sign of the camp now, although right on the shore you can see the concrete walls of the swimming pool poking their broken edges above the waves.

In 1940 a naval gunnery school and radar station were established there, which became HMS *Cambridge* in the 1950s and remained in MOD hands until it was closed in 2001. An appeal enabled the National Trust to acquire the site, and the Trust began dismantling and clearing away the ugly clutter of shoddy buildings. At the same time it also gained control of the Great Mewstone, which it has subsequently placed out of bounds to humans so that seabirds can roost there in peace.

It seems remarkable, given its extremely exposed position, steepness and bare, windswept profile, that anyone would have chosen to live on the Mewstone. For the first inhabitant, a local felon named Finn, the alternative was transportation to Australia so perhaps his decision was understandable. Finn's daughter, known as Black Joan, stayed there with her husband and children, until he fell off a rock into the sea and drowned. The last full-time residents were Sam Wakeham and his wife and their brood, who kept pigs and poultry and trapped a proportion of the numerous rabbits for sale, and supplemented their income by ferrying inquisitive visitors over from the mainland and back. The remains of their cottage are still visible on one of the Mewstone's less precipitous slopes.

The rain had finally worn itself out by the time I got to Wembury Point. Looking back from the shore my eye was taken by a pair of very striking snow-white houses perched high above the bay. They had been built somewhat in the Sandbanks idiom, with much glass and square towers, all sharply defined right angles with terraces raised up on the seaward side. I called at the first of them and found its owner at home. He told me his brother had the other – they were partners in a Plymouth-based building firm. He gestured at the window running the length of the sitting room and I had to agree: the view was simply fabulous. He said he walked the dog six miles or so along the cliffs every day, swam in the sea, fished a bit, looked out from the terrace or the window a lot.

I told him he was a lucky devil. He said he knew it. 'How could I get tired of this?' he asked, sweeping his hand across the vista from the Yealm estuary in the east to Rame Head in the west. How indeed? Yet when I looked online a while later, the house was for sale: a 5 bed semi, guide price £1,250,000. Maybe he got short of money.

Around the point towards Plymouth I ran into a group of cheery dog walkers. I asked them where, in their view, the Channel ended and Plymouth Sound began. Their opinion was that it was Channel as far as the Plymouth Breakwater, and Sound after that. I looked at the map again and decided this was clearly nonsense. I drew an imaginary line from Wembury Point across to the wedge-shaped headland with Penlee Point at its eastern edge and decided that would do for me.

21

TWO LOOES

Remember Robert Shaw as Quint in *Jaws*, grunting out the first line of 'Spanish Ladies' in one of the classic displays of celluloid hamming? Had he carried on with the song in its original form – substituting 'Boston' for 'England' makes a geographical bollocks of it, not that Quint would have cared – he would have arrived in the third verse at 'Rame Head off Plymouth', one of the great familiar landmarks for sailors returning to home waters from distant seas.

It stands out from the wedge-shaped headland west of Plymouth Sound rather like the extended head of a tortoise. There is the shell of a very ancient chapel on its summit. Behind and below is the hamlet of Rame, with its church and slim tower and spire, also very old. There is no electricity in the church, but there was no need for it on a brilliant July day, the sun streaming through the low, narrow windows.

There was someone inside rubbing linseed oil into the backs of the pew. I commended him on his community spirit and he disclosed, not modestly, that the church was not even the half of it. He did RNLI, voluntary coast watch, ambulance support, the sailing club and more besides.

'There's three kinds of people around here,' he said, rag in hand. 'There's the locals born and bred, who do nothing but moan about everything and get excited about racing their gigs. There's the immigrants – that's me. We do everything. If we don't do it, it doesn't get done. And then there's the second-homers. They think they integrate with us and the locals because we're all in the pub together, but in fact everyone hates them.'

He had come from landlocked Northamptonshire, unwillingly. 'I had roots there, I had to dig 'em up.' But his wife came from Cawsand, just around the headland towards Plymouth, and she wanted to go home – 'only they don't talk to her because she's married to an outsider. That's how they are.'

Cornwall is not like Devon – the hills are slightly less steep, for a start. Devon never had anything much apart from farming and fishing and, latterly, tourism. Cornwall is significantly more detached from the centre of things, and its people are, or were, more distinct. For a long time it had a serious industrial aspect in the mining for tin and copper and the production of china clay, as well as fishing in every littoral community. Now there is some fishing, and a lot of tourism.

A great Cornishman, Sir Arthur Quiller-Couch – who wrote under the pseudonym 'Q' – addressed the issue a long time ago. He said there had to be a debate about tourism: 'On the one hand I see Cornwall impoverished by the evil days on which mining has fallen. I see her population diminished and her able-bodied sons forced to emigrate by the thousand. In the presence of destitution one is forced to consider any cure thoughtfully suggested.' But he saw dangerous side effects in the cure. 'A people which lays itself out to exploit the tourist runs an appreciable risk of deterioration in manliness and independence. I had rather be poor than subservient.'

His solution was characteristic of him if not as straightforward as it may have sounded at the time: 'Well then, since we must cater for the stranger, let us do it well and honestly. Let us respect him and our own native land as well.'

W. H. Hudson, an outsider who loved Cornwall and spent long periods there, was struck – as visitors always were – by how unlike the rest of the country it was, both in its landscape and its people. Perhaps ill-advisedly, he attempted an analysis of Cornish character and temper. He found them remarkably and commendably free from the great nineteenth-century working-class vice, drink – except for the tin miners, who were drunk and savage. Hudson noted that the Cornish were friendly and pleasant to strangers but spiteful and vindictive among themselves. They were unreliable, given to sexual immorality and cruel to animals and birds. They went to church but thought there was nothing wrong in plundering a wrecked ship. He thought they lacked humour, and that far from being imaginative, as Celtic peoples are supposed to be, the Cornish people were defective in the creative faculty, had produced very little worthwhile art or literature and were inclined to religious fanaticism.

Hudson, like 'Q', was writing at the turn of the nineteenth century. By then the tourist tide was beginning to run strongly. The opening of the railway line to Penzance cut the journey time from London to seven hours. The service was christened the *Cornish Riviera*; one Great Western Railway poster showed a map on which the Lizard peninsula had been subtly redrawn to resemble Italy, and claimed similarities between the two 'in shape, climate and natural beauties'. Cornwall was marketed as 'the land of legend and romance'. It had coves and little beaches of dazzling sand, quaint fishing villages, wild landscapes and seascapes, old ruins and a distinct manufacturing heritage.

In fact Cornwall had everything the increasingly mobile holidaymaker and pleasure-seeker wanted, and post-1945 it became a prime destination. By 1959 the little port of Looe was said by the County Planning Department to have reached 'saturation point'. The *Shell Book of the British Coast*, published in 1983, reported Polperro to be 'so overcooked commercially that much of its original charm has disappeared'. Planners feared that 'unless carefully guarded, the holiday industry could contribute to the destruction of the very features that attract visitors.'

That clearly has not happened. The flow is running as strongly as ever, bringing seasonal visitors, second-home owners and permanent migrants like my acquaintance from Northamptonshire. Whether Cornwall has managed to retain the manliness and independence so prized by 'Q' is another matter.

There is a Celtic cross on the seaward side of Rame Church with an inscription written by Rudyard Kipling, although it does not bear his name:

This was a man who did not seek his ends
In trivial honours but content to be
Himself in all things, never failed his friends
And least of all his lifelong friend, the sea.

The subject of this rather touching tribute was an obscure London stockbroker, Barclay Harper Walton, who advised Kipling on his investments. Walton made his money in the City but his passion was sailing, and the love of his life was his steam yacht, *Bantam*, which he kept at Cawsand. Kipling joined him several times between 1905 and 1911 to cruise Cornish waters, bringing his only son John, who was to be killed on the Western Front in 1915. They went mackerel fishing off the Eddystone Rocks even though – as Kipling wrote to a friend – 'I hate yachts and nets of slimy fish flopping about the decks.' On the last occasion Mrs Kipling and their daughter Elsie came too, and Kipling wrote to Walton that they had had 'a glorious time and one which the children will never forget'.

After that the friendship lapsed. But when Walton died, unmarried, in 1931, his family approached Kipling for an epitaph. The writer obliged, but was most insistent that his lines should be anonymous, which is how it has remained.

On a clear day the lookout on Rame Head commands a view of a prodigious sweep of sea as far out as the Eddystone Rocks twelve miles away, and of coastline from Bolt Tail in the east to Dodman Point in the west. The curve of shore immediately to the west is Whitsand Bay, which at low tide has a fine stretch of sand very seductive to a perspiring cyclist on a blazing July day. But the slope behind the beach is steep and rough, and apart from a considerable peppering of wooden chalets, has remained undeveloped.

Just beyond Freathy a spur of rock known as Sharrow Point thrusts itself out from the sand. A bizarre labour of love and toil reveals itself as you scramble down. It is an excavation known as Captain Lugger's Cave (or Grotto), the officer in question having lived up the hill at Tregantle. The story goes that he began chipping it out during the American War of Independence on the advice of his doctor, who thought the exercise might alleviate his chronic gout. By the time Captain Lugger had finished, the pesky colonials had won the day and the cave was fifteen feet deep, seven high and wide enough to accommodate a stone bench on either side.

The Captain then turned to poetry, inscribing his own verses on the walls and ceiling. On the south wall he invited the traveller caught in a storm

To Sharrow's friendly grot in haste retreat
And find safe shelter and a rocky seat;
Then listen to the ocean's awful roar
And view the waves dash on its bounded shore.

The north wall offered his reflections on the war – 'By ill-judged measures Britain see / America no more depends on thee' – and urged the visitor to 'the terraqueous hall' to forget 'ev'ry jarring passion'. The lines on the ceiling celebrate the health-giving properties of the sea and, by implication, the wisdom of Captain Lugger's doctor:

To you who now enervated descend
She (the sea) will in time her kind assistance lend:
By this an exercise here oft endured
The gout itself for many years was cured.

Sadly, Captain Lugger's handiwork has been scurvily treated by the National Trust, which has the care of it. I found the entrance barred by an ugly metal gate, through which quantities of rubbish had been deposited. Far from the traveller being able to find safe shelter in the friendly grot, he was not even able to make out the lines of poetry. Wake up National Trust – Captain Lugger deserves better!

A considerable sample of the youth of Plymouth, in trunks and bikinis, was engaged in leaping from the rocks into the turquoise water. Watching over them was a muscular young man on life-saving duties. He told me he spent the summer looking at people having fun and intervening when they did something stupid – most commonly getting stranded by the tide, banging their heads on rocks, challenging the strength of the currents and losing, or hurting themselves by jumping off a rock at low tide and finding the water two feet deep instead of twelve.

The rest of the year he spent travelling, but he said he knew he was getting to the stage when he should be settling down to something more permanent. 'Trouble is, I want to stay round here,' he said mournfully. 'I went to London once. Didn't like it. But what is there around here? That's the problem.'

Charles Harper – now on to the not very catchily titled *The Cornish Coast (South)* – did not linger long beside Whitsand Bay or its settlements: 'They are quite recent collections of houses, mostly of an extremely commonplace plastered type, devoted to letting lodgings for the summer . . . their situation has nothing to recommend it for the coastline here is quite bald and uninteresting.'

Looking at Freathy, Downderry and Seaton, it would be hard

to challenge his verdict. But little Portwrinkle, with its tiny beach and miniature harbour, is very charming; in fact too charming for its own good, according to its small rump of full-time residents. More than 60 per cent of the dwellings are second homes – for instance, what used to be the old pilchard cellars, the beating heart of the village's economy and social life, is now a gated enclave of exceedingly tarted-up holiday lets, shuttered and empty for most of the year.

It is not surprising that the issue of second homes arouses such violent passions. But it is one thing to resent them, quite another to devise a way of addressing the problem. It is a fact that most second homes became so because they were sold by local people keen to get the best price they could. No one compelled them to sell, and had a cap been imposed to make them more 'affordable' there would have been howls of protest.

Speaking for myself, I have neither the money nor the desire to have a second home. But I have rented holiday homes, and stayed in friends' second-homes, and thoroughly enjoyed myself, and am reluctantly compelled to think that the business is a necessary evil. It is also true that, by virtue of their economic circumstances, second-homers tend to put more money into local economies than the locals themselves. They have boats and parties and go to restaurants to eat lobsters and crabs and drink Pinot Grigio, and buy rounds in pubs. Without them the holiday industry would totter, if not collapse altogether.

Pedalling through Downderry, where there is nothing much to look at, I pondered the marine tendency in naming villas and bungalows by the sea. I passed The Nook, The Lookout, Gun Deck, Ahoy The Sloop, Four Winds, West Wind, Sea Breezes, Sea View, Sea Drift, Smugglers' Cottage. I wondered how many Smugglers' Cottages there were along the Channel coast. It must run into hundreds. Another tendency is to bestow Cornish names on new dwellings – Gwel an Mor (Sea View), Chi an Mor (House by the Sea), An Dyji (The Small Cottage), Pol Dhu (Black Pool) and so on – as if in an attempt somehow to compensate for the erasing of Cornish particularity else-where.

There is a devil of a hill out of Downderry. At the top the lane passes the Monkey Sanctuary. Why there should be a sanctuary for monkeys in Cornwall – a county at the end of a country where there are no native monkeys – was a ques-tion I felt too worn out to tackle. There is a sharp descent into Millendreath, a holiday village which fell on hard times and is now being spruced up no end, and another ascent. Finally you look down on Looe; or two Looes, East and West.

I liked them both considerably, even though the only room I could find for the night was in a questionable guest house near the bridge. The two Looes – it is debatable whether they are two portions of the same town, or separate entities – are squeezed either side of a long, slender harbour reached from the sea by a tight neck of water. Inland, beyond the bridge con-necting the two sides, the harbour broadens. At high tide the expanse of water appears impressive, but the ebb reveals most of it to consist of quaking banks of grey oozing mud with feeble trickles between.

Looe East and West

East Looe has a little sandy beach beside the entrance to the harbour. When I arrived in the evening this was strewn with litter and looking distinctly tacky, but by morning the rubbish had been cleared and the sand swept. It and the blue sea looked tempting, but not sufficiently so for me to join the two ladies forging purposefully through the wavelets on their morning swim, suspending their powerful breaststroke every now and then to chat.

The old town was thronged with holidaymakers, who were heavily outnumbered by gulls. These birds are a menace, detested by the locals even more than the second-homers. My landlady, a tough but affable migrant from Glasgow, told me with relish that that morning she had kicked an infant gull off the gangplank leading to her boat and watched it drown. There are notices up all over the place denouncing them as a prime public enemies and urging people not to feed them. Some people, the incurably stupid, still do so, however; not that it would make any difference if they didn't, since the gulls are such accomplished raiders and swoopers on chips and sandwiches and half-eaten pizzas. The authorities have the eggs pricked when and where it is possible to get at them, but the gull is an irrepressibly fertile and resourceful creature, and short of arming the populace with orders to slaughter them or an outbreak of plague, it seems nothing can restrain them.

It is tourism that keeps Looe ticking economically, but the commercial fishing that has sustained and defined it throughout most of its history survives, and in its reduced form thrives. The skippers with the resolve to endure the black times of plunging fish stocks, combined with the imposition of quotas and stultifying amounts of paperwork have emerged, if not into a sunlit upland, at least into a viable present and future. Thirty years ago there were thirty to forty boats working out of Looe. Now there are fewer than ten, but that handful are doing all right, thanks to the growing market for fresh fish and the sustained price.

In search of more information on the subject, I called in at the office of the harbour-master, thinking he might know a thing or two. He wasn't there but his helpful secretary said the fellow I really needed to talk to was the historian of Looe's fishing industry, Paul Greenwood. As it happened I had already filleted his *Once Aboard a Cornish Lugger* and wasn't at all sure I had the time or the need for a personal encounter. 'Look, there he is,' the harbour-master's secretary exclaimed, pointing through the glass door at a distinctly sea-doggish individual with a rough, dark beard and a face as weather-beaten as a holystoned deck. 'Paul, Paul,' she cried, waving her arms, 'there's a chap here wants to talk to you.'

So off we went to have a coffee at the sea's edge, and I was soon glad that I had, as he was excellent company and thoroughly agreeable with it. I knew from his book that he had packed in the fishing. I asked him why. 'I was tired of it and I wanted to make some money,' he said baldly. 'So I got into property. Buying old cottages, doing 'em up, flogging them for holiday homes. A lot more money in that than fishing, I can tell you.'

He read the look on my face cannily. 'I know, second homes, very non-PC. Let me tell you about those old fishermen's cottages. They are poky, dark, damp, tiny and totally uncivilised. You wouldn't want to live in one; neither did they. They're all right for a week or so, very quaint and jolly, but try living there. If people like me hadn't got interested they would all have been demolished and replaced by flats, so don't go all sentimental about it.'

Looking back at the fishing that had lured him to sea at the age of sixteen, Greenwood was clear-sighted and unsentimental, not bitter. But angry, still angry, about what had happened in the 1980s when the Scottish purse-seiners came and pretty much killed off the old way of life. Greenwood had begun in the old luggers, fishing pilchards and herring. Towards the end of the 1960s Cornish mackerel fishing began to take off; throughout the 70s more and more Cornish boats caught more and more mackerel. But because the boats were small and the method – feathers or lures on hand-lines – was selective, the fishery remained entirely sustainable.

Then the Scottish boats arrived. They were large trawlers fitted with gear capable of putting out nets a mile long to encircle whole shoals of fish from the surface to the seabed. These engines of mass destruction, paid for with lavish government grants, had already cleaned out the North Sea of herring. They headed south, drawn by reports of the huge shoals of mackerel out from Plymouth and Falmouth.

One Scottish purse-seiner could catch more mackerel in one night than the entire Cornish fleet in a week. The Scottish boats were soon followed by big trawlers from Hull and Grimsby. The landings of mackerel soared, the price crashed. No one could possibly eat the enormous quantities available, so most were converted into fishmeal. The Cornish hand-liners could not compete. Fishermen gave up and the smaller ports fell silent, while out at sea the destruction of the stock continued until there was no stock left.

'The thing about fishing in the old days,' Greenwood said, 'was that we were just as greedy to catch fish, but because of the limitations of the boats and the gear, there were always parts of the sea that never got fished. They were sanctuaries. Then they got found and fished out.'

I bought copies of both his books and he gave me a crunching handshake in return. The books give a superbly real and vivid picture of the fishing life, the rigours and rewards, the comradeship, the boredom and discomfort, the thrill. His prose is as lean and hard-muscled as the flanks of a big mackerel, as bracing as a faceful of spray thrown by a stiff southwesterly breeze. Above all, Greenwood makes it possible for a landlubber like me to understand something of the power and fascination of the sea, and what it is that makes fishermen what they are: a different breed.

*

Looe is also the headquarters of that fine institution, the Shark Angling Club of Great Britain. I have never fished for sharks but plenty do, and Looe is the top spot for them. The main target species is blue sharks, which are not that big or ferocious. Occasionally they get a porbeagle or a thresher, which run bigger, and very occasionally indeed a mako, which can exceed 500 pounds. Sharks of all kinds are much less abundant than they used to be, including the blues, but the day before my visit there had been eight boats out and seven fish had been landed and released. The club secretary told me you had to get one at least seven feet long to become a member. I asked her if she liked sharks. 'Don't like fish full stop,' she said. 'It's a job.'

The Shark Angling Club of Great Britain was founded by Brigadier J. A. L. Caunter, a pillar of Looe society and an enthusiastic big-game angler. According to Paul Greenwood, the Brigadier was actually after the elusive tunny in the 1940s when he started catching blue sharks. Word got around, and the local skippers began making useful money taking anglers out to the marks. In 1953, 350 sharks were recorded by Looe boats; by 1957 it was more than 4000. The secret was in the deployment of the rubby-dubby, a mesh bag packed with pilchard heads and guts which was trailed over the side to bring the sharks in. The smell of it, Greenwood says, took the breath away, and the shaking of the bag would induce a collective groan of nausea from the anglers.

The sport and the club were very much Brigadier Caunter's pet, and each year he would make a speech at the annual dinner. At one of these events he chose to comment on the success of a new conservation scheme to fix a tag on the dorsal fin of the fish and release it, instead of killing them all. Did he really – as Paul Greenwood relates – congratulate the skippers on shagging the tarts instead of tagging the sharks? Maybe he did.

About a third of a mile out of Looe is St George's Island, more commonly known as Looe Island. In 1788 it was reported to be inhabited by a family called Finn – apparently some of the same Finns previously resident on the Great Mewstone off Wembury Point. But there seems to have been another family there as well, the Hoopers, two of whom – a brother called Amram and a sister called Jochabed – were great smugglers.

They were evidently a resourceful lot, these Finns and Hoopers, whatever the nature of the relationships between them. The nineteenth-century historian of Looe, Thomas Bond, recorded that before their arrival the island swarmed with rabbits and rats, but that these were 'now much reduced by the inhabitants catching and eating them ... a rat smothered in onions must no doubt be a delicate dish.' I'm inclined to think that it must have been this connection between rats and onions that inspired Wilkie Collins to include in his *Rambles Beyond Railways* an extremely fanciful account of the extermination of the rats of Looe Island in a great communal rat hunt: 'They were caught by every conceivable artifice and once taken were instantly and ferociously smothered in onions, then decently laid out on clean china dishes and straightway eaten with vindictive relish.'

The island was bought in the 1960s by two adventurous middle-aged spinster sisters from Surrey, Babs and Attie Atkins.

They lived there alone for the rest of their lives – Attie Atkins died in 1997 and her sister ten years later. They are buried in the corner of what was once a field of daffodils near their cottage. No one lives there any more; the island is looked after by the Cornwall Wildlife Trust and is open for two-hour tours between Easter and the end of September.

22

SKULL OF DOOM

Between Looe and Polperro is the hamlet of Talland, over-looking Talland Bay. The church there is unusual in having its bell tower standing apart from the main building, and unique in being dedicated to Saint Tallanus, supposedly a Cornish hermit who most probably never existed.

One of the tombstones records the death in 1746, in his ninety-third year, of the long-serving vicar, the Reverend Richard Dodge. According to the Looe historian, Thomas Bond, Parson Dodge was 'a very singular man ... he had the reputation of being deeply skilled in the black art and could raise ghosts or send them into the Red Sea at the nod of his head ... he was a worthy man and much respected, but had his eccentricities.'

A later vicar, the Reverend Nicholas Kendall, hired a curate to tend to Talland while he remained at his other living in Lostwithiel. This curate, who called himself Thomas Whitmore, disappeared suddenly taking an armful of church silver with him. He reappeared subsequently in the Forest of Dean and obtained another curacy, this time under the name Thomas White. He was arrested after absconding with £30 that he had borrowed from a church warden and tried for forgery at Gloucester Assizes under his real name, Robert Peacock. Despite being described as a model prisoner happy to give religious instruction to his fellow inmates, he went to the gallows. The news of his crimes caused alarm in Talland, where seven couples who had been married by him came forward to take their vows again, and eight babies were rebaptised.

All this and much else I gleaned from a brilliant little exhibition in the church. What no one can do, sadly, is to bring back what was its most extraordinary treasure: a series of medieval wall frescoes depicting, among other things, Christ on the Cross, the devil and a gallery of monsters, imps and dwarfs, a Roman centurion, and a four-masted sailing boat about to collide with a prison. When Talland Church was restored in the mid-1850s, the view was taken by some pious philistine or other that the paintings were primitive and unseemly and they were destroyed.

Polperro is a dream of a fishing village realised: a huddle of absurdly sweet old cottages and crooked houses squeezed into a cleft in the coastline beside a blissfully sheltered harbour. Its streets were intended for horses and donkeys, and for many years visitors in the summer have had to leave their cars on the outskirts. A favourite diversion for the inhabitants is the sight of a Tesco delivery van jammed on a corner between leaning walls or a hire car being reversed uphill around improbable angles accompanied by the smell of burning clutch.

My reason for lingering there was to make inquiries of, and pay my respects to, a brace of very different men who had one passion in common, a passion shared by me. One was no more than a fleeting visitor to the village. The other spent most of his long life there, and was most reluctant to travel more than a few

Polperro

miles away. One was a wanderer of the world, a spinner of tall tales, a fantasist, a boaster, something of a scoundrel. The other was a man of science and unimpeachable good character, a pillar of the community, unfailingly scrupulous in thought, word and deed.

I first became aware of the name of F. A. Mitchell-Hedges – Mitch to his friends – at least forty-five years ago, when my brothers and I got hold of a book with the irresistible title *Battles with Giant Fish*. A glance at the chapter headings was enough to set the pulse racing: *Four hour battle with a mighty tarpon – The horrors of the deep are encountered – Face to face with death – Terrific fight between shark and saw-fish – Battle with a veritable leviathan of the deep –* and so on. We were utterly gripped by these thrilling accounts of adventure and epic struggles in the waters of Central America. One of our favourites climaxed in the capture of a seventeen-foot hammerhead shark which causes Mitch's boatman to leap back yelling, 'Lord, boss! It's the devil, cut the line, boss, cut the line!'

His methods were not very sporting, involving either lowering into the sea a giant chunk of meat with a huge hook in it at the end of a thick rope and allowing whatever monster swallowed it to tow his steam yacht around until it was sufficiently exhausted to be shot; or impaling the monster on a harpoon, with the same outcome. Each episode was illustrated by photographs of the corpses of the leviathans with Mitchell-Hedges, invariably in shorts with a pipe in hand or clenched in firm jaw. We were much intrigued by the appearance in quite a number of the photographs of a companion identified as Lady Richmond Brown, her face shaded by a hat, her body wrapped up against the tropical sun.

Mitch's domestic circumstances were certainly unorthodox. Born in 1885, he married a woman called Lillian Clarke – known as Dolly – when he was twenty-one, and remained married to her until his death in 1959. He took up with Lady Richmond Brown after the 1914–18 war, in which he did not fight, went on several expeditions with her to Central America and was cited when she was divorced by her husband Sir Melville Richmond Brown in 1930. Subsequent entanglements included an apparently bigamous marriage with a chorus girl.

At some point Mitchell-Hedges acquired the artefact that made him famous, the so-called Skull of Doom. This object, fashioned by high-speed cutting instruments from a block of quartz crystal, is probably twentieth century in origin, and certainly no earlier than mid-nineteenth century. This did not inhibit him from claiming that he had found it while excavating the lost Mayan city of Lubaantun in British Honduras (now Belize) in the late 1920s, that it had been fashioned by generations of Mayan craftsmen using sand to rub down the crystal and that it was at least 3000 years old. He hinted that its sacred function was to be used by the high priest to will death on enemies and unbelievers.

After Mitch's death, the skull was inherited by his adopted daughter Anna, who shared his oblique relationship with factual reality. She insisted that she herself had found the skull, either beneath a collapsed wall at Lubaantun or in a cave in a pyramid into which her father had lowered her on a rope. She would tell anyone prepared to listen that the skull was imbued with the power to heal, deflect witchcraft and ward off the evil eye.

In fact Mitch bought the crystal skull at an auction at Sotheby's in London in 1943 for £400 (about £16,000 today), it having previously been in the possession of an antiques dealer, Sydney Burney. Mitchell-Hedges later stated that it was he who had originally sold it to Burney, which may or may not have been true. One story is that he originally obtained it from a fisherman in Belize in exchange for two sacks of flour, although how the fisherman got hold of it is not related.

All of which brings us by an admittedly wandering route to Polperro. Throughout all his escapades, Mitch stayed in touch with his wife Dolly. In 1948 she was living in Polperro at a guesthouse called The Watchers, overlooking the harbour. According to Ray Howgego, author of the definitive *Encyclopedia of Exploration* and of a website devoted to Mitchell-Hedges' colourful life, the guesthouse was run at the time by the current owners' grandparents.

This, I thought, was a golden opportunity for some first-hand research. The lady who answered my ring at the doorbell looked at me suspiciously as I embarked upon a rambling explanation of my business. Then she interrupted me: 'So it's Mitchell-Hedges, is it? Amazing how many people want to know about him.' I was dumbfounded. I had always thought that, apart from my brothers and I, no one had ever heard of him. 'I must have had a hundred inquiries about him,' she said rather crossly. 'I was even phoned up when I was on holiday in Scotland.'

Feeling somewhat crushed, I asked her if it was true – as related by Mr Howgego – that Mitch had shown her grandfather the Skull of Doom. She said he had told her that Mitch produced it at a dinner also attended by the well-known Polperro painter Fred Cook and his wife, and had rolled it along the table. I then asked her if she remembered Mrs Mitchell-Hedges, which was probably a mistake considering that she was about my own age or a bit younger. 'What is this, Twenty Questions?' she demanded. 'Look, I'm not interested, okay?' Then she shut the door in my face.

So much for first-hand research, I thought. I went off instead on the trail of Dr Jonathan Couch, supreme ichthyologist and Polperro's greatest son.

Couch was born in Polperro in 1789 and died there in 1870. He was educated at Bodmin Grammar School, became a scholar in Latin and Greek and decided to pursue a medical career. He completed his studies at Guy's and St Thomas' hospitals in London, and then returned to Polperro. There he remained, marrying three times in all – the last when he was seventy to a woman of twenty-two – and having a total of eleven children.

He was, first and foremost, Polperro's doctor. Habitually dressed in a stovepipe hat, a white neckerchief doubled over, a long black coat over dark-grey trousers and a pair of shoes with silver buckles, he ministered tirelessly to the sick and needy, regardless of class or income. His patients included the local bigwigs, the Trelawnys, old Zephaniah Job who was the financial brains behind the local smuggling syndicate and just about every family in Polperro. Couch was a man of profound learning, able to mix easily with scientists, antiquaries and ladies and gentlemen of culture, but equally at home in the dark, pilchard-infused cottages of the fishermen.

In 1837 there was an outbreak of smallpox locally. Couch vaccinated virtually the entire village, using an ivory point dipped into a pustule on someone already deliberately infected with the milder cowpox. Not a single death from smallpox was recorded and after that Dr Couch could do no wrong in the eyes of Polperro.

Hard though he worked, he had energy and time to spare. This was the golden age of Victorian discovery; all over the land doctors and clergymen and gentlemen of leisure were immersing themselves in archaeology, geology, meteorology, ancient and natural history. Couch began by examining, drawing and describing the creatures most readily available to him: molluscs, crustacea, fish, zoophytes, bats, midges and much else. He became a Fellow of the Linnean Society of London, although he managed to attend only one meeting in his life, and produced a stream of scientific papers for various journals which, over time, covered just about every subject under the Cornish sun. Shooting stars, fossils, bird migration, abnormalities in unborn babies, the behaviour of cuttlefish, common spiders, rooks, jellyfish, whales, hedgehogs – nothing was too great or insignificant to escape his searching eye.

But Couch's great labour of love and learning – and the reason why his name should be revered by fish-lovers – was his epic *History of the Fishes of the British Islands*. This was published in its final form in four volumes between 1862 and 1865, and brought together the fruits of sixty years of inquiry. The 252 coloured plates were of his own watercolour paintings, which whenever possible he executed while the subject was still alive. It is true that some of his classifications are shaky – for instance he includes four separate species of freshwater eel whereas, in fact, there is only one, *Anguilla anguilla* – but by the standards of the time it was a monumental work of scholarship which brought the Polperro doctor international renown.

I rather doubt that Jonathan Couch would have had much time for F. A. Mitchell-Hedges. He would have found Mitch's braggadocio ill-mannered and his casual attitude to the truth offensive. Perhaps if they could have gone fishing together it might have been different, but I have found no evidence of Couch having the least interest in catching fish for fun. His grandson, Sir Arthur Quiller-Couch – 'Q' – put it neatly: 'He was a patient man of science who spent his life observing the habits of fish, without attempting to teach the Almighty how to improve them.'

* * *

Once up and out of Polperro I had a glorious ride along the lane in the general direction of Fowey. It was a prime summer's day with no more than a wafting breeze from the south-west in my face. I could not see the sea; in fact I could not see very much at all in terms of vista, for these Cornish lanes – like Devon and Somerset lanes – are generally sunk deep between their hedges. The Cornish hedges are not really hedges as we Home Counties types understand the word. They are more walls of stone and slate and earth, surmounted by a tangle of bramble, hawthorn, blackthorn, hazel or whatever else manages to retain a roothold.

Their glory is the wealth of flora carpeting their steep lower sides. Foxgloves, red campion, native bluebells, violets, speedwell, pale-purple vetch and pale-yellow toadflax, primroses, yarrow, dog's mercury, nipplewort and lesser stitchwort – the

names are as seductive as the flowers – grow in the gayest abandon among the bracken and ferns and various grasses. I cruised
along at a gentle pace under the cornflower sky, ravished by
scent and colour, pausing every now and then where a gate
opened the prospect onto fields of grazing and ripening summer wheat woven into a patchwork by more distant hedges
with stone farmhouses and cottages scattered thinly about.

I passed places with pleasing names – Raphael, Windsor,
Lansallos, Trevarder and Triggabrowne. Eventually the lane
brought me back within sight of the sea: an irresistible crescent
of sand and rock fringing a bay of glittering blue water. I teth-
ered the bike and scrambled down a steep path. On a flat rock
raised above the beach to the right an entirely naked man was
doing curious exercises. Below him a girl in half a bikini was
stretched out on the sand reading a book. I changed and strode
bravely into the water. It was damn cold but not disablingly so,
exhilarating beyond belief. I would have liked to have stayed
and read my own book but the road to Fowey was summoning
me.

I spent that night in a pub near the quayside in Fowey called
the King of Prussia, where I had a decent dinner and a few pints
of decent St Austell ale. There was time before arriving and
dining to explore the peninsula between Fowey – which is not
really on the Channel by my strict definition – and St Austell
Bay. I followed an old track called the Saints Way, and wished
I hadn't as there were many gates and a luxuriance of brambles
and nettles that left my poor forearms and legs bloodied and lacerated. It was a hot, annoying slog which ended near a little
church, a so-called Chapel of Ease put there by the Rashleighs,
owners for many centuries of the famous house of Menabilly.

The name, of course, is indelibly associated with the writer Daphne du Maurier, who lived there, and her novel *Rebecca*, which she set there. Having no particular interest in either novelist or novel, I sped past the gates down to the beach at Polridmouth where the subject of the story drowned. It is an exquisite spot: a sheltered sandy cove clasped by rocky headlands, separated by a causeway from the lower of the Menabilly lakes, which has a glorious stone house beside it. Just visible on the flat top of Gribben Head is the slender outline of Gribben tower, placed there in 1832 to guide ships towards Fowey.

Rootling around in a local studies section of one library or another, I had come across a Cornish anthology which included a potent passage about the bay. It was taken from a privately printed and anonymous memoir simply entitled *Michael*, which I think must have been written sometime in the 1930s by Pamela Jekyll, the wife of Sir Reginald McKenna, who served during the 1914–18 war both as Home Secretary and Chancellor of the Exchequer, and later as chairman of the Midland Bank. They had two sons, the elder of whom died in 1931, and the memoir recalls family holidays at Menabilly:

'Michael loved to go up to the Gribben alone and would spend hours there, stretched at full length on the fragrant turf, gazing down the cliff-side where gulls and jackdaws kept up a flying commentary . . . One day, when he came back to the rest of us down in the cove below, he confided to me very secretly that it was on the Gribben when he was there alone that he saw visions.'

That last sentence still haunts me.

* * *

I gave the Saints Way a miss the next morning and took the main road to Par. It brought me to the entrance of an enormous caravan park which is above Par's main attraction, its even more enormous sandy beach. The morning was grey, the water also grey, the tide three-quarters in. I talked for a while to three women who were walking their dogs. 'I bring her here every day,' the eldest of the women said. 'She loves it. I love it. I have salt in my veins, I have to be near the sea.'

Why Par, I asked? 'Simple. Couldn't afford anywhere else. It's all right, nothing special but friendly enough.' One of the others had migrated from Seaford in Sussex to be near her daughter. 'I wouldn't go back to Sussex,' she said firmly. 'Everyone's in such a hurry there.' What, in Sussex? She read my look. 'It's true. Down here people take their time over things.'

To the south-east, towards the Gribben and the fields behind, the view is a delight. But scenically Par Sands is blighted by the presence, bang on the western shore, of its china clay works. This complex comprises a harbour, a network of private roads, batteries of warehouses, storage facilities, ancillary buildings, waste tanks and steel towers, miles of piping, conveyor belts and chutes, all gathered around a cluster of gigantic concrete and steel chambers for drying the clay.

This was all fine when hundreds of local people worked there. But since 2006 the whole site has been progressively decommissioned by its owners, the French company Imerys. The harbour was shut and its business switched to Fowey, and production of clay was slashed with the loss of most of the jobs. There is a grand plan – naturally – to transform it all into a marina, biomass energy plant and 'eco-town' of 500 houses, but the company behind the project says it has been forced by the state of the property market to scale back its ambitions. Meanwhile the china clay works continues to moulder and rust away, left to the multitudes of gulls roosting in the tops of the drying chambers and the advancing walls of brambles and buddleia and ivy consuming it from the margins.

The footpath took me around the perimeter of this industrial graveyard and between the cliff edge and the greens and fairways of a golf course until I came to a spectacle even more dispiriting than the china clay complex. This is Carlyon Bay, once – and not that long ago – a prime destination for funlovers throughout south-west England, now looking more like part of Sarajevo at the end of the Bosnian civil war.

It began as the New Cornish Riviera Lido, and over time added bars, restaurants, a ballroom, sauna, solarium, amusement arcade, mini golf, boating and a premier arena for live music known as the Coliseum. By the 1990s, though, the Lido had long gone and the Coliseum was on the skids. The buildings were getting tatty, tastes were changing, competition from elsewhere was hotting up. In 2003 it was closed.

By then Carlyon Bay was owned by a property company which had plans – big plans, bold plans, money-making plans – to turn it into a complex of 500 beach-side apartments with bars, restaurants and leisure facilities. It secured planning permission and stuck up a hideous wall of sheet metal to protect the site from the sea. Apartments were advertised at up to £800,000 each, but mysteriously none were built. In fact nothing much happened, apart from the partial demolition of the complex, leaving the Coliseum to rot into a roofless ruin surrounded by a wasteland of rubble and rubbish, and the rapid rusting of the metal defence wall.

I have no idea who is most to blame for this scandal. Local people blame the developers, the developers blame the locals for being difficult, both blame Cornwall County Council for being either too complaisant or obstructive. Meanwhile the savagery of the winter storms of 2013–14 has underlined the need for improved sea defences, which will be hugely costly. The developers say that they need more time to lay their hands on the necessary cash to proceed, and that they 'hope' to start building in 2016 – twenty-five years after the scheme was first approved. No one is holding their breath.

Poor St Austell! What has it done to deserve two such disasters on its doorstep? But at least no one has yet devised a way to ruin the jewel gleaming on its southern flank, the perfectly preserved Georgian seaport of Charlestown.

My first reaction on seeing the square-riggers moored on the clear blue water of its superbly picturesque harbour, with the rows of whitewashed cottages and stone storehouses wrapped around, must have been extremely common. I've seen this before, I thought, and I had, several times over. In my case it was the TV series *The Onedin Line*: Peter Gilmore as James Onedin, ruler-straight sideburns and jaw as square as one of his own sheets of canvas; Captain Baines with even more luxuriant whiskers; long-suffering plain Anne and totally seductive Elizabeth; the sweeping theme tune borrowed from Khachaturian's *Spartacus*; and the ships, those glorious ships with their billowing clouds of sail.

That was 1971, but long before that the location had been used in the original Hitchcock *Rebecca* with Olivier and Joan Fontaine. It was used again in the 1997 remake, and in scores of other films and TV dramas with a seafaring strand. For the past twenty years or so this has been Charlestown's chief business, feeding the appetite for make-believe, yet it was built for hard-headed commercial reasons, to handle exports of copper and of Cornwall's newest industrial product, china clay.

The man behind the project was Charles Rashleigh, one of the Rashleighs of Menabilly, a lawyer, land agent and banker with an entrepreneurial bent. He commissioned the great engineer of the time, John Smeaton, to design the harbour, which was built from granite in the 1790s. To run the harbour, Rashleigh appointed his trusted man of business, Joseph Dingle, whom he had rescued from the St Austell workhouse at the age of twelve. The closeness of their relationship, given their disparate social backgrounds, caused comment. Charlestown Harbour prospered for a while, but Dingle was a wrong 'un and systematically helped himself to rents and port dues to the tune of £25,000. In the end Rashleigh took legal action against him, and a marathon succession of court proceedings worthy of Jarndyce and Jarndyce ended with Dingle being declared bankrupt and Rashleigh financially disabled.

Copper smelted on site continued to be a mainstay of the Charlestown Harbour until the 1870s, when the reserves of ore began to run out. By then more than 30,000 tons of china clay, dried in kilns close by, was being shipped out each year. There was also a ship-building yard, and a range of ancillary businesses, including salting pilchards, a brickworks, net and rope making and the assembly of casks and barrels. But through the twentieth century business dropped off, with most of the china clay exports being switched to Fowey and Par, and by the early 1990s Charlestown was hardly used at all.

It was then that Robin Davies, the boss of a company called Square Sail, specialising in film and TV work, stumbled upon it and bought it as a base for his operations. Since then the little harbour and Mr Davies' tall ships have featured in scores of sea-faring films and TV dramas, and the locals have become used to pulling on antique costume to appear as extras. But now the future of the perfect little harbour is surrounded by uncertainty. It and Square Sail were put up for sale by Mr Davies some time ago. Two out of the three tall ships were disposed of – one, according to local reports, to the inevitable 'Russian oligarch', with the idea of sailing to Brazil for the 2016 Rio Olympics.

23

THE TRAIL OF THE SEA MONSTER

The dark granite snout of Black Head closes off St Austell Bay in the west. There is a memorial on the path to the historian and supreme Cornish egotist A. L. Rowse, with the inscription: 'This was the land of my content.' Rowse was born in poverty in a china clay village near St Austell and lived for forty years at Trenarren House, inland from Black Head, where he spent his time among his books, kept the lower orders at bay and proclaimed his contempt for the second- and third-raters of the academic world.

In *A Cornish Childhood*, Rowse recalled Sunday school outings to the beach at Pentewan, taking the little train that serviced the harbour there. The track cut through the edge of Kings Wood beside the St Austell River, so closed in that 'the honeysuckle reached into the truck and tickled your neck.' At the beach they paddled – 'hardly anyone bathed in those days,' Rowse recalled – and played games and quarrelled. Then there was tea – 'an enormous, round, golden saffron bun, corrugated with currants and flavoured with lemon-peel.'

The railway has long gone, but to compensate there is a fine cycle track to Pentewan. The village is clustered around the edge of what Rowse remembered as the harbour. But after his time, and long before mine, the harbour was cut off from the sea by a sandbar which extended across its mouth from the long beach to the west. Behind the beach, covering the grassy bowl where Rowse and his little friends played, is a whopping great holiday park. These days Pentewan's chief function is to service the needs of the holidaymakers. As with many of these coastal settlements, its past seems somehow richer and more colourful than its present.

It owed its development as a port to Christopher Hawkins, a member of an old Cornish family with extensive estates around St Erth, further to the west. By all accounts Hawkins was an exceptionally greedy and tight-fisted individual. He was a great collector of rotten boroughs – at one time controlling six, each returning two MPs to Westminster – and had no scruple about destroying the homes of those who dared oppose his candidates and bribing the rest. His reputation was summed up by an anonymous notice pinned to the gates of his mansion at Trewithen, near Truro:

A large house and no cheer,
A large park and no deer,
A large cellar and no beer,
Sir Christopher Hawkins lives here.

Pentewan's port was bedevilled by the stream that brought down the silt and waste from the mines and clay workings around St Austell and deposited them on the seashore. Between 1818 and 1826 the new harbour was constructed with a deepened basin, new quays and gates, a breakwater designed to keep the mouth from being silted up and a reservoir upstream to trap the waste. A horse-drawn tramway ran from the harbour to St Austell, and Pentewan itself more than doubled in size.

Although it never realised Hawkins' ambition to challenge Fowey and Charlestown, the volume of trade did grow steadily before and after his death in 1829. In the 1850s Pentewan was handling almost a third of Cornwall's exports of china clay, and a major refurbishment combined with the introduction of steam locomotives kept it in business into the twentieth century. Eventually, however, the accumulation of silt blocked the free passage of vessels; the requisitioning of the locomotives and the track to assist the war effort was another blow, and the port became largely moribund after 1918.

The agency of its downfall is obvious today. Hawkins' harbour basin is still there, holding water. The gates – installed as recently as 1945 – sag motionless, the quays are crumbling, the bollards poke rusted heads above shattered concrete. Railway lines emerge from the ground for a few yards, then vanish. The shape and structure of the complex are clear and intact, but between the harbour gates and the sea is a barrier of sand at least a hundred yards wide, a silent reminder of the limitations of human endeavour.

I had supper, hog's pudding and mash, in the Ship Inn. It was a Sunday evening, the first weekend of the school holidays, and the place was packed with large men in black tee-shirts exuding noisy bonhomie. Over the fireplace was a colour photograph of a smiling David Cameron, a memento of a flying visit a few years ago when the village was flooded. But most of the pictures around the walls – and in my B & B and in the souvenir shops and cafés – were in black and white and recalled aspects of Pentewan's more distant past.

There were fishing boats and grimy cargo vessels heaped with china clay and slabs of stone, fishermen in caps and heavy sweaters, steam trains puffing down the line from St Austell, pilchard girls in long skirts, village dances, donkeys, farmers – a great gallery of images from another world. For centuries the people here fished and farmed, and later worked in the mines and clay pits and at the harbour. They were born and lived and died here and most knew no other place or life. And then the old ways were swept away. The harbour died, fishing diminished to almost nothing, farming much the same. Tourism came and thrived and swallowed up everything.

The images retreated onto the walls of pubs and into display cabinets in museums. My landlady told me there were just two Cornish families left in Pentewan.

In the late evening I wandered along the beach into the holiday park. It was laid out in bands: mobile homes and chalets at the back, caravans in the middle, tents at the front. There were lots of fluttering flags: Welsh dragons, skull and crossbones, Wolverhampton Wanderers FC, the inevitable Cross of St George. Every pitch had its own power point and there were notices advising what to do if the satellite signal failed. But in fact hardly anyone was watching TV. They were socialising around barbecues, sauntering along with infants in buggies or on shoulders, the older children running about or playing football in the fading light. A few hardy souls were still in the sea. Lads with fishing rods balanced on the rocks near the harbour, hurling spinners far out into the water.

Today no one would come to Pentewan in summer in search

of tranquillity and unspoiled scenic beauty. A. L. Rowse's childhood playground is covered by caravans, chalets, tents, 4x4s, kayaks, bikes, windbreaks and assorted clutter, and seethes with a host of ordinary, decent, peaceful families having fun. The great Cornish snob would doubtless have averted his eyes and curled his lip, but I thought the scene was rather heartwarming.

Hardly had I taken a last lingering look at the caravans of Pentewan than an extremely narrow and twisty lane was carrying me at alarming speed into Mevagissey. Joseph Hammond, who was Vicar of St Austell in the late nineteenth century and wrote an affectionate history of the town and its environs, said of Mevagissey that the county contained few places more thoroughly Cornish and primitive. It was, he said, bizarre, picturesque, smelly and insanitary – 'the odour of fish which pervades the place has led some profane persons to christen it Fishagissey,' he records with a clerical chuckle.

In spite of the advent of electricity and other modern conveniences, Mevagissey remains resolutely fishy. It accommodates yachts and pleasure boats, but declares that it is first and foremost a fishing port. Having survived the familiar peaks and troughs, it is now doing quite nicely, landing around £2 million worth of fish a year, the mainstays being mackerel and the now proud Cornish sardine.

But they are a curious lot, fishermen. On one side of the harbour I got talking to a thoroughly curmudgeonly mackerel man in a pair of yellow waders extensively stained by blood and fish juices. He'd been out at four and was back at eight thirty with a couple of boxes of fish to pack in ice and send off to market. He had been a trawlerman once, with his dad – 'I hated it' – and now went out when he felt like it. I asked him about Mevagissey. 'Bloody horrible dump. Full of drug addicts and pissheads from Liverpool and Manchester.' How come? I asked, and he embarked on a lengthy grouse about north-western rejects being offered homes and lavish benefits in the village.

Dispirited by his want of charity, I cycled around the granite harbour walls to where a sturdy blue fishing boat, *Ocean Harvest*, was taking on ice for her next trip. She is operated by a father-and-son team; I buttonholed the son, shovel in hand. They were hard at it, out at midnight, fishing for eighteen hours, back in to unload and catch a few hours' kip, out again. The catches were good: plenty of haddock, lemon sole, Dover sole, premium John Dory and monkfish, some squid, although not as much as there should have been. They were making up for a dreadful late winter, when the persistent freezing-cold easterlies had restricted fishing to six days in six weeks. You had to take it when it was there, he said.

What about Mevagissey? 'It's a great place to live. 'Andsome, as we say. One thing you notice is that Mevagissey people who move away as often as not end up coming back. That tells you something.' What about all these Mancunian and Liverpudlian cast-offs? He pulled a face. 'What bollocks.' And the fishing life? 'Couldn't do anything else. Now the catches are good and the prices have stayed up, it's worth it. I'll never make a fortune but so what? There's more to life than that.'

A 1920s photograph of Portmellon, the next cove to the west, shows a tiny settlement of grey stone cottages huddled at the sea's edge. The cottages are still there, all smartly whitewashed with brightly painted shutters; what used to be the fields behind are covered in a rash of white and pale-grey bungalows and villas. It was once celebrated for boat-building, but Percy Mitchell's yard – where generations of sturdy luggers and sleek yachts were handcrafted and launched – closed in the 1980s, and these days Portmellon is as somnolent as Mevagissey is vivacious.

Up the hill is the handsome farmhouse of Bodrugan Barton, the successor to a much older and grander establishment from which the ancient Cornish family of Bodrugan directed their affairs. The most notorious of them was Sir Henry, who backed the losing side in the Wars of the Roses and was attainted for treason by the winner, Henry Tudor. The story is that he was pursued to Bodrugan by his old foe, Sir Richard Edgcumbe, but managed to slip out of a back door and make his way to the cliff edge at Turbot Point, below which a boat was waiting to take him to France, or possibly Ireland.

With Sir Richard's men at his heels, Sir Henry had no time to make his way down to the beach, so he leaped from the top. He landed safely on a patch of soft turf near the water and made his escape, leaving Edgcumbe seething behind. The Cornish poet Charles Causley wrote some stirring lines:

He rode him down the valley
He rode him up the steep
Till white as wood Bodrugan stood
Above the Cornish deep.

South from Bodrugan's Leap, Dodman Point thrusts out into a dangerous stretch of sea. There have been many disasters off the Dodman, the most recent in August 1966 when a Falmouth pleasure boat, the *Darlwin*, disappeared on the way back from an outing to Fowey. Thirty-one people were drowned, and the cause was never established.

There is a great granite cross on the summit, 330 feet above the sea. It was put there by the Reverend George Martin, who was Rector of St Michael Caerhays between 1893 and 1898, both as a landmark for mariners and an expression of hope for the Second Coming. Mr Martin was a strange, saintly man who found his true vocation after leaving Cornwall and abandoning his ministry to take a job as a porter at Borough Market in Southwark and devoting himself to helping the poor.

Dodman Point is a spot to encourage solemn and sublime reflection. Anne Treneer, a schoolteacher whose parents ran the school in nearby Gorran, wrote in one of her books of Cornish memories: 'Dodman absorbs the blackness of winter . . . something in it subdued us. We never played there.' It was sombre, even on a warm, sunny July day. The views – east past Looe Island to Rame Head, west to Nare Point with the dim outline of the Lizard beyond – were tremendous. The sea was empty except for a single yacht beating west through the crests of the waves, its sail bulging and as taut as a drum. To the west, headland after headland dropped into the sea, the dark-grey rock edges sharp against the foaming surf.

I looked again at Mr Martin's inscription – 'in the firm hope of the Second Coming of Our Lord Jesus Christ and for the encouragement of those who strive to serve Him.' The wording seemed short on confidence; there was hope, not expectation, and a need to encourage those who strove to serve rather than served. It felt like a place for faith to be tested.

*

The Church of St Michael Caerhays stands beside a road a little way inland, isolated, with no village anywhere near. The road there from Dodman Point passes the sea end of a thickly wooded valley whose little stream was dammed long ago to make a lake and other water features. Looking out to sea, with the woods behind it, is Caerhays Castle, one of the more outlandish creations of that great enthusiast for grand-scale pseudo-Gothic, John Nash.

As so often with these follies, there was a perfectly respectable mansion there beforehand which had served the Trevanion family well enough since the Middle Ages. But it was not grand enough for an impressionable John Bettesworth, who inherited the estate through his mother at the age of twenty-one. He added the Trevanion to his surname, and required a castle to go with it. Towers and battlements and castellations, chamfered doorways and arches and parapets and other nonsense sprouted in profusion; but when the bills for Nash's wild fancies poured in, the young squire found himself financially embarrassed.

Over the years after the completion of the castle in 1810, Squire Trevanion's debts mounted. His hopes of being bailed out by his enormously wealthy mother-in-law were dashed when his dog bit her footman, and he came to depend heavily on his attorney, Edward Coode of St Austell, to keep him out of the clutches of his creditors. Mr Coode's office overlooked the yard of the White Hart, where the London coaches stopped, and he kept a sharp eye out for anyone with the look of bailiff about them. On the occasion of his client's final disgrace, Mr Coode appropriated the fly ordered by the bailiffs and reached Caerhays just in time to persuade the Squire to flee to Brussels.

By the time he died in Belgium in 1840, the castle had

revealed itself to be no match for the Cornish weather. The roof, deprived of its lead, leaked so freely that a visitor found ducks paddling around the floor of the drawing room. All the fixtures and fittings were removed, even the bells and the wiring, and it remained a decayed shell until 1854 when it was bought by a mining and banking magnate, Michael Williams. It remains in the family's ownership today and the gardens are world famous for magnolias, camellias and rhododendrons.

Many generations of the Trevanions lie at peace in the churchyard of St Michael's. The official church history makes no mention of the saintly George Martin, but much of a predecessor as rector, the Reverend William Willimott. He was there for twenty-five years, and was evidently a resourceful and energetic man. When the church was restored soon after his arrival, Willimott carved the screen and the chancel stalls, made the tiles for the chancel floor and produced designs for the stained-glass windows. He brought in a harmonium and introduced *Hymns Ancient and Modern*, which was considered very High Church and radical.

He was a great fellow for pets, Mr Willimott, with a menagerie that included a bull terrier called Rock, an otter, a lamb, a white rabbit, two badgers and several peregrine falcons which he trained to take gulls off the cliffs. In old age he wrote down his memories of Caerhays, illustrating them with his own water-colours. 'What happy days I have had,' he wrote, 'rejoicing in God's good gifts of health, strength, wholesome food, pure air, walks, rides, flowers, birds, pleasant companions, kind neighbours and higher blessings than these.'

* * *

At the beginning of February 1914 the German cargo ship *Hera*, carrying a cargo of Chilean guano, was making her way in thick, dirty weather for the Lizard. At about half-past ten at night the mate reported breakers ahead. The captain ordered the *Hera* to be put about, but she struck the outer edge of Gull Rock, a notorious hazard a mile or so out from Nare Head. At once she listed steeply to starboard. The order was given for the lifeboats to be launched, but two out of three broke away. All but the captain and three seamen piled into the third, which was swamped by the surging seas. Several men were washed away, but nine managed to cling to the lifeboat mast.

Distress flares had been fired immediately after the impact. The coastguard at Portscatho alerted the Falmouth lifeboat, which reached the scene at half-past three in the morning. In the darkness the crew could not locate the wreck, but they heard a whistle being blown by one of the survivors clinging to the mast of the half-sunk boat. Five men were rescued. Next day wreckage and bodies were washed ashore between Portloe and Portholland.

On 3 February Joseph Johns, the sexton at the nearest church, at Veryan, was told to make ready a grave for the victims of the disaster. The result was Veryan's Long Grave, a continuous burial ground seventy-five feet in length. The next day between six and seven hundred Cornish men and women gathered for the funeral of the twelve Germans whose bodies had been recovered. Later three more were found and added to the grave. Three bodies were never found; that of the captain was returned for burial in Germany. The names of the dead were engraved on the marble headstone, the youngest of them Herbert Bahr, aged sixteen.

Six months later the two nations represented at this ceremony were at war.

Gull Rock and Nare Head separate Veryan Bay from its western neighbour, Gerrans Bay. Portscatho is the main village on Gerrans Bay; Gerrans itself is immediately behind, although to the visitor uninformed about ancient local rivalries they compose a single settlement.

Portscatho is typical of many south-west coastal villages. It consists of a cluster of old cottages and one or two more substantial houses around the harbour, with successive generations of housing spread behind, initially along the roads out of the village and subsequently across the spaces between the roads. The harbour is small, and is protected by a breakwater shaped like a crooked finger. There is a sandy beach flanked by rock.

Its past – fishing to the front, farming behind, a tightly bonded community between – is clearly written; its present – second homes, tourism, retirement, the servicing thereof – equally so. It has a village store, very much better than the average, and a decent pub, the Plume of Feathers. In holiday time Portscatho brims with life. The rest of the year it is just as pretty but as quiet as an old-fashioned Sunday afternoon. Its history has been chronicled with exemplary love and thoroughness by a local enthusiast, Chris Pollard, and I hope he will forgive me for observing that it is full of character and incident but short on major sensations.

Portscatho does, however, have its sea monster. Or had. Or may have.

In the late evening of 10 July 1985, Sheila Bird, a local historian from Falmouth specialising in books about hauntings and other paranormal happenings, was walking with her brother along the cliffs near Portscatho when they saw a creature close to or on the surface of the sea. She described it as being mottled grey in colour with an elongated neck, a trunk twenty feet or so long and a large tail. 'It glided swiftly with a swan-like motion,' she wrote. 'We watched it for several minutes with two other passers-by and then it submerged like a submarine.' According to reports in the local newspapers, Mrs Bird consulted 'two independent palaeontologists' who told her the monster was 'probably' descended from plesiosaurs, which most scientists believe became extinct at least seventy million years ago.

Mrs Bird expressed irritation with suggestions that the monster may have been an optical illusion, or an invention. There have been other sightings of abnormal sea beasts in the area. A Mr Bosisto wrote to the *Royal Cornwall Gazette* in April 1876 to report the capture – no mere sighting this! – of a sea serpent by crab fishermen in Gerrans Bay. They had found it coiled around the buoys marking their pots, disabled it with a blow to the head from an oar, dragged it ashore and killed it – and then threw it back in the sea.

A hundred years later a creature sounding very much like Mrs Bird's monster made several reported appearances – one off Pendennis Point near Falmouth, one in the Helford River further south, two off Rosemullion Head and at least six others at various locations as far away as the Isles of Scilly. A Falmouth newspaper printed two photographs of the Morgawr (Cornish for sea monster) sent in by a 'Mary F' who said it was at least eighteen feet long, long-necked and small-headed, with lumps on its back. Subsequent inquiries into Mary and the provenance of her photographs proved inconclusive.

That was all in the hot summers of 1975 and 1976. Since then, after Mrs Bird's sighting, the one reported encounter with the beast was in 1999, when a holidaymaker took a somewhat indistinct image of something dark with what might be a head and neck sticking up while filming his wife swimming off Portscatho. As it happens I have a dear friend who was brought up in Portscatho, and whose parents still live there. Her dad has spent a great deal of time along this stretch of shore in his own and other people's boats and knows the waters intimately. On my way through I dropped in for a cup of tea and raised the subject of the Portscatho sea monster. Had he ever seen it? No. What did he think it might have been? Reply unprintable. He is a man of strong views forcibly expressed.

I didn't see it either as I cycled along the eastern prong of the Roseland peninsula towards Falmouth. The conditions were reasonable for monster-spotting, calm and clear, and I kept an eye out for the Morgawr whenever the sea was in view, although I accepted that the odds against it surfacing when I happened to be passing were remote. It was a lovely ride through a rolling patchwork of fields and woods, with the odd farmhouse or hamlet nestled in the folds and the open sea never far away. The lane turned into a track which took me past the gates of Rosteague, an Elizabethan house whose formal gardens have been lovingly restored by its owners after many years of neglect.

A little way beyond Rosteague is a path which leads to one of the treasures of Roseland, Towan Beach. The Cornish writer Winston Graham, creator of the Poldark stories, remembered it as 'a lovely small rock and sand beach where there is no surf but endless brilliant rock pools full of tiny fishes and shells . . . one of the few places in Cornwall where cowries can be found.'

To his dismay he witnessed the arrival there of caravans, and did not return for several years. When he did, he was astonished to find that it had not been blighted by development; instead, the National Trust had got it. There were no caravans, and people were outnumbered by cows. 'What we in England, and people in Cornwall especially, owe to the National Trust is beyond computation,' Graham reflected gratefully.

Towan Beach is quintessential National Trust. There are no facilities, but there are rock pools and rocks and sea and sand. On a summer's day there are dogs, and dads in shorts and polo shirts and mums in sensible swimming costumes carrying picnic boxes and fold-up chairs and children with buckets and spades and bodyboards.

The scene highlights the unmistakable class division between the family that takes a cottage in Roseland and uses Towan Beach, and the family that takes a caravan at, say, Pentewan. The Pentewans do not care to tramp considerable distances through gorse and brambles to reach a beach devoid of any diversion not provided by nature. If they go somewhere they like to drive and be able to leave the car in a car park close enough to permit the transport of much clobber. They do not mind being cheek by jowl with other families, smile tolerantly if someone has a radio going, like a café to get a bacon sandwich and an ice cream. They need a phone signal, are happy with throwaway barbecues and bought burgers. On wet days they have no inhibitions about staying inside watching TV. They are not members of the National Trust.

The Towans are all members of the National Trust – in fact they are the National Trust. They rent stone cottages with low ceilings and crooked staircases. On wet days they play board games and put on waterproofs to walk the dog. They do not go to amusement arcades. If they camp, it is likely to be somewhere rustic with teepees around. They do not care for caravan parks. They talk a great deal about their children's education and are well-informed about which parts of the country have retained grammar schools. The Towans are just as fond of their children as the Pentewans, but not so demonstratively. They ration sweets and never swear in front of them.

The Towans like to shop in local butchers and greengrocers and buy artisan bread if they can find it. They are delighted to buy fresh fish direct from a real fisherman, although they are sometimes slightly taken aback by how much goes in gutting, beheading and filleting. They would regard Dexter cattle as more appropriate to the landscape and 'better for the environment' than fat-uddered Holsteins. They would consider buying a second home, while regarding it as a serious moral issue.

I confess that, by inclination, I am more a Towan than a Pentewan. But I hope very much that I do not consider myself superior for that. We need both, and diversity is good.

There is a very different National Trust attraction at the tip of the Roseland peninsula, a reminder of distant times when we looked across the sea for our enemies. The battery at St Anthony Head was installed in 1897. It and the batteries at Castle Point near St Mawes and at Pendennis Castle on the far side of Falmouth Bay were designed to guard the entrance to the vital deep-water anchorage at Falmouth itself. Subsequently the armaments at St Anthony Head were upgraded and the battery was enlarged to include a camp, officers' quarters, storerooms and workshops. It remained in commission until 1952, when the nation's Coast Defence was given up.

St Mawes

The National Trust acquired the site in 1959. By then much of
the network of underground chambers and emplacements had
been filled in, in the belief that an era in our history was over
and no one would be interested again. How wrong! They did

not reckon with the heritage hunger. Over the years volunteers have excavated and cleared the subterranean warren constructed of cheap brick and utilitarian concrete with as much loving care as if it had been the Tomb of the Kings at Paphos. Visitors may now peer into the rusted hatch through which the shells were lowered, stroke the remains of the tubular range finder, descend into one of the emplacements and inspect the racks on which the firing-pins were stored. It's even possible to book a holiday in what was the officers' accommodation block.

The Channel shore is peppered with these abandoned installations left over from ancient conflicts and invasion scares. The Martello Towers are the most obvious relics, but the coast of Cornwall – never a prime target for would-be invaders – is dotted with castles, forts, fortresses and batteries established over the course of a thousand years to keep our enemies out. When the panic over Napoleon's ambitions was at its height the defences overlooking Plymouth Sound were massively expanded, and batteries were either newly constructed or greatly strengthened at (west to east) Mousehole, Penzance, St Michael's Mount, Falmouth, Mevagissey, Charlestown, Fowey and Looe. Many of these were maintained until the 1939–45 war, while others – such as the St Anthony Head battery – were added.

How infinitely remote those anxieties seem to us now. We cannot enter into the minds of those who saw – rather than imagined – close and present danger from over the sea. In that sense, of the sea as our prime protector, it no longer matters. The notion of the island race, separated from neighbours by the Channel and other seas, is redundant. Our encirclement by water has long since ceased to be of any strategic significance.

Our enemies, whoever they may be, are within, or so far away as to seem faintly unreal. Sentimentally we may still call ourselves – even to a degree think of ourselves – as an island people, defended and defined by our seas. But over time, surely, the place of the sea in our self-image will fade until it disappears altogether.

In the meantime the battery at St Anthony Head – which of itself is no more than an unsightly clutter of storage facilities and useless holes in the ground – becomes a heritage asset, a monument to times and conditions that our parents or grandparents knew and that we cannot.

24

GABBRO AND SERPENTINE

I arrived that evening at Mawnan Smith, with a puncture. The village is well inland and has a rather boring late nineteenth-century church. A much older and more interesting church is some distance away, overlooking the sea. It was locked when I got there the next morning, so I had a sit-down beside the granite slab placed inside the lychgate for coffins to be rested on. There is a legend in Cornish over the gate that is translated as 'It is good for me to draw nigh unto God'.

A lady arrived to clean the church. She told me she had spent most of her adult life abroad, and had come to this out-of-the-way corner of Cornwall thirteen years before. 'I needed to be near the sea,' she said, in the manner of someone stating the blindingly obvious. She walked beside it every day, but had never seen the Portscatho sea monster and was clearly sceptical about it.

When Charles Harper steered his trusty bicycle down here a century and more ago, he found the church 'lavishly decorated in texts and admonitions in the old Cornish language' which, he snorted derisively, had become extinct so long ago that 'nobody outside the ranks of scholars has the least recollection of it.' He was further displeased by a notice advertising something called The Society of King Charles the Martyr, and concluded his considerable rant thus: 'We say Charles was absolutely untrustworthy and a danger to the nation and that he deserved his fate.'

I could find no trace of the texts and admonitions, and nothing about Charles I. Nor did I get even a fleeting glance of the resident cryptid – meaning creature unrecognised by science – known in crypto-zoological circles as the Mawnan Owlman. This winged beast was first spotted in the summer of that highly paranormal year, 1976, flying around the church tower. It was later described as being five feet tall with black feet and glowing eyes. Paranormal researchers speculated that it might be a manifestation of 'earth energy'. Sceptics pointed out that most of the evidence for its existence had been collated by a Falmouth paranormalist and self-confessed hoaxer also involved in the stories about the Portscatho sea monster.

The student who piloted me across the Helford River had at least heard of the sea monster, although I did not get the impression she believed in its existence. The Helford River is not a river at all, but another of the many rias – flooded river valleys – that interrupt the cyclist's progress along the coast of Devon and Cornwall. It is one of the largest, reaching far inland to Gweek, and with its many associated creeks and absence of bridges has kept the bulge of land between it and Falmouth to the north largely unblighted by holiday invaders.

Helford itself is remarkably insignificant considering it is a ferry port. I made my way inland through glorious countryside up to Manaccan and then down to the sea at Porthallow. The situation of the cove there is appealing; curved, sheltered, with a gently shelving beach flanked by rocky headlands. But the once golden sand of Porthallow has long been overlaid by a thick layer of grey grit washed along from the neighbouring quarry at Porthkerris. On a grey, overcast day the blending of grey beach, grey sky and sea, and dark-grey cliff faces created a deeply sombre effect. There were a few small fishing boats pulled up on the beach, but no sign of fishing activity, and it was too early for the pub, the Five Pilchards, to be open.

But there was life in the little arts-and-crafts shop close to the seafront. It was run by a potter and former art teacher who had migrated from Cambridge. She told me she had always yearned for a pottery by the sea, which I suppose is understandable if you live in Fenland. She liked Porthallow because it was not – not yet – a fully fledged holiday village. 'It's not especially pretty,' she said, 'but it is friendly, which matters a lot more.' I asked how many Cornish families were left. 'Not many. They tend to sell to incomers and then moan about them.'

A slab of stone on the sea wall marks the halfway point on the South-West Coast Path. From Porthallow it is 315 miles to Poole and 315 miles to Minehead. One side of the slab is inscribed with a kind of communal poem under the title 'Fading Voices', listing the names of boats and wrecks and reefs and rocks and long-departed fishermen and other aspects of the history of Pralla – the local contraction of Porthallow. It ends: 'That's How It Was / That's How We're Like We Are', but there are precious few Prallians or Porthallowians left to remember how it was.

A mile north of Porthallow is Nare Head, another jagged hazard to shipping named with a muttered curse by mariners of old. On that dreadful March night of 1891 that saw the SS *Marana* and the *Dryad* come to grief off Start Point, the SS *Bay of Panama* – a four-mast square-rigger carrying Indian jute bound for Dundee – was in trouble further down the Channel. She had been driven far off course by the pitiless, snow-laded easterly gale and in the early hours of the morning was smashed onto the rocks just off Nare Head. Her lifeboats were swept away and as she sank the crew dragged themselves into the ice-encrusted rigging. Several froze to death before the rescue boats arrived. Others had to be prised off and were carried down still hunched and bent in the positions they had taken against that terrible wind.

South of Porthallow, just out from its coastal neighbour Porthoustock, are the Manacles, perhaps the greediest ship-swallower along the whole Channel shore. The name applies to a reef of saw-toothed rocks spread over an area of one-and-a-half square miles, some exposed at low tide, some just hidden, all potential killers. The roll call of wrecks is enormous, and takes no account of the many vessels that were shattered and lost before records were compiled.

One of the most infamous of all shipping disasters occurred here in May 1855. The *John* was a Plymouth-based barque chartered for the transport of impoverished families from Devon and Cornwall seeking a new life in Canada. She had left her home port for Quebec with 154 adult passengers on board, 114 children and infants, and a crew of nineteen. She weathered Rame Head and the Dodman, steering for the Lizard, but on the night of 8 May the mate reported to Captain Rawle that he could not see the Lizard lighthouse and that he thought they were too close to land.

According to the evidence given at the subsequent inquiry, Captain Rawle, whose family owned the *John*, 'pooh-poohed' the notion. Shortly afterwards the barque struck the outer ring of the Manacles under full sail. Her momentum carried her through, and although fatally holed, she carried on until she struck again, settled and began to break up. Of the four lifeboats only one was usable. The captain and several members of the crew appropriated it, but Rawle returned to the vessel when it was discovered that the boat had no plug. A passenger took his place and ingeniously thrust his pipe into the hole, enabling the one lifeboat to make it to shore at Coverack.

In the meantime the crew left on the *John* – most of them drunk – ignored the passengers and scrambled high into the rigging as the ship sank in a rising tide. Most of the passengers were washed off the decks before the coastguard rescue boats could reach them. Altogether 193 of them were drowned, and the bodies of a hundred children and babies were laid out on the beach at Porthoustock to be identified. Captain Rawle was tried for manslaughter and acquitted, although he served a short prison sentence for incompetence. Two locals were also jailed for robbing a corpse of ten sovereigns. It was a bleak, shameful episode.

Porthoustock is even more deeply grey than Porthallow. On one side of the cove is a stark concrete mill built for crushing quarry stone into aggregates, now disused. On the other side is a wharf where barges and bulk carriers take on the hard greenish diorite extracted from the quarry next door, used – among other things – for road-building and sea defences. In between, the beach is smothered in a layer of gabbro spoil.

The lane out of the village led to another lane and then another, until I found myself crossing Main Dale, a wild tract of heather and gorse with lumps of gabbro scattered all around, and descending into Coverack. The sun had come out and the cove, its sand undefiled by quarry waste, looked distinctly picture-book. Flotillas of kayaks were scudding about and a handful of brave swimmers were breasting the waves. The village looked very neat, the slopes thickly covered with whitewashed bungalows and villas. The village noticeboard advertised a range of wholesome activities – beach clean day, RNLI day, the Coverack regatta, the Coverack Singers performing *Anything Goes*, a sale of unframed pictures at the Arts Club.

A constant fear and intermittent menace along this whole coast in distant times were the predations of the Barbary pirates – often referred to in contemporary accounts as 'Turks' although they mostly came from North Africa. During the seventeenth century hundreds of fishing boats and other vessels were ambushed by the dreaded xebecs and galleys, and thousands of fishermen and seamen were captured and sold into slavery in Tunisia, Morocco and especially Algeria. Most were never seen again.

The chronicles of the village of St Keverne refer to repeated incidents of boats fishing off the Manacles being seized and emptied of their crews 'to the sorrowful complaint and lamentable tears of their womenfolk'. Witnesses deposed that 'these Turks daily show themselves ... and the poor fishermen are fearful not only to go to sea but likewise lest these Turks should come on shore and take them out of their houses.'

They were right to be fearful. A petition smuggled from Algiers in 1640 and delivered to Charles I said there were five thousand English slaves in 'miserable captivity undergoing most insufferable labours ... suffering much hunger and many blows to their bare bodies by which cruelty many have been forced to turn Mohammedans.' It's estimated that between 1580 and 1680 as many as a million Europeans were enslaved in North Africa, the great majority from fishing communities too poor to pay ransoms. The slaving raids continued throughout the eighteenth century and into the nineteenth. In 1816 a naval force led, on his final command, by that great Cornishman Edward Pellew – by then ennobled as Lord Exmouth – put Algiers to flames and forced its Bey to renounce the enslavement of Christians.

* * *

Every slog has its champagne and *foie gras* – or ale and pork scratchings – moments. I had one when I first laid eyes on Kennack Sands. I had bumped down a long track to a farm, Trevenwith, with the sun in my face. The path went through the farmyard and down the side of two sloping meadows. I stopped at a gate where the path was squeezed between banks of hawthorn.

To the west the glittering sea was roughly edged by one headland after another. The Lizard was the last, shaped like a reptile's head lain flat on the sea, its tongue the white foam breaking on the rocks. Long breakers rolled slowly against the twin hemispheres of Kennack Sands, divided by the Caerverracks, a broken jumble of black rocks reaching out into the sea. The sand was pale and ribbed, gently inclining into water so clear that every stone and dab of weed was visible. A gang of kids was messing around with bodyboards where the waves crashed down. Further out two or three more serious surfers bobbed about biding their time until a significant crest showed itself.

A band of heather, gorse and hawthorn, littered with pale, lichen-spotted rocks, stretched behind the beach, with green meadows beyond. Everything glowed in the sun, beneath a soft blue sky.

A slim, blonde woman in beach gear came up the path towards me. She was on her way back to Trevenwith, where she lived, leaving her sons and friends on the beach. I asked her about the farm. More of a smallholding, she said. They did beef cattle and some sheep, not enough to make a living, so she worked in Penzance for social services, helping 'problem families'. There was no shortage of families or problems: generational unemployment, abundant drugs coming through the port at Newlyn, crime, hopelessness. She said it was the end-of-the-line syndrome. People just washed up in Penzance with no further to go.

'Then I come back to this,' she said looking back at Kennack Sands. 'It's a paradise. I'm so lucky.'

Coming out onto the beach my peripheral vision registered a change in the texture of the light to the west. I looked that way, initially puzzled as to why the fields should look different. Then I realised: it was the gleam off the roofs of caravans, massed ranks of them in wavering lines, crescents and triangular blocks across the downslope of the western flank of the valley. In all there are four holiday parks, shoulder to shoulder. A lane crept down from the nearest to a car park close to the beach. The car park was full and the lane was lined with cars.

There was a café awash with families chomping and slurping. The sand was thickly peopled.

From the café I looked back to where the roof of Trevenwith Farm peeped above the trees. The fields behind were spotted with livestock, noses down in the rich grass. Paradise was a restricted area.

Close to Kennack but entirely hidden from it is Carleon Cove, a dark, rock-strewn refuge overshadowed by beetling cliffs. Next to the beach is a roofless round stone building which housed the capstan used to haul the pilchard boats up from the sea. Behind it, considerably restored by the National Trust, is a warehouse – the one substantial relic of what was the thriving heart of the Lizard Serpentine Company a century-and-a-half ago.

Serpentine – or serpentinite, to give it its full geological dignity – is found in significant deposits on the Lizard and nowhere else in Britain. It is deep, dark green in colour, veined with white, red and yellow; soft enough to be worked easily into vases, candlesticks, lampstands, paperweights and a host of other decorative objects. In 1846 Queen Victoria and Prince Albert sailed into Mount's Bay in the royal yacht – rather unimaginatively named *Victoria and Albert* – and were taken on a tour of Penzance, where the Prince was much taken by a display of serpentine in the museum. A selection of objects was then ordered for Osborne House on the Isle of Wight, which set off a boom in Cornish serpentine production led by an enterprising Londoner, Jabez Druitt.

Druitt acquired several serpentine quarries and established workshops and a showroom at Poltesco, just above Carleon

Cove. The little stream was fitted with a water wheel to power circular saws to cut the stone into manageable blocks. A wharf was constructed in the cove for the finished articles to be barged away for export. For a time Druitt's enterprise prospered. Mrs Dinah Craik, an eager tourist of the 1880s, included a detailed description in her *An Unsentimental Journey Through Cornwall*. She noted the 'monotonous hum of the machinery' which 'mingled oddly with the murmur of the stream'. The appearance of some of the vases she considered 'quite Pompeian', while in the faces of the workers she detected neither stupidity nor servility, 'but a sort of dignified independence'.

Jabez Druitt watched over his little empire from Carleon House, a sturdy residence up the path which now houses National Trust volunteers. The artefacts were dispatched as far away as India and even Australia, and the company maintained showrooms in the Strand. The Bank of England had pillars of serpentine, serpentine mantelpieces were installed at Hampton Court and Chatsworth, and churches all over the place acquired fonts and lecterns of the green stone. But it had a fatal flaw. It was fine for smallish objects, useless for architectural features. Over time the water in the veins caused it to crack, or if the water dried out, to crumble. Demand waned, profits slumped, and the Poltesco works closed in 1893.

25

LIZARD TALES

A while back BBC Two showed a series about the fishermen of Cadgwith, which featured and was presented by an amiable, hulking ex-Royal Marine, Monty Halls. If you ask me, most BBC Two is tosh, but this was not, mainly thanks to the personality and charm of its presenter. He did not try and lord it over the locals and was commendably unafraid of making a bit of an ass of himself. I did not catch all the episodes, but there was a memorable one in which Monty forsook his own inshore crabbing boat for the big trawler for a day out in heavy seas. Monty went green, he went grey, he spattered the deck and the sea with vomit, and ended up prone on the deck while the skipper, grinning evilly, speculated as to whether he would survive at all.

The series succeeded in teasing out something of a necessarily closed society: the rivalries, the interdependence, the slyness, the jealousies, the prickliness, the subtle distinctions in rank, the suspicion of outsiders. It also captured the extreme hardness of the life, too much at times for tough guy Monty Halls. His declared intent at the start was to pay his way, to show that it was possible for someone not bred to the life to learn it and make a living from it. It wasn't; much easier, he discovered, to make TV.

Cadgwith is a working fishing village in a way Coverack no longer is, although tourism still dominates its economy. Its beach is divided by an outcrop of rock known as the Todden, with the fishing boats occupying the eastern part. Behind is the old village: low-roofed cottages with thick walls and tiny windows, smartly thatched and whitewashed these days, converted pilchard cellars, boathouses, pub. The usual mix of modern bungalow and villa creeps up the slopes behind.

One of the most absurdly picturesque of the ancient dwellings is Dolphin Cottage, which sits at right angles to the sea behind what was the customs watch house. Its well-groomed thatch descends to head height, nestling over a white porch embraced by climbing roses with a tiny, scent-heavy cottage garden in front. Inevitably it is now a holiday let, but in the 1950s, it is said to have been the home of the pianist Harriet Cohen.

She was a great star in her day, although she is now pretty much forgotten, except by vintage recording enthusiasts. She was much admired as a performer and equally celebrated for her beauty and her personal life. Cohen was tall, slender, raven-haired, statuesque. She never married, but for many years was the mistress of the composer Arnold Bax. Other composers and artists were stirred by her looks and magnetism, among them Vaughan Williams, William Walton and D. H. Lawrence. Ramsay MacDonald and Lord Beaverbrook were mesmerised by her. She counted Elgar, Arnold Bennett and Einstein among her close friends.

Reading about this extraordinary woman, I was amazed by the range of her repertoire. Harriet Cohen had small hands, which precluded her from playing much of the nineteenth-century virtuoso classics. She adored Bach and championed early English keyboard masters such as Purcell and Gibbons when no one else was much interested in them. She was an equally passionate advocate of contemporary piano music. She gave the premier of Vaughan Williams' piano concerto, played de Falla and Turina, travelled to Moscow to perform Shostakovich and Kabalevsky, and introduced the music of Bartók, Honegger and Kodály to London audiences.

Her career waned after a mysterious accident involving a tray of glasses left an artery in her right wrist severed, although she continued to give recitals well into the 1950s. One wonders how they managed to squeeze a piano through the door and into the tiny cottage in Cadgwith, but it is pleasant to think of the rough-handed, weather-beaten Cadgwith fishermen tending their nets and sorting their catch with the strains of a Bach Prelude and Fugue, or perhaps the *farruca* from Turina's Danzas Fantasticas, wafting over their heads.

The Lizard and its lighthouse

Lizard Point is the southernmost extremity of the British mainland. It follows that Landewednack Church, half a mile or so inland, is the southernmost place of worship. The church is at one with the landscape: rugged, forceful, devoid of elegance, its curiously chequerboard granite and serpentine tower standing four-square against the tempests, its graveyard filled with salty seafarers and wind-blasted farmers. According to one of Cornwall's historians, Sir William Borlase, the last sermon in the Cornish language was delivered at Landewednack in the 1670s, although it should be recorded that at least two other Cornish churches claim that distinction.

The road past the church leads in one direction to Church Cove, once a great place for pilchard landings, and in the other to the settlement known variously as Lizard, The Lizard, Lizard Village or even Lizard Town. Charles Harper was scornful of its urban pretensions, noting that the combined population of it and Landewednack was 683. It is bigger now, but retains a distinctly haphazard feel about it, as if it had been allowed to follow its inclinations by growing away from the village green like ivy or bindweed.

The light was fading when I got to Lizard Point. The sea surged and moaned and roared in a restless, hungry fashion like a tiger awaiting feeding time, the noise blending with the cry of gulls in a desolate duet. The rocks, black, ancient gneiss, raised jagged serrations into the foam lines as if seeking prey. I peered down in wonder at the old lifeboat station at the bottom of the cliff, which was closed off because of a recent rock fall.

When it was first established in 1859, the boathouse was at the top of the cliff and the boat was run down a track with a hairpin bend in the middle and a sheer drop to the sea at the end. In severe gales the lifeboatmen had to crawl down on hands and knees for fear of being blown away. Later the boathouse was repositioned with a slipway down to the water, where it did duty until 1961, when a new station was opened around the head to the east at Kilcobben Cove.

The Lizard lifeboatmen were busy volunteers. Among the many wrecks, one stands out – that of the White Star liner *Suevic*, which was homeward bound from Australia when she struck off the Lizard in March 1907. The Lizard lifeboat was quickly on the scene, followed by those from Cadgwith, Coverack and Porthleven. Over the next sixteen hours all the 524 passengers and crew were rescued, making it numerically the most successful rescue in RNLI history.

The Lizard lighthouse is just along the point to the east. The light, from a single 400-watt bulb, is visible twenty-five miles away in clear weather, and when the cloud and mist roll in, it is backed up by a foghorn blast every thirty seconds. The first lighthouse there was originally proposed to James I by Sir John Killigrew of Falmouth, and strongly opposed by the locals, on the grounds that it would affect their proceeds from plundering wrecks. Trinity House, supposedly the protectors of the nation's shipping, also objected on the interesting grounds that a lighthouse would attract pirates and was anyway unnecessary because there was a sea wide enough for careful mariners to avoid the Lizard if they kept their wits about them.

Sir John persisted and built the tower. His agreement with the government stipulated that the cost of the coal for the light and for manning the tower would be defrayed by a charge of a halfpenny a ton on shipping passing it. But most of the ship owners simply refused to pay. The maintenance of the light became haphazard, and Sir John bombarded the King's advisors with letters of protest and supplication to no avail. Eventually his losses became intolerable and the light was extinguished for good and the tower demolished.

Cycling back up Lighthouse Road in near darkness, I followed a badger for a time, which trotted along without any evident care in the world before disappearing into a bramble patch. Murk and mist were closing in, and by the time I went to bed in my B & B the lighthouse foghorn was sending forth its mournful caution. It kept it up all night and was still sounding when I left early and breakfastless in the morning.

I headed for the most famous beauty spot on the Lizard peninsula, Kynance Cove. Many feet more eminent than mine have trod its shelf of pale-yellow sand, and eyes more far-seeing marvelled at its singular rock formations and the play of sunlight on the blues and greens and purples streaked through the pinnacles and stacks of serpentine. Tennyson's for one, George Bernard Shaw's for another, Wilkie Collins' for a third. It was bad luck for me that the tide was in over the sand and the shroud of mist was so thick that I could hardly tell where land ended and sea began.

Returning the way I had come I passed a filthy Land Rover close to a marquee standing incongruously in a field. There was a hefty young man inside the vehicle, talking on his phone. When he'd finished I asked him about the marquee. Party, he said. Bit out of the way, isn't it? I said. That's the way they wanted it, he replied, suggesting heights and depths of wildness and depravity.

It turned out he was the local farmer, Lizard born and bred. He worked entirely on his own – 'can't afford to pay no one, can I?' He had beef cattle grazing a wide area of extremely poor-quality land, courtesy of Natural England which paid him something to keep it all pristine. The serpentine that underlies the plateau is pretty much devoid of nutrients, making the thin layer of soil capable of sustaining nothing more than heather, gorse and scrubby grass, and tiny orchids and other undemanding wild flowers.

The farmer had spent his whole life hereabouts. A generation ago there had been thirty farms around the village. Now there were two. He loved the life, he said, wouldn't have any other, but he didn't think it would suit everyone. He asked me where I was heading. The answer was actually Penzance, but that seemed a long way off. Mullion, I said, and asked if the footpath could be cycled. He looked doubtful. There were several tracks into the heath, all of which were soon swallowed by the mist. One of them might get you there, he said cheerily.

I went back to the one main road and pedalled vigorously north, thinking of breakfast. As a result I missed the long, wriggling, highly indented stretch of coastline between Kynance and Mullion Head; without much regret, as my appetite for savage cliffs and surging seas had been amply satisfied for the time being. I reached Mullion within the breakfast time zone, with just enough slack, I judged, to have a look at Mullion Cove first. It was a long, swift descent which made me think of the long, slow ascent that must follow. I parked my bike and walked down to the wall of the little harbour with my right trouser leg still tucked into my sock. A voice inquired as to whether I was a Freemason, and we fell into conversation.

He was a Mullion man but had been away a long time. I asked him why he had come back. 'I ask myself that. I knew I would have to sometime, when I was ready. I need something to wonder at, you know, which for me is being able to see as far as I can. You can't get that anywhere else.' He took his hand from his pocket and extended his arm towards France. 'There's no end to your world here. Does that make sense?'

It did. He had an inshore boat for crabbing but had a mind to get something bigger. 'The fish are out there,' he said. 'Dover sole, lemon sole, turbot, the lot. Last winter off Newlyn the boats were finding big herring. I mean, big. So why not give it a go?' He pointed out his partner, Barry, who was attending to pots in the open boat. 'Barry looks after the crabs. I like diving. Had some luck, too.' He gave me a crafty look. 'A hoard of Portuguese gold coins. 1743. Not half a mile from here. I've only managed to recover half of 'em.' I asked him what he'd done with them. 'That's my pension. Under the bed, so to speak.' And the rest? 'Barry knows where they are.' What about your wife? He laughed uproariously. 'Tell her? She might go off with some other bloke.' I wondered if he'd made the whole story up.

I got to the Old Inn in Mullion at ten past nine, legs trembling from the strain of the ascent from the harbour, stomach begging for sustenance. They said they stopped serving breakfast at nine. There must have been something in the look on my face, or maybe it was my howl of despair, that melted the landlady's heart. Opening hours were extended, the chef went to work, eggs and bacon and black pudding and mushrooms and toast and coffee were produced, and the smile was firmly replaced on my day.

What a superb pub! And it has long been so, according to the records. In Queen Victoria's day the landlady was Mary Mundy, and her fame extended far beyond Mullion. Kilvert stayed there and found her to be 'a genuine Cornish Celt, impulsive, warm-hearted, demonstrative, imaginative and elo-quent.' Mrs Dinah Craik described her as 'a bright brown-faced little woman with the reddest of cheeks and blackest of eyes.' The immensely eminent Greek scholar and Scottish national-ist, Professor John Stuart Blackie, left a tribute to her in verse in the visitors' book running to fourteen stanzas, of which this is a sufficient sample:

> 'Twas on Saturday afternoon
> That I was trudging, a weary loon,
> To spend at the Lizard my Sunday,
> When thro' the corner of my eye
> A happy sign did I espy
> OLD INN by MARY MUNDY

When Charles Harper came to the village, Mary and her brother were no longer running the pub. He refers to them being 'jockeyed' out of their house and being 'old and poor'. But rather annoyingly he gives no why or wherefore, saying darkly 'they will tell it in Mullion.'

One of Harper's many powerful prejudices was against golf. 'It is a scourge,' he thundered, 'that has devastated the once beau-tiful wild sandhills and heaths and reduced them to the titivated promenading grounds of the wealthy bounders who generally used to confine their energies to the billiard room.' Whether John Betjeman could be classified as a wealthy bounder is doubtful, but he certainly loved what Harper disdained as 'that desolate game'. It is claimed that after playing the Mullion course, Betjeman coined the term 'mullion' to mean a duff shot caused by the distraction of the sea view. Among others to have mullioned or been mullioned there was Arthur Conan Doyle, who in 1901 played the course regularly while on holiday with his wife at what was then the Poldhu Hotel.

Doyle also explored the area and – as was his way – soon found a place for his famous detective in it. In *The Adventure of the Devil's Foot* Holmes and Watson take a holiday in a cottage near Poldhu, but Holmes is diverted from his burgeoning interest in the possible links between the Cornish language and the arrival of Phoenician traders by a tangled tale centred on the vicarage in the nearby hamlet of Cury. The tale – of murder, jealousy, greed, thwarted love and the ingenious use of poison vapour from the root *Radix pedis diaboli* – is untangled, of course, and the murderer allowed to go free on the grounds that his victim richly deserved his fate.

The Mullion course rolls up and down and around the clifftops between Poldhu Cove and Church Cove. Close to the eleventh tee and almost on the beach of Church Cove is a minute church dedicated to Winwaloe, a Breton saint who is said to have worn goatskins and a hair shirt every day of his adult life, and to have subsisted on a diet of barley bread mixed with ash. The church appears to be half buried in the sand; the visible part dates from the fifteenth century, although it has been necessarily much repaired and restored.

One night in 1787 a Spanish ship was wrecked at the foot of the cliffs beside the Church of St Winwaloe. The fate of the crew was not recorded, but stories that she was carrying an

enormous weight of silver dollars continued to stir greedy interest long afterwards. There were several attempts at salvage, one
of which involved a gang of tin miners being hired to dig a shaft
under the wreck; they had got ten yards when the roof fell in.
Small quantities of silver coins continued to turn up, and in
1872 a team attempted to use an industrial mining pump driven
by an agricultural threshing machine to suck the treasure from
the hold, but all they recovered was sand and more sand.

26

LEGENDS OF MOUNT'S BAY

St Winwaloe's is the church of Gunwalloe, a parish consisting for the most part of a treeless tract of reclaimed moor and heathland. The settlement of Gunwalloe itself is at the northern end and is so inconsequential that even at cycling speed you may blink and miss it. It stands just back from the eastern end of the Loe Bar, a great sickle blade of pale, flinty grit which at its centre holds back the waters of Cornwall's largest natural lake, Loe Pool.

The coastal path runs along the top of the bar, sea to one side, freshwater to the other. It is a lovely place, and often lonely. On a calm sunny day it looks like a perfect deserted beach, and those who do not know it may wonder at the absence of car and caravan parks and cafés. But the bar is deadly. The seaward slope is steep, and if you look closely you can see the undertow working where the waves break. There are no boats, and no sensible swimmers; as recently as New Year's Eve 2013 a young man who went in up to his knees was plucked away and drowned.

It is also not a good place to steer a ship. In December 1807 HMS *Anson*, a frigate with orders to join the blockade of the

French Channel ports, was crossing Mount's Bay when she was caught in a typical south-westerly gale and driven towards the bar. Captain Charles Lydiard tried to anchor her but the ropes parted. He saw the pale, apparently unobstructed stretch of sand in front and steered for it, but struck a hidden reef close in. The *Anson* turned sideways and went over, her mainmast almost reaching the shore. Some of the crew scrambled along it and reached safety, urged on by their captain from the wheel. When his turn came he stopped to try to help a terrified midshipman and was swept away. Altogether sixty men were drowned that night.

Nearly three hundred years earlier, in January 1526, the same reef accounted for a Portuguese ship, the *San Antonio*, setting off one of Cornwall's most protracted treasure-hunting sagas. According to documents stored at the Public Record Office, she was carrying silver bullion, precious stones, gold and silver ornaments, musical instruments, a suit of armour intended for the King of Portugal and much else – the most startling items being two thousand barber's basins. The depositions state that three leading local clan leaders – Thomas St Aubyn of Clowance, John Milliton of Pengersick and William Godolphin of Godolphin – arrived with their retainers and seized most of the treasure. St Aubyn denied the accusation, maintaining that he and his fellow squires had tried to help and that the treasure was lost with the ship. No charge was ever proved.

For a long time the wreck was believed to be close to St Winwaloe's Church. It was not until 1981 that the correct site was identified after a copper ingot was recovered. More copper ingots were found, as well as a silver one weighing seventeen pounds. Other items, including copper candlesticks, can be seen in local museums. The wreck became a protected site, to be explored only under licence. Over the years more copper and lead artefacts have been found, but no more silver, suggesting that St Aubyn and his cronies probably did help themselves, although the fate of the barber's basins remains a mystery.

Geomorphologically Loe Pool has much in common with Slapton Ley, but it is even more lovely and mysterious. It is formed of two branches, one reaching towards Helston and the other, Carminoe Creek, deviating east to nowhere in particular. Woods spill down to its margins with farmland behind, and there are only isolated houses beside it. Historically Loe Pool was noted for its fat and delicious trout. A sixteenth-century source referred to it breeding 'a peculiar kind of bastard trout in bigness and goodness exceeding such as live in freshwater' – which was nonsense, as it is fresh water and they were ordinary brown trout grown fat on an abundant diet.

The development of mining around Helston during the nineteenth century turned Loe Pool red and killed off much of the plant growth. More recently it suffered badly from sewage being flushed down from Helston, and the enthusiastic use of chemical fertilisers by farmers, leading to severe eutrophication. The land around is now managed by the National Trust and water quality is improved, although whether the trout are still there I have no way of telling, since no one seems to fish it any more.

The path leads up from Loe Bar to a lodge perched on the cliff edge commanding amazing views of the Lizard, Loe Pool and the whole of Mount's Bay. Half a mile further on are the first bungalows and 'executive-style' houses of Porthleven. The old town is gathered around the eastern side of the harbour, which was built of great granite blocks between 1810 and 1820. For much of the nineteenth century Porthleven did well enough on fishing, boat-building, net-making, exports of china clay and imports of coal and timber for the mines but subsequently the familiar slide took hold.

These days it retains a residual small-scale fishery but – as elsewhere – tourism has become the insecure mainstay of a shaky local economy. A report carried out in 2009 for a Cornish charity revealed that 14 per cent of the population of 3100 were classified as 'economically deprived' – i.e. poor. A fifth had no car and a fifth of homes had no central heating. To add to Porthleven's problems, the harbour and seafront took a tremendous battering in the storms of February 2014, leaving boats smashed and sunk and a repair bill exceeding £100,000.

The Lizard peninsula ends at Porthleven, but the character of the coastline – harsh fissured cliffs tumbling into a surging sea – continues as before as far as Praa Sands. The hinterland of this wide expanse of safe, gently shelving beach is now annexed by car parks, caravan and camp sites, clusters of chalets and rows of bungalows and holiday apartments. Behind all that are the remains of Pengersick Castle, which is not a castle at all and never was, but a fortified manor house of which the castellated tower remains.

Assorted paranormalist cranks and charlatans have been keen to promote Pengersick as a gathering place of ghosts and demons. Absurd tales of devil-worship, monk murder, phantoms of drowned sailors, a wandering woman in white, alchemy, a demon hound and so on have been peddled online and even on television, much to the disgust of scholarly super-naturalists who complain that their own serious research into Pengersick's attested top-class spirit energy has been brought into disrepute.

To be honest, I am not that fascinated by ghost stories. Nor, at this stage in my journey, was I gripped any more by tales of smugglers and smuggling. I had passed uncountable Smugglers' Lanes, Smugglers' Cottages, Smugglers' Retreats and Smugglers' Haunts and more than enough Smugglers' Inns and Smugglers' Arms. I had been buffeted on all sides by stories of whiskered, warm-hearted seafarers dodging flint-hearted excisemen, of torches on moonlit beaches and boats nudging into deserted coves, of the rolling of kegs and the creaking of carts on stony paths, of the parson turning a blind eye to the goings-on in his belfry.

In the hands of the heritage people, the clichés have been heaped one on another until whatever the hard reality once was is buried in a flabby heap of bogus romanticism. Inconvenient facts – that many of these men were squalid and violent crim-inals, that, then as now, the collection of tax was essential for effective government – have been lost in a flood of sentimen-tal make-believe.

It is therefore dutifully rather than with great enthusiasm that I record that Prussia Cove – which is tucked into the eastern side of Cudden Point – was the headquarters of the most famous of all Cornish smuggling enterprises. Suffice to say that it was run jointly by three of the eight sons of a local farmer, John, Charles and Harry Carter; that the leader was John, the self-styled King of Prussia, who built himself a stone residence on the cliffs above the cove from which he directed operations;

that Harry became the gang's agent across the Channel in Roscoff and in 1809 wrote or dictated a memoir giving a colourfully sanitised account of his own and his brothers' activities.

Charles Harper was as bad as anyone when it came to romanticising the exploits of the smugglers and obscuring their more vicious crimes. He wrote a whole book on the subject whose full title – *The Smugglers: Picturesque Chapters in the Story of an Ancient Craft* – gives his game away. When he arrived at Prussia Cove on his Cornish trip, John Carter's house had just been pulled down to make way for a road. Harper was affronted by what he called 'the barbed-wire squalor' and by his encounter with 'a good-looking man with a beard and an undefinable air of being a retired officer of the Royal Navy' who was raking stones and declared himself to be the owner of the road and the land and the destroyer of the King of Prussia's palace.

Harper identifies him as 'the locally famous Mr Behrens' who – far from being a retired naval officer – was in fact a rich German coffee dealer of pronounced Anglophile tendencies. He and his English wife, Emily, née Tunstall, had fallen in love with the cove – then known as King's Cove – and bought it in order to settle there. The 'uninviting residence' referred to by Harper must have been the first version of Porth-en-Alls, which was subsequently remodelled by Philip Tilden (designer of the never-built Hengistbury Castle in Dorset) into a rather lovely stone and reinforced concrete house in the English vernacular revival style. Replete with dormer windows, gable ends, courtyards, balconies, arcades, moulded doorways and any number of arts-and-crafts touches, Porth-en-Alls fits snugly against the steep rocky slope, its amazing garden reaching down to the edge of the rocks above the limpid blue water.

* * *

St Michael's Mount

Looking west from Cudden Point, the eye is pulled irresistibly to the extraordinary spectacle of St Michael's Mount. A local history of 1820 said, quite correctly: 'It is one of those rare and singular objects which impress the mind with sensations of veneration, pleasure and astonishment the instant it is seen.' The modern history of the Mount dates from the late eleventh century, when it was donated to the Benedictine monks of Mont St Michel in Normandy to serve as their priory. It was much fought over in subsequent centuries, and during the Civil War was held for the King until its surrender to Parliamentary forces in 1646. Colonel John St Aubyn was appointed its governor, and some years later he bought it. His descendants still inhabit the castle, although the National Trust administers the Mount as a whole.

Our friend Harper – in common with Sherlock Holmes and a hatful of other incurable romantics – was much attracted by the notion of the ancient Phoenicians (from present-day Lebanon and Syria) arriving in Cornwall to obtain tin and using the Mount as their trading post. In the absence of any supporting evidence of any kind, Charles Harper merely asserted their presence – 'that foreigners in times long before the Romans came to Britain were accustomed to resort to this neighbourhood has directly been shown – and that they were Phoenicians is certain.' They weren't; at least no reputable modern scholar thinks they were. Trade in tin there was, between Cornwall and Gaul, but the Phoenicians went to Spain for theirs.

Another tale about St Michael's Mount – more recent, but on the face of it equally fanciful – is that Hitler's foreign minister, Joachim von Ribbentrop, had earmarked it as his official residence once Germany had conquered Britain. As ambassador to London in the 1930s, Ribbentrop came on holiday to Cornwall with his family and became fond of its distinctly un-Teutonic wildness. According to the contemporary Cornish artist Andrew Lanyon, he boasted that Hitler had promised him the county as a reward for his loyalty, and that he would live on St Michael's Mount. Fortunately for almost everyone concerned, Germany lost, Ribbentrop was executed as a war criminal and St Michael's Mount remained in English hands.

It is the fate of Marazion to be regarded, and always to have been regarded, primarily as the stepping-off point for the Mount. It is very old and was once a market town and fishing port of some importance. But it was long ago eclipsed commercially by the development of Penzance and spiritually by St Michael's Mount. When I was there it was heaving with cars and swarming with people filling in time before they could get across the causeway to the Mount, or just filling in time. I left on the cycle path that runs between the railway line and the beach to Penzance Station, and made good speed, encouraged by an early sighting of my train at the platform emitting plumes of blue diesel smoke indicative of an imminent departure.

Penzance has, or should have, so much going for it. Its position, looking towards St Michael's Mount and the Lizard across the great sweep of Mount's Bay, is superb. It has its railway station, five-and-a-half hours from London. It has its harbour and docks and beach. It has some fine public buildings and many delightful town houses and cottages arranged in terraces along little streets and around squares enclosing gardens. It has a splendid promenade and a more than splendid lido, the Jubilee Pool, whose triangular walls are washed by the sea. It has an excellent public library as well as the beautiful Morrab Library, the great depository of Cornish culture and literature.

The local history of 1820 sang Penzance's praises to the skies: 'The temperature of the atmosphere, the mildness of the seasons, the beauty of the prospect and the exhilarating purity of the gentle breezes that play upon the bosom of the waters and scatter health upon the shores, have conferred on Penzance and its vicinity a degree of celebrity which few persons who have visited this neighbourhood will think injudiciously bestowed.' Steady on there! W. H. Hudson, a regular visitor ninety or so years later, was not so smitten. He found the streets 'mean and commonplace' and the market 'curiously mean'. But he was favourably struck by the sobriety of the people and 'their singularly happy disposition, lively and sociable, with a very intense love of their families and homes.'

Of late Penzance has become something of a byword for social deprivation, drunkenness, drug addiction, yobbishness, crime and disorder, generational unemployment and general hopelessness. Its people are said to smoke more, drink more, inject more heroin, abuse each other more, work less and have less to spend than almost anywhere else in the land. The retail heart of the town – particularly along Market Jew Street – has an air of struggle about it, with an abundance of charity shops and empty premises. The harbour is in acute need of investment to keep the ferry link with the Isles of Scilly going, and the helicopter service has ended because of heavy losses. The wonderful Jubilee Pool has been starved of public money and shows it, and took a fearsome mauling from the storms of early 2014.

But those who care about Penzance are doing their utmost to bring it round. Compared with so many soulless town centres, it has a wealth of independent shops which are fighting hard to stay alive and prosper. The local chamber of commerce has got itself organised, and campaigners have managed to prise £2 million from central government to rescue the Jubilee Pool from years of penny-pinching neglect. And on a fine summer's day it is a pleasure to linger in Penzance. The seafront and the old part of town are utterly delightful – nowhere more so than the sub-tropical Morrab Gardens, with its quaint bandstand, its luxuriant banks of berberis, camellias and azaleas, its acacia trees and Japanese quinces.

Penzance has few literary sons and daughters to boast of. One was a most wretched young man, John Thomas Blight, who worked for a while as an assistant at the library. Blight was a precociously gifted artist, as seen from the illustrations for his book *A Week at the Land's End*, which – despite having been published 150 years ago – remains an essential guide. He was twenty-five when it appeared; a few years later he had a severe mental breakdown and became obsessed with the belief that the ancient Druids had infiltrated the Church of England and were intent on reintroducing their savage pagan rites. In the end the poor fellow was confined in the lunatic asylum at Bodmin, where he died as late as 1911.

Perhaps there was something in the Penzance air. Another writer hailed as a genius and subsequently forgotten came to a ghastly end there. For a time in the 1890s, the Glasgow-born John Davidson was a bright light in the London literary scene, crossing swords with the young Yeats, consorting with Swinburne, being lauded by Shaw. He wrote abundantly: plays, novels, poetry, philosophy, much of it inspired by his desire to 'aid in the overthrow of the rotten financial investment called Christianity'. A brief flowering of celebrity and success gave way to critical hostility and public indifference, particularly to his great labour, a dramatic verse epic called *God and Mammon*.

In 1908 Davidson moved to Penzance, where he sank into deeper and deeper despair. He wrote to his publisher 'the time has come to make an end', then waded out into Mount's Bay and drowned himself.

27

A Different Place

On the map Penzance runs seamlessly into Newlyn, but the two are very distinct. Because of its harbour and its fishing fleet and its particular history, Newlyn seems to have a stronger sense of itself and what it is for. Only Brixham among English ports lands more fish than Newlyn, and as at Brixham, the smell of fish is in the air. Newlyn fishermen have seen bad times and good, and these days the times are pretty good.

The fishermen have been there for ever and a day, as long as Newlyn has been Newlyn. The painters came much later. Yet the two – the painting and the fishing – combined to give the port a uniquely dual image: of a man in a boat with a net, and an artist with an easel, both braving whatever the south-west and its winds could throw at them.

The artistic migration from London was initiated at the end of the nineteenth century by Stanhope Forbes. He had studied in Paris and learned to paint from nature and real life in Brittany, and found its English equivalent by the sea at Newlyn. The living was cheap, the scenes were vibrant with drama, the models were there for the painting. 'Unflinching realism', as Forbes characterised it, was the creed. They placed their canvases and palettes among the fishing people, who thought it all very strange at the start but became accustomed to these bohemians in their midst.

A Newlyn school was born, made up of Forbes' friends and pupils, among whose leading lights were Laura Knight and her husband Harold. One of Harold Knight's many portraits is of a slim young man in a fawn suit and bow tie sitting at a table in dappled sunlight with a book in one hand and a cigarette in the other. The subject was Alfred Munnings, who came to Newlyn in 1911 and became a central figure in the artists' colony. Munnings paid court to one of Stanhope Forbes' most fetching students, Florence Carter Wood, and married her with tragic consequences. She attempted suicide on their wedding night and killed herself with cyanide two years later, an event which Laura Knight said 'put an end to all our joy.'

Munnings erased her from the official version of his life, and went on after the 1914–18 war to become rich and famous as a painter of horses and paddock scenes, and notorious for his violent hostility to 'modern art', in particular that of Picasso. In 1949, as President of the Royal Academy, Sir Alfred Munnings shared his views on the subject with distinguished guests at the annual dinner. 'I myself,' he declared, 'would rather have a damned bad failure, a bad, muddy old picture where somebody has tried to set down what they have seen than all this affected juggling.'

Around Penlee Point from Newlyn is Mousehole with its sweet, hemispherical harbour, steep twisting streets and granite cottages. Now chiefly a tourist hotspot with a handful of working fishing boats, Mousehole once rivalled Newlyn in importance. In 1595 it was put to fire and sword by a force of Spanish pikemen and musketeers who arrived unexpectedly from Britanny. Having torched Mousehole, they sailed round to Newlyn and Penzance and repeated the trick, and escaped across the Channel before ships sent from Plymouth could intervene.

The simple creed of Methodism expounded in the fields and by the roadsides and on the seashore by John Wesley found a ready audience in Mousehole, as elsewhere in Cornwall. A fine new chapel was built in 1784 and later enlarged to accommodate new converts. Among them was a group of Mousehole fishermen whose convictions were so strong that they were persuaded to turn from casting their nets in Mount's Bay to trawling for souls on the other side of the world.

The man who did the persuading was Captain Allen Gardiner, a disappointed naval officer turned missionary zealot. He must have known what he was letting these simple Cornish lads in for when they sailed from Liverpool for Tierra del Fuego in September 1850. He had already been to that famously grim place twice before, declaring that he would turn the savages from their heathen ways to the light of Christ, and on neither occasion had received any encouragement of any kind. But Gardiner was one of those fanatics whose impregnable faith in his own righteousness made him both immune to reason and a danger to those around him.

The mission was doomed from the start. Apart from Gardiner and the three Mousehole men, it consisted of a surgeon, a carpenter and John Maidment, described as a 'catechist'. There was no one who could speak a word of whatever language the natives spoke, or with a notion of how to survive in one of the most barren, storm-blasted wastelands on earth. They landed in two open boats on Picton Island, at the southern tip of the

Tierra del Fuego archipelago, on 5 December 1850, with basic provisions sufficient for six months.

The natives were antagonistic and missed no opportunity to steal from the provisions store. Whatever attempts may have been made to get them to pay attention to the Word of God were soon abandoned in favour of a hopeless struggle to stay alive. John Badcock of Mousehole was the first to die, after six months, of scurvy and starvation. His comrades survived a little longer by eating mice, a dead penguin, a dead fox and half a rotten fish washed up on the shore, but by the end of August 1851 only Gardiner himself was still alive.

His remains were found by a rescue team the following January beside one of the boats. He was dressed in three sets of clothes and had his hands thrust into woollen socks. His Bible was beside him, with many passages marked and underlined. The bodies were buried and the leader of the rescuers ordered a volley of musket fire – 'the only tribute of respect I could pay to this lofty-minded man and his devoted companions.'

Mousehole will always be associated with the Penlee disaster of December 1981, when its lifeboat and eight crew were lost trying to rescue those on board a cargo vessel disabled by hurricane-force winds in Mount's Bay. A less melancholy claim to distinction is that Dolly Pentreath – 'the last speaker of Cornish' – lived there. Her accomplishments were revealed by a well-known antiquarian, Daines Barrington, who visited Mousehole in 1768 and found her in a hut 'maintained partly by the parish and partly by fortune-telling and gabbling Cornish.' She was said to be eighty-seven years old, short and bent with age, but 'so lusty however' that she thought nothing of walking the three miles to Castle Horneck and back in a day.

In a report for the Society of Antiquaries, Barrington said she had told him that in her youth Cornish had been well understood by everyone, 'even the gentry', but that now 'there is neither in Mousehole nor in any other part of the county any person who knows anything of it.' On that basis Barrington declared Dolly to be the last Cornish speaker, and the label stuck. However, its factual basis was examined in formidable detail by the Celtic language scholar Peter Berresford Ellis, in his 1974 study *The Cornish Language and its Literature*, and was found – not surprisingly – to be wanting.

According to Ellis the language was in headlong retreat from the mid-sixteenth century onwards, for various reasons including the lack of a proper alphabet and a translation of the Bible, and its long-standing association with Catholicism, now outlawed. By 1650 it had retreated to the far west where it clung on in a handful of rural parishes and fishing villages, including Mousehole. Although various gentlemen enthusiasts endeavoured to keep the flame alive by collecting a meagre store of written records and sources and writing a vocabulary, by the end of the eighteenth century Sir William Borlase declared 'this language is now altogether dead so as not to be spoken anywhere in conversation.'

Not spoken in conversation perhaps, but not quite dead either. Dolly Pentreath died in 1777, but Peter Berresford Ellis shows that she was survived by several Cornish speakers. One of them was a fisherman of Penzance, William Bodener, with whom Dolly was reported to have talked Cornish for hours on end. Neither of Bodener's two sons spoke it, but another resident of Penzance, John Nancarrow, did; and he claimed there was 'an inhabitant of Truro' who had it as well.

As Ellis comments, 'a language does not die suddenly, snuffed out with its last remaining speaker ... it lingers on for many years.' And thanks to him and other scholars and linguistic activists, Cornish has been exhumed and resurrected to the extent that UNESCO has ruled that the label 'extinct' no longer applies to it. It lives on rather in the manner of a kidney patient on dialysis, taught in some schools, used on road signs and dutifully promoted by the county council.

As for Dolly Pentreath, she was buried in the churchyard at Paul, the village above and behind Mousehole. A century later a somewhat grandiose monument to her was fixed in the churchyard wall, paid for by Prince Louis Lucien Bonaparte, a nephew of Napoleon and a great enthusiast for obscure and moribund European languages. The stone bears an epitaph from Exodus: '*Gwra perthi de taz ha de mam: mal de dythiow bethenz hyr war an tyr neb an arleth de dew ryes dees* – Honour thy father and thy mother that thy days may be long in the land the Lord thy God giveth thee.'

The perceived 'otherness' of Cornwall evinced by its language has long been a key element of its appeal to outsiders. Laura Knight wrote that it was no use comparing it with anywhere else – 'an atmosphere prevails which takes away any sense or belief you have ever had, and you don't know why but you aren't in England any more.'

The further west, the more distinctive the landscape seemed. W. H. Hudson compared it with Connemara in the west of Ireland: 'This coast country is the most desert-like and desolate ...

the black, frowning, wave-beaten cliffs on the one hand, the hills and moors on the other, strewn abundantly with granite boulders, rough with heath and furze and bracken, the summits crowned with great masses of rock resembling ancient ruined castles.'

A painter of a later generation than Laura Knight, Ithell Colquhoun, felt a sacredness in west Cornwall. She saw human and animal forms in the rocks, likened trees to limbs and stacks of rock to phalluses, and considered stone circles and holy crosses to be 'geysers of energy'. She settled for a time in the Lamorna valley beyond Mousehole, living in a tin hut with a corrugated roof and no power or plumbing. Lamorna was then and still is a place as lovely as its name, a long dale shaded by sycamores and ash, its green banks luxuriant with bluebells and wild garlic; and through it a bright, lively stream that races over miniature waterfalls and slows through clear, gravelly pools before charging over a final barrier of boulders into the cove itself.

No wonder the painters loved it, and love it still. It was 'discovered' in the 1890s by John Birch, who was dubbed 'Lamorna' Birch by Stanhope Forbes to distinguish him from the Newlyn painter, Lionel Birch. Lamorna Birch had a house perched above the cove where his grandson still lives. Another migrant, much influenced by Birch, was Stanley Gardiner, who lived beside the stream at Lily Cottage. When I stopped there I met an elderly man who turned out to be Gardiner's son Keith – another painter and author of a memoir of Lamorna and its artists, *A Painter's Paradise*. I asked him about painting the sea. 'Easier than landscape, at least it is to me,' he said. 'You have to be quick to catch it.'

The cove is rough and rocky, clasped by cliffs of granite. Before the painters arrived, Lamorna was known for its granite, used in buildings as various as New Scotland Yard and the Café Monico in Piccadilly, as well as for piers and breakwaters and lighthouses – anything where extreme strength and durability were wanted. The cove had its own pier where the barges were loaded, and horse-drawn carts piled with stone clattered up the road to Penzance.

The quarry on the east side of the valley was owned by the St Aubyns of St Michael's Mount, and that on the west by the Paynters of Boskenna. The Paynters also owned most of the houses in Lamorna as well as much land and many farms inland. They lived in style at Boskenna, a seventeenth-century manor house a couple of miles west of Lamorna. Colonel Camborne Paynter liked having artists around, and encouraged Laura Knight and her husband as well as Alfred Munnings to come and live in Lamorna.

The Colonel's daughter, Betty Paynter, was a lively girl who was much admired at a tender age by the Italian pioneer of radio and enthusiastic fascist, Guglielmo Marconi. He used to bring his yacht around from Poldhu on the Lizard – from where he transmitted his first transatlantic radio message – to Paynter's Cove to pay court to her. Newspaper reports that they had become engaged despite a thirty-seven-year age gap roused the Colonel to brandish his whip at a squad of reporters who turned up for a meet of the local hunt.

Other visitors were made more welcome – T. E. Lawrence, D. H. Lawrence, Augustus John, any number of painters from Lamorna and Newlyn. A friend of Betty Paynter, Mary Wesley, came to live at Boskenna during the 1939–45 war and later placed 'the great house in the west' in several of her novels, including *The Camomile Lawn*. Colonel Paynter died in 1948, leaving the estate to Betty, who by then was married to a solicitor called Paul Hill. Patrick Marnham, in his biography of Mary Wesley, refers to allegations that the will naming Betty as the heir rather than the Colonel's granddaughter was forged by Hill. True or not, Betty and her husband worked their way through the inheritance at speed, and in 1957 the estate and Boskenna were sold, ending three centuries of family connection.

It is the granite that gives this stretch of coastline its adamantine character. The cliffs are not high compared with elsewhere on the Channel shore, but they are unyielding. The assaults of the sea have battered and scarred them, but never broken them. They are fissured and holed and their feet are strewn with the casualties of war, but they do not surrender.

The granite ramparts are broken by coves aplenty, but most of them are very steep and inaccessible and not that much more comfortable than the headlands beside them. Penberth is an exception, with its clump of cottages and a beach which once accommodated twenty fishing boats. But for sand and somewhere to stretch out a deckchair you must go to Porthcurno, beyond the famous Logan Rock which the foolish Lieutenant Goldsmith caused to be tumbled down from its age-old perch, thereby inflicting on himself disgrace and a hefty bill to have it put back (£130 in all, a very considerable sum in 1824).

Charles Harper came here expecting seclusion but found, to his dismay, that the sands of Porthcurno displayed the imprints of many feet. These belonged to the 'young barbarians' employed by the Eastern Telegraph Company (later Cable and Wireless), which had chosen Porthcurno as the hub of its burgeoning global network of undersea cabling. By the time Harper got there, this extended to North America, Australia and India – it was said, quite truthfully, that it was far easier for someone in Porthcurno to communicate with someone in Bombay than with someone in Penzance. In 1940 the telegraph station was considered at high risk of being targeted by German bombers, and a platoon of tin miners was brought in to blast tunnels into the cliffs where the vital equipment could be hidden from sight. The station finally closed in 1970, although engineers continued to be trained there for another twenty years.

Up the road, standing out very visibly, is a white house originally built by Cable and Wireless for the widow of one of its operatives who had been drowned laying cable at sea. It was acquired in the 1920s by Dora and Bertrand Russell, who changed its name from Sunny Bank to Carn Voel and fitted on the front a porch with pillars and a curved roof suggestive of the Orient. They were intent upon a simple, outdoor life for their infant son and daughter – 'we talked much that summer about bringing up children,' Dora Russell wrote in her memoir *The Tamarisk Tree*. The words are poignant because domestic peace with Russell was inevitably short-lived, and he proved to be an appalling father to poor John Russell (there is a chilling account in Ray Monk's biography of the philosopher taking the boy kicking and screaming into the sea to teach him to swim, and holding his head under to 'cure' his fear of water).

Russell was famously short on humour, but there is a droll and revealing anecdote about him asking his wife to tie a parcel for him. She, busy with chores, suggested he do it himself. 'I have never tied a parcel in my life and I am not going to start now,' the great thinker declared.

After Russell left her for the children's governess, Dora kept the house and continued to live there, on and off, until her death in 1986. In the later years she looked after John Russell, by then diagnosed with schizophrenia. Towards the end her daughter Katharine came to live there as well, and she remains there with her son. Although she is in her nineties, she still works two days a week in the Oxfam bookshop in Penzance. I called at Carn Voel one morning; when she answered the door I was taken aback by her resemblance to the photographs of her father. I explained my business and she said she saw no reason why she should talk to me about him. As I couldn't either, I went on my way.

Penwith did not make much impression on Bertrand Russell, but – like many others – Dora Russell identified something exceptional in this wild place. 'Nowhere better than down here,' she wrote, 'can one feel the mysterious link between man and the whole of his planet down to the very substance of its rocky foundations. Here I have my share in eternity.'

And beyond is the Land's End.

In the 1970s a man called Charles Neave-Hill became the owner of the 115 acres of rock and heathland that included the south-west extremity of the British mainland, Land's End. He had inherited it from his father, William Neave-Hill, who had inherited it from his mother, born Minnie Vingoe

Toman Trahair. How it came to her is a very tangled tale – suffice to say that it had been the property of one Vingoe or Toman or Trahair or other (they were all cousins) since the mid-1600s.

After the railway reached Penzance in 1859, the Tomans began, somewhat hesitantly, to exploit the tourist potential of their patrimony. There was already an inn, the First and Last, which was expanded. A teahouse was opened, followed by what became the Penwith Temperance Hotel. Refreshments and postcards were dispensed from a little shop on the cliff edge. So it went on until the outbreak of war in 1939, when the area was requisitioned. Post-1945 the facilities remained in a deplorably run-down condition for years.

In 1982 Charles Neave-Hill put Land's End up for sale. The National Trust bid for it, but he chose to sell it to a Welsh property developer, David Goldstone. It was a black day for anyone who cares about Britain's coastline. Under Mr Goldstone's stewardship, various low-grade visitor attractions were added, and a charge was imposed on visitors who wished to walk through. Five years later Mr Goldstone sold Land's End for £6.75 million to the property magnate and entrepreneur, Peter de Savary. He spent lavishly on his new acquisition, and in questionable taste, turning it into a King Arthur theme park replete with 'audio-visual experience', expanding the hotel and adding various tacky extras. De Savary's business empire collapsed in the 1990s, and the complex was eventually acquired by the current owners, a Jersey-based 'private discretionary trust', Heritage Great Britain, which also owns John O'Groats, the top of Snowdon and other 'leisure assets'.

Land's End

Why come to Land's End?

Wilkie Collins, who visited it in the 1850s, said there was something in the very name that stirred us all, which he likened to the magnetic pull of Jerusalem.

Half a century later W. H. Hudson witnessed the daily arrival of pilgrims from all parts of the kingdom. They came in all weathers and seasons, determined to set their feet on 'this little rocky promontory' and look out upon the sea. Some were very old, wrapped in greatcoats, scarves and comforters, sitting – Hudson observed – in dejected attitudes 'silently gazing in one direction beyond that rocky foreland with the same look of infinite weariness on their grey faces and in their dim sad eyes.'

One day in May Hudson counted more than 1200 trippers arriving at Penzance Station in four trains, having spent twenty-six hours getting there from various cotton towns around Manchester. He talked to them and found none who wanted to see Penzance or the dramatic scenery of Penwith. They came to see Land's End and Land's End only, and they had seven hours to get there and back before the trains took them home.

Both Collins and Hudson made the same observation that has occurred to countless other visitors and pilgrims – that visually there is nothing exceptional about Land's End. There are many other headlands that are bolder, wilder, more dramatic, more rugged, more beautiful, just as violently assaulted by the sea. Hence the sense of anti-climax, the blank look that frames the question put by Hudson: 'Is this the Land's End? Is this all?'

Even before it acquired its clutter of commercial enterprises, Land's End often disappointed observers; or worse, panicked them into solemn bursts of adjectival flatulence, everything stupendous, awful, sublime, colossal and generally displaying what one termed 'the glorifying impress of multiplicious beauty'. You had to choose your time to avoid the crowds and dodge the clichés. Hudson recommended dusk on a stormy winter's day to experience 'the raving of the wind, the dark ocean, the jagged isolated rocks rising in awful blackness from the spectral foam ... the hoarse sounds of the sea, with throbbing and hollow booming noises in the caverns beneath.'

The poet and author of fairy tales, Ruth Manning-Sanders – who lived near Land's End most of her life – agreed: 'It is then that the sense of the primordial, the strange and the savage, the unknown, *the very long ago*, fills the dusk with something very akin to dread.'

But today you may not do as Hudson, Collins, Dickens, Tennyson, John Wesley and everyone else did, and scramble down to the sea's edge. It is all fenced off: too dangerous, the owners say. Instead you may, if you wish, submit yourself to the

Arthur's Quest interactive experience or sit back in the special-effects cinema and feel – literally feel – wind and spray in your face as Ned plunges down in *20,000 Leagues under the Sea*. You may thrill to the recreation of a real air-sea rescue, or feed a real pig at the farm and watch real Cornish craftsmen at work engraving glass and tooling leather. You may – not to be missed – have your photograph taken in front of the 'totally iconic' Land's End signpost.

But you may not feel like doing any of these things, as I did not. Instead I ordered a cream tea in the hotel and wondered how it could be that this famous place had been allowed to become and remain such a trashy dump. I repented every unkind thought I had ever had about the National Trust, and every unkind word I may have written. A hundred years ago that singular and melancholic observer, W. H. Hudson, ended his book *The Land's End* with a plea for it to be cleared of all the rubbishy, tacky shops and cafés and bungalows and the rest, and placed into public ownership. I wished for the same.

My cream tea arrived. The scone was stale and powdery but I ate it anyway. I thought about how far I had come from Dover, and all the ups and downs and the blessed flat stretches. I had not solved any great mysteries nor uncovered any startling truths. I had seen much and learned much, but I was sure I had overlooked plenty as well.

Listening and watching the sea often has the effect of emptying the mind of clutter and concentrating it on simple matters. After a little time I stopped thinking about myself and my journey, and surrendered myself to the sound of the waves breaking insistently against the rocks below.

BIBLIOGRAPHY

Ashley, Harry, *The Dorset Coast*, Countryside Books, 1992.

Baker, Denys Val, *A View from Land's End*, Kimber, 1982.

Baring-Gould, Sabine, *Cornish Characters and Strange Events*, Lane, 1909.

Barrett, J. A., *The Seaside Resort Towns of England and Wales*, University of London, 1958.

Bates, Robin, and Scolding, Bill, *Five Walks Around Ruan Minor and Cadgwith; Five Walks From The Lizard; Five Walks Around St Keverne; Five Walks Around Mullion*, Cornwall County Council.

Bird, Eric, and Modlock, Lillian, *Writers on the South-West Coast*, Ex Libris, 1994.

Blight, J. A., *A Week at the Land's End*, Longman,1861.

Boddy, Maureen, West, Jack and Attwooll, Maureen, *Weymouth: An Illustrated History*, Dovecote, 1983.

Bond, Thomas, *Topographical and Historical Sketches of the Boroughs of East and West Looe*, J. Nicholls, 1823.

Booker, J. A., *Blackshirts-on-Sea*, Brockinday, 2000.

Cannadine, David, *Lords and Landlords*, Leicester University Press, 1980.

Cattell, Raymond, *Under Sail Through Red Devon*, Alexander Maclehose, 1937.

Collins, Wilkie, *Rambles Beyond Railways*, Richard Bentley, 1861.

Connolly, Cyril, *Enemies of Promise*, Routledge and Kegan Paul, 1949.

Craik, Dinah, *An Unsentimental Journey Through Cornwall*, Macmillan, 1884.

Croft-Cooke, Rupert, *The Green, Green Grass*, W. H. Allen, 1977.

D'Enno, Douglas, *Sussex Coast Through Time*, Amberley Publishing, 2012.

— *The Saltdean Story*, Phillimore, 1985.

Dunn, Mike, *The Looe Island Story*, Polperro Heritage Press, 2005.

Eastwood, John, *The Story of Burton Bradstock*, www.burton bradstock.org.uk

Elderwick, David, *Captain Webb – Channel Swimmer*, Brewin, 1987.

Ellis, Peter Berresford, *The Cornish Language and its Literature*, Routledge and Kegan Paul, 1987.

Feigel, Lara, and Harris, Alexandra, *Modernism on Sea*, Peter Lang, 2009.

Ferry, Kathryn, *Beach Huts and Bathing Machines*, Shire, 2009.

Finlayson, Iain, *Writers in Romney Marsh*, Severn House, 1986.

Fox, Sarah Prideaux, *Kingsbridge and Its Surroundings*, G. P. Friend, 1874.

Fry, Helen, *Music and Men: The Life and Loves of Harriet Cohen*, History Press, 2008.

Gilbert, Edmund W., *Brighton – Old Ocean's Bauble*, Methuen, 1954.

Gray, Fred, *Designing the Seaside*, Reaktion, 2006.

Greenwood, Paul, *Once Aboard a Cornish Lugger*, Polperro Heritage Press, 2006.

— *More Tales from a Cornish Lugger*, Polperro Heritage Press, 2011.

Grimson, John, *The Channel Coasts of England*, Hale, 1978.

Haigh, Gideon, *Shute the Messenger*, www.themonthly.com. au, 2007.

Hardy, Dennis, and Ward, Colin, *Arcadia for All*, Five Leaves, 2003.

Harper, Charles G., *The Kentish Coast*, Chapman and Hall, 1914.

— *The Dorset Coast*, Chapman and Hall, 1905.

— *The South Devon Coast*, Chapman and Hall, 1907.

— *The Cornish Coast (South)*, Chapman and Hall, 1910.

Harrison, Shirley, *The Channel*, Collins, 1986.

Hawthorne, Paul, *Oldway Mansion*, Torbay Books, 2009.

Hern, Anthony, *The Seaside Holiday*, Cresset Press, 1967.

Howgego, Raymond, *F. A. Mitchell-Hedges*, www.howgego.co.uk

Hudson, W. H., *Nature in Downland*, Longman, 1900.

— *The Land's End*, Hutchinson, 1908.

Jefferies, Richard, 'Sunny Brighton' and 'The Breeze on Beachy Head', www.readbookonline.net

Johns, C. A., *A Week at The Lizard*, Christian Knowledge Society, 1848.

Jones, Victor Pierce, and Walton, Robin, *A Guide to Hayling Island*, 2005.

Lawrence, William, *The Autobiography of Sergeant William Lawrence, A Hero of the Peninsular and Waterloo Campaigns*, Sampson Low, 1886 (available through www.gutenberg.org).

Legg, Rodney, 'The Loss of the Halsewell', from *Dorset Life*, 2010.

Lewer, David, and Calkin, J. Bernard, *Curiosities of Swanage*, Friary, 1971.

Longhurst, Henry, *My Life and Soft Times*, Collins, 1983.

Lucas, E. V., *Highways and Byways in Sussex*, Macmillan, 1907.

Manning-Sanders, Ruth, *The West of England*, Batsford, 1949.

Maxwell, Gavin, *The House of Elrig*, Longman, 1965.

Melville, Nigel, *Abbotsbury*, Odun Books, 1999.

Morgan, Nigel J., and Pritchard, Annette, *Power and Politics at the Seaside*, University of Exeter Press, 1999.

Muggeridge, Malcolm, 'Bournemouth' from *Beside the Seaside: Six Variations*, Stanley Knott, 1934.

Nash, Paul, 'Swanage, or Seaside Surrealism', from the *Architectural Review*, 1936.

Orwell, George, 'Such, Such Were the Joys', from *A Collection of Essays*, Mariner Books, 1970.

Parker, Derek, *The West Country and the Sea*, Longman, 1980.

Payne, Tony, *Peacehaven Then and Now*, SB Publications, 1999.

Pollard, Richard, *Hastings: Looking Back to the Future – a Tribute to Sidney Little*, Richard Pollard, 2011.

Pulman, George, *The Book of the Axe*, Longman 1875 (available through www.archive.org).

Robinson, Adrian, and Millward, Roy, *The Shell Book of the British Coast*, David and Charles, 1983.

Ryan, Sheila, *Untold Stories: Beachy Head*, SB Publications, 2010.

Scarth, Richard, *Echoes from the Sky*, Hythe Civic Society, 1999.

Skinner, B. G., *H. F. Lyte: Brixham's Poet and Priest*, University of Exeter Press, 1974.

Smelt, Maurice, *101 Cornish Lives*, Alison Hodge, 2006.

Smith, Bernard, and Haas, Peter, *Writers in Sussex*, Redcliffe Press, 1985.

Smith, John Wilson, *Elias Parish Alvars: King of Harpists*, Teignmouth Museum and Historical Society Monograph 9.

Soane, John, *Fashionable Resort Regions*, CABI Publishing, 1993.

Spence, Edward F., *The Pike Fisher*, A & C Black, 1928.

Sprawson, Charles, *Haunts of the Black Masseur*, Jonathan Cape, 1992.

Stafford, Felicity, and Yates, Nigel, *The Later Kentish Seaside*, Kent Archives, 1985.

Stanier, Peter, *Cornwall's Literary Heritage*, Twelveheads, 1992.

Tait, Katharine, *Carn Voel*, Patten Press, 1998.

Thwaite, Ann, *Glimpses of the Wonderful: The Life of Philip Henry Gosse*, Faber, 2002.

— *Edmund Gosse: A Literary Landscape*, Secker & Warburg, 1984.

Travis, John, 'Continuity and Change in English Sea-Bathing', from *Recreation and the Sea*, Exeter University Press, 1997.

— *The Rise of the Devon Seaside Resorts 1750–1900*, Liverpool University Press, 1997.

Treves, Sir Frederick, *Highways and Byways in Dorset*, Macmillan, 1906.

Troak, Malcolm, *Peacehaven and Telscombe Then and Now*, New Anzac Publications, 2004.

Troyat, Henri, *Tolstoy*, Penguin, 1970.

Unwin, Peter, *The Narrow Sea*, Headline, 2003.

Urry, John, *The Tourist Gaze*, Sage, 2001.

Walton, John K., *The English Seaside Resort 1750–1914*, Leicester University Press, 1983.

— *The British Seaside: Holidays and Resorts in the Twentieth Century*, Manchester University Press, 2000.

— (ed) with Patrick Browne, *Coastal Regeneration in English Resorts*, www.coastalcommunities.co.uk, 2010.

West, Ian, *Geology of the Wessex Coast*, www.southampton. ac.uk/~imw/

Whyman, John, *The Early Kentish Seaside*, Kent Archives, 1985.

Williamson, J. A., *The English Channel*, Collins, 1959.

Willimott, William, *Parson Willimott's Cornish Sketchbook*, St Michael's Caerhays Parochial Church Council, 2010.

Wilson, Viv, *Teignmouth Then and Now*, Tempus, 2004.

Wolters, N. E. B, *Bungalow Town*, Wolters, 1985.

Young, Gerard, *History of Bognor Regis*, Phillimore, 1983.

Acknowledgements

The idea that led to this book was Harry Marshall's, and I am most grateful to him for letting me run with it. My friend Jason Hawkes has provided the pictures out of the goodness of his heart, and I owe deep gratitude to him. My agent, Caroline Dawnay, has yet again shown that no writer could have a better friend and supporter. I am also very appreciative of the support given to me by Mike Jones, who was instrumental in commissioning the book on behalf of Simon & Schuster. Jo Whitford has been patient and responsive in seeing the book through to publication. I would like to thank Garry Walton for his uplifting cover, and Colin Midson for his map and much else. The final text owes a great deal to the forensic copy-editing of Sally Partington, who has given me much invaluable help. Any blunders that survive are my fault, not hers.

I would have been lost without our wonderful public libraries and their local-studies sections, and all the help given to me by their courteous and well-informed staff.

I owe more than I can say to my wife, Helen. Without her support and forbearance, this book and its predecessors would not have been written.

INDEX

Index

Index